Also by James J. Cramer

Jim Cramer's Stay Mad for Life:
Get Rich, Stay Rich (Make Your Kids Even Richer) (with Cliff Mason)

Jim Cramer's Mad Money:
Watch TV, Get Rich (with Cliff Mason)

Jim Cramer's Real Money:
Sane Investing in an Insane World

You Got Screwed!
Why Wall Street Tanked and How You Can Prosper

Confessions of a Street Addict

JIM CRAMER'S
GETTING BACK TO EVEN

JAMES J. CRAMER
WITH CLIFF MASON

Simon & Schuster
New York   London   Toronto   Sydney

Simon & Schuster
1230 Avenue of the Americas
New York, NY 10020

Copyright © 2009 by J.J. Cramer & Co.

First Simon & Schuster hardcover edition October 2009

SIMON & SCHUSTER and colophon are registered trademarks
of Simon & Schuster, Inc.

For information about special discounts for bulk purchases,
please contact Simon & Schuster Special Sales at
1-866-506-1949 or business@simonandschuster.com.

The Simon & Schuster Speakers Bureau can bring authors
to your live event. For more information or to book an event,
contact the Simon & Schuster Speakers Bureau at
1-866-248-3049 or visit our website at www.simonspeakers.com.

Design by Rhea Braunstein

Manufactured in the United States of America

1   3   5   7   9   10   8   6   4   2

Library of Congress Cataloging-in-Publication Data
Cramer, Jim.
Jim Cramer's getting back to even / James J. Cramer with Cliff Mason.
p.   c.m.
Includes index.
1. Stocks—United States.   2. Investments—United States.   3. Finance,
Personal—United States.   4. Financial security—United States.   I. Mason,
Cliff.   II. Title.   III. Title: Getting back to even.
HG4910.C73   2009
332.63'220973—dc22   2009027131

ISBN 978-1-4391-5801-2
ISBN 978-1-4391-6354-2 (ebook)

To Ben "Better Late Than Never" Bernanke,
who, after a slow start, is doing his best
to save the Western financial world and could go down
as the greatest Federal Reserve Chairman in history.

CONTENTS

1. Don't Give Up!   1

2. Crossing the Stock Market Minefield   13

3. Putting the Pieces Back Together   40

4. Dividends: The Best Offense Is a Good Defense   71

5. How to Invest in the Recovery: Twelve Stocks to Watch   108

6. The Next Big Thing: Regional Banks Poised to Grow   140

7. Getting Back to Even Like a Pro:
       Using Options to Replace Stocks   163

8. Taking Options to the Next Level: Advanced Strategies   188

9. How Your Generation Should Respond to the Crash   205

10. Twenty-five New Rules for Post-Apocalyptic Investing   233

11. Coping with the New World Disorder   302

Afterword   335

Acknowledgments   339

Index   343

JIM CRAMER'S
GETTING BACK TO EVEN

1

DON'T GIVE UP!

Getting back to even? What happened to making yourself and your family filthy rich? Could I possibly be aiming any lower? Have things really gotten so bad that you should drop all your hopes and dreams and just struggle to stay solvent?

Absolutely not. But before you can get ahead, you have to get back to even, and in difficult times that's the hardest and most important goal of all. For the last eighteen months we've watched in excruciating horror as first our homes and then our stocks have plummeted in value. Make no mistake, the stock market crashed in the second half of 2008, and this was a crash to rival anything we've seen since the Great Depression. It was the worst year for stocks since 1931. In 2008, Americans lost more than a quarter of their retirement savings in 401(k) and IRA plans, and millions more saw their retirement funds cut in half. For many of you, it's as though your money simply vanished into thin air. I'm here to show you how to get it back, one dollar at a time.

Ever since the housing bubble went bust and the stock market fell apart like a wet paper bag, we've been deluged with books that promise to help you weather the downturn and get back on your feet. But most of them either offer up the same old tired and often discredited teachings wrapped in a new, panic-filled package—sell all stocks now and cut up those nasty credit cards—or are full of advice that could have saved you a lot of pain if the books had been written two years ago. Wonderful timing. That's not what you'll find in this book. Hindsight is twenty-twenty, but you need foresight if you're trying to rebuild your savings, and especially if you're trying to claw your way back from the ground up.

I can teach you how to protect your money in a downturn. I know how to avoid a stock market crash and even how to take advantage of one. I was entirely in cash for the crash of 1987, and in fact that's actually what put me on the map professionally in the early days of running my hedge fund and allowed me to pulverize the market in the fastest decline from peak to trough in history. I also hope that if you read and followed the advice in my earlier books *Real Money, Mad Money,* and *Stay Mad For Life,* you were able to escape the worst of the carnage. But the sad truth is that other than gold, which does well in chaotic times, and U.S. Treasurys, the safest of securities, every single asset class from stocks to corporate municipal and mortgage bonds to commodities has just been hammered. Stocks took an especially severe beating that they've only just begun to recover from. In 2008, the two most important bellwether indices that track the health of the overall market, the Dow Jones Industrial Average and the much broader Standard and Poor's 500, fell by 33.8 percent and 38.49 percent, respectively. The damage has already been done, the money's been lost, and none of these new books filled with old boilerplate bromides about investing will help you get it back. Most of what you'll find on the personal finance and investing shelves is authors giving you an ounce of prevention, when what you really need is a pound of cure. But then again, they are just writers who have never managed money, not even in a bull market, let alone the vicious bear that romped through Wall Street, eating up and crushing the defenseless eggs that you thought were safe in your nest.

Anyone can see that these aren't ordinary times. This is still a moment of financial crisis, and I'm not just talking about the mess that Wall Street got itself into or the near collapse of our banking system. I mean the individual financial crises that millions of Americans are dealing with every single day: how to keep your home, how to pay for college when the college fund's gone dry, how to retire when your retirement money's been wiped out. This is the cash you were counting on, and rebuilding it is our first priority.

This book is your financial first-aid kit, an emergency room for your portfolio complete with epinephrine shots and paddles—think "Clear!"—to bring your pocketbook back to life. I can help you stop the bleeding and start putting your financial life back together. The new strategies, rules, and disciplines in this book will help you hang on to what you have and rebuild everything you've lost.

It won't be simple or quick or easy. I'm not making any false promises here. But the good news is that it can be done, that you can exercise some control over your financial future. Whenever we're in dire economic straits it's all too easy to fall prey to the belief that nothing can be done to make things better. Millions of Americans are losing their homes, their jobs, and their savings, not because of anything they did but because a relatively small number of people in the financial industry made bad decisions while the government was asleep at the wheel or worse, promoting the reckless driving that got us into this mess. We're all at the mercy of forces beyond our control, to some extent or another, but that's no reason to throw up your hands and stop trying. The absolute worst thing you can do is get caught like a deer in headlights and turn yourself into a pure victim of circumstance.

On the other hand, you have to recognize that this isn't business as usual. If you've lost lots of money that you need, then the stakes have never been higher, both for you and for your family. So how the heck do you deal with that kind of crisis? I can tell you the specifics, new investing strategies that incorporate everything we've learned about what works and what doesn't from the crash and its aftermath, and how you should vary your approach depending on your age. But first you need to make sure you're on an even keel.

Everyone remembers that famous quotation from Franklin Roosevelt's first inaugural address, "the only thing we have to fear is fear itself," but you hardly ever hear the rest of that sentence, the most important part, expanding on this fear: "nameless, unreasoning, unjustified terror, which paralyzes needed efforts to convert retreat into advance." Now, obviously, if you've just had your retirement fund shredded or are in danger of losing your house, you have more to fear than fear itself. Fear is a great motivator but not when it paralyzes needed efforts to convert retreat into advance. We've been through nasty recessions before, and believe it or not, it's possible to overcome the problems they create for you personally, and even to profit from the broader crisis and come out wealthier than ever. But to do that, you have to recognize that in extraordinarily difficult times, the stock market doesn't always operate according to ordinary rules. However, there are new rules, and rules I have pioneered to help you navigate your way through these brutal times. I can teach you how to learn from and play by these new rules and win while everyone else is trying to show you how to avoid a crash that already happened.

Why should you listen to me, and what makes this book so different from the standard fare? I'm a stock guy after all, and aren't stocks what got us into this mess in the first place? Look, I have been at this for thirty years. Unlike the usual peddlers of financial advice, I actually made myself rich by investing in the stock market and managing the money of my wealthy clients at my old hedge fund, Cramer Berkowitz & Company, including cleaning up during the devastating crash of 2000, when my fund was up 36 percent, while the Dow Jones Industrial Average took a 6.18 percent hit, the S&P 500 fell by 9.1 percent, and the NASDAQ plummeted 39.29 percent. I know how to make money in bear markets and during recessions. But beyond that, I've also been where you are right now. I know what it's like to lose a vast amount of money in a short period of time. I know how it feels to have my very future on the line. I understand the stress and the fear, but I also understand how to come back.

I still keep a memento of one of the lowest points in my life tucked into my wallet, and carry it with me wherever I go. It's a little piece of paper, a cutout from my daily portfolio run on the single worst day my hedge fund ever had, October 8, 1998, a date that, at least for me, will live in infamy. With less than three months left until the end of the year, my hedge fund, which was supposed to be managing $281 million, at the time was down $90,915,674 or 32 percent, because I'd made a series of boneheaded bets in the market. That's the kind of loss that would destroy most hedge funds, like the hundreds of funds that were brought low by 2008. It wasn't just my money that was at risk, it was my job and my entire career, too, not to mention my reputation, as virtually everyone I knew had written me off as a failure. Even *The New York Times* had written my premature financial obituary.

I was in the very same position that most of you are probably in right now. My investments had cratered and my future was in jeopardy. Practically everyone around me urged me to quit and head for the hills, wherever the hills might be, since I live in a Jersey suburb of New York City. So you see, I know exactly how you feel. But I'm not telling you this to show that I feel your pain. Empathy is great, but it won't make you money. You need concrete solutions and this book is filled with them.

Between October 8, that dark day when I was down almost $91 million, and the end of the year, I did what I'm going to teach you to do in this book. I got back to even, and actually finished the year with a small profit of 2 percent. I buckled down and in less than three months I made back $110 million, averaging $1.4 million in profits every single day. Not only is it possible to come back from devastating losses, but also, if you're lucky, you can even do it quickly. Now, in one respect you're in a much better position than I was in 1998: you don't have to worry about arbitrary time constraints the way a hedge fund manager does. No clients are trying to pull out money while you try to rebuild your capital, nor is anyone even looking over your shoulder, forcing you to get back to even by the end of the year. You can afford to be patient. Of course some of you have less time than others. If you're on the verge of retirement or you're about to send a child off to an expensive college that you're paying for, then you can't be as patient as someone who's in their twenties with no dependents and no big, unavoidable expenditures on the horizon. But you still have a heck of a lot longer than I did at the end of 1998, and that makes things easier.

On the other hand, I also recognize that this is not 1998. The rules of the game have changed, and it's become harder to make money in the market. Not everything that used to work for me when I was running my hedge fund still works today. Many money managers have given up and returned to other professions, too baffled or fed up with a stock market they perceive as intractable or inscrutable at best, and downright malevolent at its worst. Ideas that were common sense or conventional wisdom even just a year and a half ago can now seem downright insane. I have always believed that putting part of your income in stocks is the best way to augment your paycheck every month, that anyone can make themselves rich by investing wisely. I still think that's true, but we also have to come to terms with some harsh new realities.

First and foremost is the fact that for many people the stock market feels broken, a totally justifiable attitude. The market has taken on a level of risk that makes it a much more dangerous place to keep any money that you think you'll need to make a major purchase any time in the next few years. And beyond that, many of you probably feel betrayed by stocks. I don't blame you! Instead of being a time-tested vehicle for wealth creation, stocks have come to be viewed as the reason why people are forced to postpone retirement or take on a second job. Stocks that were once considered "blue-chip" investments, household names that lots and lots of people owned, such as General Motors, Bear Stearns, Lehman Brothers, Citigroup, AIG, and Kodak, just to name a handful, have been bent, spindled, mutilated, and then mutilated some more. This is not like the aftermath of the dot-com bubble, where the stocks that lost people money could all be written off as overvalued, overhyped, speculative junk. These were considered real companies, revered time-tested institutions, part of the bedrock of the market—and if you owned them you got killed.

So why should you believe that investing in stocks, which got us into the mess we're in, can also get us out of it? Why not just cut your losses and stick your money in a traditional savings account where you won't have to worry about it? First of all, because you'll never get back to even that way, and second, because there is a world of difference between owning stocks, which has caused so much wealth to disappear, and trying to *make money* in stocks, an approach that at the very least lets you sidestep some of the pain. You can get back to even if you follow the latter course. Most peddlers of financial advice, even after the wealth-shattering crash of 2008, preach the virtues of owning stocks just for the sake of owning them. They will still tell you to buy and hold, an investing shibboleth that I have been trying to smash for ages. The buy-and-hold strategy, if you can even call it one, is to pick a bunch of good-looking blue-chip companies, buy their stocks, and hang on to them till kingdom come. Selling is strictly forbidden. It's considered a sign of recklessness, of "trading," which all too many supposed experts think of as a dirty word. Same goes for the once-sacred mutual funds, with managers who adopted the same careless buy-and-hold, one-decision philosophy.

If you had practiced buy and hold over the last decade, you would have gotten exactly nowhere. The major averages have literally fallen back to levels they first hit ten years ago. That means, for example, that if you'd contributed a little bit to your 401(k) each month, the way most people do, then most of your buying was at much higher prices. The results are in and this philosophy has lost more people more money than anything save gambling, and frankly, it's hard for me to see the difference between gambling and deciding to permanently own stock in a company that could change its stripes at any moment. It's investing blind, and investing blind is no different from investing dumb.

That's why my philosophy is "buy and homework." For every stock you own, you must spend at least an hour a week checking up on the underlying company, and that's in addition to the research you ought to do before buying a new stock. I know it sounds daunting, but I'm talking about a block of time that's shorter than an NFL or an

NBA game, and certainly shorter than just about every Major League Baseball contest, even without the commercials. It's less time than you'd spend seeing a movie, and I know you've never made a dime going to the movie theater, especially not with the way they rob you at the concession stand. The homework, like taking your car in for an occasional maintenance inspection, lets you know if everything is still working under the hood, or if it's time to sell and trade the stock in for a different model. Doing the homework lets you avoid holding on to the stock of a troubled company as it meanders closer to zero like AIG and GM, or sinks all the way down like Lehman Brothers or Fannie Mae and Freddie Mac. It lets you stay on top of what's blue chip and what's been downgraded to red or white or no chip at all.

Just owning stocks because that's what you're supposed to do won't help get you back to even. But doing the homework, and owning stocks not for their own sake but for the sake of making money, definitely can. How important is the distinction between buy and hold and buy and homework? It's the difference between passively accepting whatever hand the market deals you and taking control of your own destiny.

Let me give you an example. On my television show, *Mad Money*, where I teach viewers how to be better investors, help make sense of the market, and tell you which stocks I would buy and sell, I made a call, based on my homework, back on September 19, 2008, recommending that people sell at least 20 percent of their portfolio because I expected the market to go lower. On that day the Dow Jones Industrial Average had closed at 11,388. Then, a little more than two weeks later, on Monday, October 6, with the Dow a thousand points lower at 10,332, I went on NBC's *Today* show, and in a much-derided appearance told viewers to take any money they thought they'd need over the next five years out of the stock market because I believed it had become too dangerous and too risky. That call earned me more scorn and criticism than anything else I had ever said in a career that's been full of scorn and criticism. It was also one of the best calls I've ever made, as the market went on to have its worst week in history. You avoided a 33.6 percent decline in just two months if you heeded my first clarion call, and a 26.8 percent decline with the second. A simple sidestep into cash would have kept your savings from disappearing and thus keeping you from having to work for many more years than you had probably thought would be necessary just a few weeks before these calls were made. And I helped you get back in at the lows in many stocks using the methods detailed here, methods you can use without me after I teach you their rudiments, which will allow you to rebuild your savings and make even more money. Basically, I hit the investing equivalent of a grand slam.

Now that the market's bounced back, there are those who say my philosophy of dodging the declines is flawed versus a buy-and-forget-'em method. But these uninformed critics are ignoring the colossal difference between a rally that makes up some of your losses and a rally that actually makes you money because you sidestepped the losses in the first place. In doubt? Consider the difference between someone who avoided the decline starting September 19, my first sell call, and then got in on March 9 when I said the worst of the downside was over and it was time to come back in, *versus* the buy-and-hold method. The buy-and-hold philosopher with $100 in the market who ignored my September 19, 2008, sell call saw his portfolio drop to $57.50 on March 9. If he then caught the 40 percent gain through the end of July 2009, he would have $81.

Now compare the person who listened on September 19 and sold his $100 and then got back in on March 9, when I said the coast was clear. By sidestepping the loss and then getting in near the bottom he would have been able to make $40 on that $100 and would finish his round-trip at $140. The person who actively managed his money and avoided the worst part of the crash by selling on September 19 has 72.8 percent more money than the buy and holder at the end of July.

How about the October 6 sell call? The buy and holder who slept through the call saw his $100 turn to $63.50 on March 9 but would be back to $88.90 at the end of July. The person who sidestepped and got back in on my suggestion would have that $140, or 57 percent more than the buy and holder. And all of this arithmetic presumes that you didn't panic out at or near the bottom when the declines became too painful to endure. How can anyone in his right mind compare the returns and say that buy and hold makes more sense?

But in print and on television I was taken to task for being reckless and irresponsible and for causing a panic with these calls. Allegedly cooler heads responded that it would be more prudent to stay the course. But nobody said I got it wrong. They didn't care. These people thought it was more important that you own stocks than that you make money in them. The whole industry is biased toward keeping you in at all times, rather than preserving your capital so it can live and appreciate another day. Your broker, your financial advisor, they want to prevent your account from going to cash at any costs. I was a broker once and I know that the instructions were "keep people in," because brokers get paid on commission, and they will never make any money if people decide to leave the party. When you sell, they will keep calling you about new opportunities so they do not lose your money to the sidelines. And the mutual fund managers are even worse. They are totally fee based. They don't earn a fee for making you money, they just take a cut of everything that's invested with them, whether they make money or lose it. Buy and hold is perfect for them because it keeps your money in their funds, generating profits for them, even if it creates losses for you. When you retreat to the sidelines and put your money in a savings account, the whole brokerage and mutual fund industries get crushed.

The sidelines, as smart and attractive as they can be, are derided as stupid by these people, but only because they're the kiss of death for any financial professional. Except, that is, for me. I don't want your assets or your commissions, I just want to give you honest advice. And as someone who has worked on commission and run a fee-based hedge fund, I know what I'm talking about. Too many people advocate buy and hold because it makes *them* money, not because it makes *you* money.

Their approach might eventually get you back to even, although I doubt it and it might not happen within your lifetime. Last I looked, that time frame surely mattered. But if it does get you back to even, it will be because of dumb luck and not anything you've done right. I have a different view: I believe that selling is the responsible thing to do when you think the stock market is headed much lower. In some ways, I wish I could have gone on *Today* and told them to "stay the course," if only because I didn't want to scare people, particularly when they are going off to work or getting the kids dressed for school. Not only would it have been easier for me to be bullish from a public relations standpoint, but I also genuinely want stocks to go up, not down. Unfortunately, all the signs I follow pointed to a big decline, so optimism would have been gravely misplaced. Instead I had no choice; I had to do the equivalent of shout fire in a crowded theater, because there was a massive conflagration raging behind the scenes that was about to consume everyone who stayed inside, oblivious to the disaster I knew was about to occur.

To get back to even, you need to know what to look for in a stock to figure out if it can deliver in a time when the market is busted and the economy has gone bust. I am no perma-bull, someone who always believes it's a good time to buy and to own stocks, although I do believe that you can almost always find good stocks to buy. I was literally screaming about the financial crisis starting in the summer of 2007, warning anyone who would listen that our entire financial system could come crashing down because our policymakers didn't have a clue about the true depth of the banks' problems. You can still see my "They Know Nothing" CNBC rant on YouTube, meant as a last-ditch attempt to save the banking system from its regulators. The call, obviously, was not heeded. I'm not telling you this to boast. I've made plenty of mistakes, too, mistakes I own and call attention to regularly so that we can all learn from them. My point is that I am not relying on some misguided faith in the idea that stocks will always go higher eventually to help you restore the money you've lost and make even more. I have some new investing strategies, including one that relies on dividends—yes, dividends—that will help you generate both income and potential upside while protecting you from the downside.

If you want to know how to make the best of a bad situation, resist the fear, keep your house, not to mention your shirt, and turn a profit, too, keep reading. I will tell you what the deadly combination of a credit crisis, stock market crash, and a global economic slowdown means for you, depending on whether you're young or old, rich or middle income. For young people, a market crash is a great long-term investing opportunity, but a big economic slowdown makes it much harder to find work. If you're older, you need to focus on rebuilding the money that you've lost in order to pay for your retirement. This is not a one-size-fits-all book. For whatever situation you're in, I'll tell you what pitfalls to avoid and how to deal with your money troubles so you can get back to even, and then get ahead. I'll tell you everything you need to know about rebuilding your retirement fund using your 401(k) plan and IRA as well as using the downturn to invest for your children.

I've also created twenty-five new rules for trading and investing based on the crash and its aftermath to help make you a better investor. Plus, because the government has such a major effect on the economy when we're in trouble, I'll go through the latest rules and regulations from the feds that can help you and your family save money. Getting back to even also means knowing how to tell the difference between a legitimate money manager and a con artist. Hard times tend to bring scammers out of the woodwork, and when we're in desperate situations we're more likely to jump at deals that are too good to be true. Bernie Madoff and his $50 billion Ponzi scheme is just the biggest of them. You don't want to be the victim of the next Madoff—something that the regulators seem blind to, but I can sniff from miles away. Finally, I'll tell you how to spot a genuine recovery, in the market and the economy, and how to make money from it.

No matter what, don't give up. These are frightening, and occasionally infuriating, times, but with a little help you can stop being scared, stop getting mad, and start getting back to even!

2

CROSSING THE
STOCK MARKET MINEFIELD

How are you, as an individual, supposed to cope with the worst economic catastrophe since the Great Depression? How do you get by, let alone get back to even, when virtually everything that could be stacked against you *is* stacked against you? Where are you even supposed to begin when your retirement fund has lost half its value, your college savings are nearly wiped out, your house is now worth less than the mortgage you took out to buy it, and anything else you had invested in the stock market has all but evaporated? Sound like a bleak picture? If you don't have at least one of these problems, consider yourself very lucky.

And losing vast sums of money is really just the tip of the iceberg. The real catastrophe is seeing all of your plans for the future, to say nothing of hopes or dreams, unravel in the span of a few short but incredibly painful months. A year or two ago you might have been contemplating early retirement, and now you're grateful just to be working. At least from a financial perspective, the life you'll actually be living will look a whole lot different from the one you expected before the market came crashing down and the economy bit the dust. It doesn't have to be this way. You may have to take some short-term hits to your standard of living, but if you play your cards right you can turn what seems like a radical life-altering financial disaster into something much closer to a momentary hiccup. The way things are now doesn't have to be the rule; you can make it the exception. You can make back everything you've lost and more.

But before you can even start thinking about replacing the part of your wealth that's been obliterated, you must do everything in your power to keep what you still have. If your portfolio is still hemorrhaging money, then we need to stop the bleeding. If you're taking too many of the wrong kinds of risks, and you probably are because the rules of the game have changed and nobody sent you the new instruction manual, I'll let you know where the dangers lie. There are myriad mistakes that even the most disciplined and experienced investors tend to make during bear markets, and we're just starting to emerge from the worst, most unforgiving bear market of my entire lifetime. In fact, by some metrics, the crash that began in 1929 and precipitated the Great Depression was more benign than what we've been through. In cases where you can make direct, apples-to-apples comparisons, when you have a stock that traded during the crash of 1929 to 1932 and is still around today, you can find plenty of examples of stocks that took a worse beating in 2008 and 2009. US Steel (X) and General Motors (GM) both fell further in our crash than they did from the top in 1929 to the bottom in 1932, and it took them much less time. While the crash of 1929 got off to a much faster start, the crash of 2008 and 2009 eventually caught up to it. By the way, if you want to understand the dynamics of this market, then John Kenneth Galbraith's *The Great Crash* is required reading, particularly the parts where he talks about those who told investors to stay the course, voices that included many who were themselves selling, even while still mouthing these words of conventional—and fatal—financial "wisdom." Staying the course has never been my style when the course is suicidal for your wealth, as anyone who watches my appearances on the *Today* show or my regular gig on *Mad Money* knows.

What do you need to know in order to keep yourself safe? First of all, if you don't feel as though you have been betrayed by stocks in general then you haven't been paying attention. As the market repealed ten years of gains, we also repealed decades of conventional wisdom that said equities were the best place, the only place, to invest your money for long-term "capital appreciation," which is just a piece of Wall Street gibberish that means growing your money. But in a market where a key average like the S&P 500 can get cut in half in less than two years, where General Electric (GE), the company you see when you look up the phrase "blue-chip" in the dictionary, can trade under $10 and Citigroup (C) for less than $1, as they did at their lows, you wouldn't be crazy if you felt like stocks had stabbed you in the back.

Remember, at the very same time as stocks began to be heralded as the face of future prosperity, the 401(k) and IRA retirement revolution came into full force. Over the course of the 1990s American businesses moved away from traditional defined-benefit pension plans, where employers would pay their retired workers the same amount of money every month based on a set formula, and began increasingly to adopt 401(k) plans and make use of individual retirement accounts, or IRAs, which function like 401(k) plans, but which anyone can open (they're not tied to a job). The greatness of the 401(k) and IRA is that they allow workers to invest their own money with tax-deferred income, letting them direct their own investments and choose how much money to set aside for retirement. But as 401(k)s and IRAs replaced traditional pensions, neither the companies that provided them nor the government that made them possible made any serious efforts to teach people how to manage their retirement money. At times it's been even more nefarious; the institutions that we entrusted to help us with our 401(k)s often steered us into fully invested products, meaning funds that were 100 percent invested in stocks—no cash on the sidelines—with high fees, most of the time never offering anything that was truly conservative or that allowed managers to sidestep declines. Sure, I've gone out of my way to educate anyone who's willing to listen, and we certainly have more than enough talking heads who are eager to offer their own advice, much of it harmful to your financial health, but there's no way to make anyone listen if they don't want to. Combine that with the dogma that stocks should be bought and held at all times, no matter the price or the economic backdrop, and you have a recipe for disaster.

The crash has turned 401(k)s and IRAs, two great innovations for wealth creation, into veritable fifth columns working for the forces of wealth destruction. Stocks turned out to be much higher risk propositions than the general public had assumed. To be fair, equities were far from alone in getting hammered, as every asset class other than gold and Treasurys have been beaten like unloved stepchildren in the course of this crash. Only thirty-year Treasurys, the most plain-vanilla asset around, considered risk free the world over, made you any serious money. What set equities apart from, say, commodities as an asset class was the public's widely and confidently held belief that stocks were practically the only way to go to grow your money over time without taking on too much risk. And now there's a whole cohort of retail investors, meaning individual investors as opposed to institutional money managers, who have been burned by stocks and may never be enticed back into the market.

Plenty of people are now questioning the old conventional wisdom that it's always a good idea to own stocks. But there's another idea, something else that gained widespread acceptance during the greatest bull market in history, the one that ended in 2008, and still goes almost unquestioned by many intelligent people: no one should pick their own stocks. In fact, it's practically an article of faith among the punditocracy that ordinary people have no business investing on their own. We're constantly told that actively managing a portfolio of stocks, choosing yourself what to buy, when to buy it, and when to sell it, is something that's best left to the professionals. According to this absurd consensus, regular people can't beat the market; you cannot consistently earn returns that outperform the S&P 500. Timing the market, they say, is impossible, so don't try.

The best you can hope to do, if you listen to numerous advocates of this philosophy, is stay even with the market by owning an index fund, a mutual fund that mimics the market by owning all of the stocks in a broad-based index like the S&P 500 or the Wilshire 5000, another popular one. Countless folks who have never owned stocks, never invested, and don't claim any particular expertise will nevertheless tell you that owning individual stocks is a sucker's game and that index funds are the only responsible, appropriate investment for everyone who isn't a professional. Even though this premise is transparently bogus, huge swathes of the press mindlessly parrot it over and over again. These same people condemn me as a charlatan and a wild-eyed "trader"—their equivalent of financial curse words— because I attempt to keep you out of severe rough patches and vicious declines. My message is considered heretical by most of the industry, yet based completely in common sense. Their orthodoxy has been discredited by the numbers but is still given credence by an uncritical media and an industry that can't afford to admit its own weaknesses, lest it lose your business forever, even as, perhaps, it should!

I know from personal experience that this mindless "buy and forget"—I am no longer using the term "buy and hold" because that presumes what you "hold" doesn't go to zero, wishful thinking in retrospect—is a form of recklessness that can no longer be tolerated as a serious way to manage your money. If you have the time and the inclination to research stocks, then you can absolutely do better than you would by parking your money in an index fund. At my hedge fund, I managed to deliver an average annual return of 24 percent to my clients, and that's after all fees, a much better return than the 10 percent annually that you'd expect to get from the market in general, and the 8 percent annually that you would have earned if you had chosen an index fund during the time when I toiled in my turret. Of course, most people like you can't invest money in hedge funds. They are almost exclusively the province of rich people who can afford to take big risks. But that doesn't mean you can't apply to your own portfolio the lessons I learned at my fund, and everything I've learned subsequently by managing a charitable trust, which you can follow at www.ActionAlertsPlus.com, and coming out every day to give regular people investing advice on my show *Mad Money* and on the website, www.TheStreet.com. Not only can you beat an index fund, I believe it's possible for you to do better than I did at my hedge fund, because you don't have to answer to a horde of rich clients who demand short-term results, sometimes at the expense of longer-term gains. You don't have to make money every year, or every quarter, or even every day, as many of my old clients practically demanded of me. The only person you have to answer to is yourself.

As we know from the comparisons given earlier between those who bought and held through my sell calls of 2008 and my buy call of 2009 versus those who took my advice to sidestep the decline and buy back in near the low, actively managing your money is clearly the safest and least reckless way to go. When you invest your own money, you are in control. You can sell when things look dangerous and save yourself a lot of pain. I am constantly mocked and called irresponsible, even dangerous, for espousing this view, but that's because it threatens the status quo, where the companies that operate these index funds make fortunes, even though the funds have relatively low fees and the managers of actively managed funds make even more money. These people have a vested interest in keeping you ignorant. They want you in your chains, fully invested in some fund at all times, and incapable of thinking for yourself. That's not to say that all the people in the industry are bad guys; they're definitely not, and you can find plenty of professionals who truly do want to help you make money. Nevertheless, you have to understand that because of the way the system is structured, most professionals have strong incentives to keep you invested so they can take your fees or your commissions. They're just doing what's best for them, but that's not what's best for you. Only you care enough about your money to be entrusted with running it. Everyone else, even those who are truly on your side and completely honest, is still trying to take your money. As someone who taught brokers how to bring in assets at Goldman Sachs, I can tell you that the lesson was simple: get them invested, and once they are all in, they will never leave. As an investing professional, I certainly thought I could do a better job for people than if they did it themselves. I certainly didn't want to "sucker" people in, but many brokers and mutual fund companies care more about bringing you in and getting you fully invested, because that's what their firms want them to do, regardless of whether it's good for you or not. As someone who is actually willing to tell the truth about the way it really works, I know that the mantra is still the same: keep 'em in, and if they get burned, find more of them to take their place. Believe me, you are simply "more of them" to many people in the financial industry, and not much else.

The last thing they want you to do is sell, to take your money out from under their management and do it yourself. That doesn't mean everyone should pick their own stocks. It doesn't mean index funds are a bad thing. I think an index fund can be a terrific tool if you don't have the time or the interest in stocks to do it yourself. If investing is all too much for you, then index funds are definitely the right way to go.

But for those of you who want to take control of your own finances, who want to be able to avoid the kinds of enormous declines that we saw in 2008 and January and February of 2009 and get in at better prices, then do not believe the index fund propaganda. You can do it yourself. You are not outclassed by the professionals. In fact, you have an enormous advantage that money managers do not have: you're nimble. Size is a major handicap for the pros. A fund that's managing billions of dollars simply cannot buy or sell a significant position in a stock without changing the price of that stock. That makes things much harder for them. You are vastly more flexible than the big boys.

We have now learned from the brutal bear we have lived through that both individual stocks and the entire asset class should be approached with newfound skepticism and a healthy dose of fear. Now

I am in no way denouncing or renouncing stocks. You need stocks if you want to get back to even, and they're still my favorite asset class if you have more than four to five years to sit with them. Nevertheless, it is imperative that you recognize how much tougher and more risky investing in them has become. The stock market can be like a minefield, and you must avoid stepping on the land mines, something that's easier said than done. Take the health-care stocks, a group that usually outperforms during times of economic weakness. They outperformed all right, right up until President Obama announced his budget and decided that health companies should either have less profits or be nonprofits. Then they got poleaxed because many of these companies are heavily dependent on government spending, and Obama decided to rein in what he perceived to be runaway health-care costs even as the companies touted their products as lifesaving and essential. They, like many other stocks in the 2009 rallies, came back but got nowhere near where they started from. You can never be totally immune to this kind of thing, but you can take steps to minimize the damage. With that in mind, let me give you six rules for protecting the money you have and making sure you have the money you need.

RULE 1: Stocks are no substitute for a savings account. This is a quick and easy rule of thumb for when the market's lousy that could save you a lot of pain and heartbreak. Do not keep all the money that you think you'll need to spend over the next four to five years in stocks. In other words, sell enough stock in order to raise much of the cash you'll need for any major outlays in that time frame. Of course, as stocks go down they become less risky. Stocks do get less expensive, and that was another reason I wanted to get you out before the crash when I urged you to sell in October, 2008, so you could buy them more cheaply, as we did in the spring of 2009. But we recognize now that the asset class can be dangerous, particularly when it gets expensive. The buy-and-forget crowd never believes stocks are expensive;

that's the fatal flaw of their logic. But you have to become more bullish as they go lower, because you don't want to miss a potential once-in-a-lifetime buying opportunity, especially when it comes to the stocks I highlight later in this book, those with accidentally high dividend yields and those that can consistently raise their dividends. Stocks came down for so long and so hard that today they are less dangerous than when I made my big sell calls, even if the economy continues to falter or just flatlines, with occasional spurts up.

When you know the market's difficult, you just do not want to have all of that money tied up in stocks. The risk that it won't be there when you need it is simply too great. There are some chances you shouldn't be willing to take. By all means, go ahead and put these dollars somewhere safe like a nice certificate of deposit, a savings account, U.S. Treasurys, or even your mattress despite the lack of yield, as long as it's not in stocks. Okay not the mattress, but home safes have done a brisk business since the banks started falling like flies. That's too paranoid for me, and I'm a pretty paranoid guy. This is not 1933. Do not be afraid to keep your money in an FDIC-insured bank account. There is no reason not to keep up to $250,000 in any one account at these banks, $250,000 being the upper limit for FDIC insurance. If you have more than that, you can break the money up into multiple accounts at the same bank, and you'll be fine. FDIC-insured certificates of deposit are just fine, too, but only invest your money in the short-term kind. Interest rates could change and go much higher when things get better, so you don't want your money to be stuck in a low-yielding certificate of deposit for more than two years' time. Just be sure you never buy a CD from a bank that is not FDIC insured, because that's begging for trouble. Ask the people who bought incredibly high-yielding CDs from Stanford bank. They forgot to look for the FDIC label and got robbed. I have spent a considerable amount of time with the FDIC and its chairman, Sheila Bair, and despite many questions I receive on *Mad Money*, I can tell you in no uncertain terms that this program is among the best run of all federal programs and will never run out of money to protect you or the value of your assets, something that can never be said about stocks.

If you have a child whom you're sending to college sometime in the next four years and you're planning to pay for it, do not risk most of her tuition money in the stock market. I took out mine for my eldest daughter when I told people to raise cash if they needed it for a major purchase in the near future. This was after I had lost her senior year tuition money in my mutual fund, and I wasn't going to lose the junior, sophomore, and freshman years to boot! I wasn't going to tell you to stay the course when I was frantically calling Roger at my local Fidelity office and telling him to pull out.

If you plan on buying a home in the same period of time, something I think is actually a good idea after the brutal decline real estate has had, particularly in areas of the country where property values have fallen 40 percent or more, which has produced bottoms in every single instance, don't take too many chances with the dough you'll need for the down payment. Retiring in the next four years? Then make sure not that much of the money you need to fund your retirement through 2013 is invested in the stock market. When stocks feel unreliable, you'd be nuts to rely on them. Need to buy a new car— and I stress the word *need* here, because when times are tight you don't want to splurge—take much of that money out of stocks, too. I know this may sound disheartening, but it won't always be this way and if they retreat again to dramatically lower levels, naturally I will become more positive. The lower the market goes, the more money you can safely invest in it. People tend to panic as stocks go lower, but that's when you should be less fearful. We have to be careful not to lose lots of money, but we also don't want to be blind to the opportunity when the market's been totally hammered. Stocks are only as resilient as the companies and people behind them. They are less risky if you look at them over the long term because they have other attributes: they can be taken over, they can pay dividends that you can reinvest—40 percent of a stock's increase in value over time comes from the compounding income stream created by reinvested dividends—and economies can recover. But all three might not happen in the next four to five years, so we need to be cautious with those near-term financial demands.

I'm not saying you should sell immediately everything you'll need to finance your big outlays over the next few years. You have to be disciplined. Try to wait for a rally to sell into strength. Please don't panic and dump all your holdings after a huge decline in the Dow Jones Industrial Average. You can take some time and be patient about it, waiting for a rally such as in the summer of 2009. But don't take too long, not when stocks have this level of risk and you know you need that money for a big acquisition. Stocks are not cash!

What if your portfolio has huge losses and you don't want to lock them in by selling? Tough cookies! If you need the money to pay for something serious in the next four years, you cannot risk keeping it in stocks. We do not care where stocks have been, we care where they are going, and I am telling you that over the next four to five years they might not go anywhere, or, in some cases, they could be wiped out. If Lehman Brothers and GM can be wiped out, why can't some of what you own be demolished? In this market you're likely to lose even more money by sitting around waiting for your stocks to get back to even. Unlike the brokers and mutual fund managers, who endlessly defend picks no matter what the performance because of the buy-and-hold canard, you have to realize that losses are losses, whether you've realized them by selling or not, particularly because we have learned that severe losses occur when businesses falter and never recover or just outright fail. It's never a good idea to hang on to a stock just because you don't want to acknowledge the loss, but it's an especially bad one when you're dealing with money that doesn't belong in stocks in the first place.

And remember, the reasoning here is twofold. On the one hand you want to be sure you'll be able to cover any large outlays in the near future. On the other hand, when you think we're in for a big decline, of course you'd want to sell. Only an absurd buy-and-forget fanatic, and there are a lot of those, would tell you to stay in stocks no matter what.

RULE 2: Never, ever be afraid to sell when things look like they're headed down the tubes. But never (hardly ever) sell everything. One of the easiest mistakes to make after a bear market that's already torn you apart limb by limb is to sell everything and sit on the sidelines, entirely in cash, and wait until it gets easier. The problem is that you will most likely miss the rebound and a lot of great opportunities, like some of those we have had since the March 2009 lows. There was a sustainable rebound after the Great Depression, so there will certainly be a rebound from this severe downturn.

The trick here is to divide your investments into two streams: the longer-term retirement stream that sends money into your IRA and 401(k), and the short-term discretionary stream that you use for everything else. When you're selling stock to pay for any big outlays over the next five years, it should be stock from your discretionary portfolio. Why? Because your discretionary portfolio exists to cover shorter-term outlays, and because saving for retirement should always be your top priority. No matter what, you know you're going to have to retire someday when you can't work anymore. Plus, pulling money out of a tax-advantaged 401(k) or IRA to plug a hole in your discretionary portfolio will cause you to get banged with a 10 percent early withdrawal fee on top of the income tax you're already paying. You don't need that money anytime soon, so don't run the risk of liquidating it now only to find six or seven or eight years from now that we have a brand-new bull market that you missed out on because you couldn't take the short-term pain. Short-term pain is terminal if and only if you need the money within the next four to five years. But if your time frame is much longer than that, the pain is manageable as the price you pay to wait for better times.

The time frame is different depending on whether you're talking about a 401(k) for retirement, or a 529 plan, for example, which allows you to reap tax-deferred profits in order to help pay for the cost of sending your kids to college. I'll go over different strategies that you should pursue depending on your age and your priorities later in the book, but there are a couple things you need to know about protecting yourself from losses right now. A 529 plan with a good chunk of change in it will often be set up too close for college comfort. You might be contributing to your 401(k) for thirty or forty years, but a 529 has a more limited life, since you've only got the eighteen or so years before your child goes to school and then the (hopefully) four years when they're in school to pour money in. Plus, when you're dealing with a retirement fund, you're spending that money over the course of a third of your lifetime, while money in a 529 gets gobbled up quickly to cover the cost of college tuition. You can roll over money from one child's 529 plan into another, but that doesn't help you if there's no money left to roll over.

Unless you're planning to retire in the next four and a half years, you don't want to sell most of your stocks, even in a hideous bear market, because your retirement portfolio has a much longer time horizon. That doesn't mean you shouldn't sell something to sidestep a big decline if you see one coming, but it does mean that once that decline happens, you should put your retirement money back in stocks. If you aren't close to retiring, this money should be earmarked for the market, almost always. If you're retiring in twenty, thirty, or forty years, a chance to buy stocks at prices well below levels of just a few years ago, is a pretty solid long-term opportunity. You always want to keep some stocks in your retirement portfolio even if financial Armageddon or a second great depression is upon us, as the best of stocks produced bountiful returns coming out of the Great Depression. But you have to be very careful about which stocks you own.

That said, having a long time horizon is not a license to own bad stocks or an excuse not to worry about your holdings. Yes, you can afford to take more pain in your retirement portfolio, but that doesn't mean all pain is worth taking. All too often, stocks that go down stay down, and countless investors have been crushed while waiting for a bottom that never comes. That's why you should never buy into the notion that "it's too late to sell." You may feel that way after a stock has fallen 60, 70, or even 80 percent, but under no circumstances does that make it true. The "too late to sell" philosophy is a real money killer.

Consider the last bear market, the dot-bomb collapse from 2000 to 2003. The NASDAQ Composite peaked at 5,132 in 2000 and only stopped falling when it hit 1,108 in late 2002, a 78 percent decline. All the way down the right move was to sell. The declines were enormous: Intel down 82.7 percent, Cisco down 90.1 percent, Yahoo down 96.6 percent, Microsoft down 66.4 percent, and Oracle down 84.4 percent, and these were the legitimate companies that eventually recovered, although not to anywhere near their 2000 peaks.

As bad as it was, these tech stocks still didn't go down in a straight line. Every time they would blip up, an endless procession of commentators on TV would proclaim that the tech bottom was at hand, the agony over, the time to buy just around the corner. But then the stocks would go down even more. Instead of being afraid of losing more money, too many of the people who owned these stocks were afraid of missing the turn, worried that they had missed their opportunity to sell. They owned these stocks for no better reason than that they had already taken huge losses. So they held on and their stocks went down 80 or 90 percent, and if they were undiversified they were never heard from again.

When the outlook is terrible, your bias must be to sell. It's never too late. The people who rode these stocks all the way down never made it back to even. Don't let the same thing happen to you because you own the wrong stocks and you can't bring yourself to dump them into a big rally. Keep reading and I'll tell you how to identify the right stocks, both for long-term investments and to capture quick trading gains in the current environment.

But knowing that you should sell some, even most stocks, when the market is giving you a beating doesn't mean you should be blind to opportunities. That's why there are very few circumstances when it makes sense to simply dump everything. You have to be able to distinguish between damaged stocks and damaged merchandise after the market has taken a real beating. I'll help show you how later in the book, but let me give you two examples from the tech collapse of 2000 to 2003 to illustrate the difference: Apple, which fully recovered from the crash, and Dell, which never got you back to even. Apple went from $38 in December 1999 to $7 in December 2002, and as I write, it's a $160 stock, and that's after being severely bruised in the big decline. If you'd bought Apple at the worst possible time, right before the 2000–2003 tech collapse, you still would have had more than a 180 percent gain, double that if you got out before the most recent crash. If you'd held on to Apple at the bottom or bought it there, the gains would have been even more spectacular, a 1400 percent win. Dell? It went from $52 at the end of 1999 to $22 at the end of 2002. Where is Dell as I write this? It's at $13, which is 40 percent lower than where it was at the bottom of the tech collapse, and 75 percent lower than where it was at the end of 1999.

How do you tell the Dells from the Apples ahead of time? How do you tell them apart after they've already crashed and you're deciding what to keep and what to throw away? I'll give you much more guidance on this later in the book, but here's what you need to know for now: Back in 1999, Dell was considered the much more exciting story. Michael Dell was haled as a visionary, while Apple's Steve Jobs was, at best, seen as questionable by the Street. In the end, however, it was Apple that recovered. Apple was worth owning, while Dell should have been sold as fast as possible. Apple was always seen as a company that had great computers, but then it came roaring back with terrific management and superior products like the iPod and then the iPhone. Dell, on the other hand, was a one-trick pony. Everyone copied its delivery gimmick where you could customize your computer and order it for a lower price than what the competition offered, and in the end it was just making plastic boxes with Intel processors and Microsoft software that was sent by mail. Dell went from being proprietary, meaning it had something that no one else was offering—in this case its business and distribution model—to commodity, meaning it was making a product that anyone else could duplicate. That's exactly what the competition did. Apple, on other hand, became even more proprietary, selling iPods, which became so popular and ubiquitous—the only MP3 player anyone wanted to own—that people, including my daughter, the one who pointed out this trend to me, were buying multiple iPods as fashion accessories. Meanwhile Apple came up with a totally revolutionary business model for selling music, movies, and television shows, the iTunes store, and then followed that with the incredibly successful iPhone.

It can be difficult to tell what companies are worth owning after their stocks have been savaged by a crash, but you want to find companies that have the ability to launch more and more proprietary products, stuff that can't be copied. That makes the company special and better than its competitors, especially when you're dealing with tech. Dell never really had that capacity. It was always going to become a commodity because it had no edge in innovation. Apple, as we've seen, had it in spades. Most of the tech stocks that got crushed from 2000 to 2003 never came back, and even Apple was worth selling at the top, but only so you could buy it back later at lower prices. Still, there are stocks that will get you back to even, stocks like Apple, and I'll teach you how to find them. For now you should understand that there are a lot more Dells than there are Apples.

Never be afraid to sell nearly everything when the market and the economy seem to be falling apart, but don't let that permanently blind you to the opportunities that are out there. They'll present themselves, believe me. Historically the best time to buy stocks has been when they're feared and hated, and the most dangerous times when they're worshipped. In 2009 we entered "fear and hatred" territory, and if you have money that you won't need in the near future, then it's probably a good idea to put it to work in stocks. You just have to find the right ones and be mindful that the market always overshoots and it could take years for it to recover from its recent trauma.

RULE 3: Skip the first four stages of portfolio grief: denial, anger, bargaining, and depression. When you know your stocks have been hammered and you're facing big losses, it's tempting to do just about anything to avoid acknowledging that fact. A lot of investors will go through something similar to the five stages of grief and end up wasting precious time that could be used to start cordoning off the damage. Listen, I know investing can be absolutely gut-wrenching. But it's better to face things head-on instead of embracing the usual dodges. Just ask the people who held on to all their tech stocks from 2000 to 2003, or those who decided to hold on to their stocks, instead of selling, as the S&P 500 took a 53 percent fall from its high in 2008 to its low in early 2009. These are periods that blew out a lot of people because they couldn't come to terms with the damage quickly and cut their losses before taking more of them.

First there's denial. That's when you stop opening your statements, turn off the TV, and stop checking up on your stocks on the Web because it's just too painful too watch. Totally natural response, but the longer you wait before even looking at your losses, the longer it will be before you can start hammering your portfolio back into shape. A lot of what I do on my television show, *Mad Money*, is to try to prevent people from drowning in denial by keeping it light and making sure the medicine tastes better on the way down so you stay engaged with your money. After denial comes anger, usually in the form of lashing out at whoever's handy, be it short-sellers, incompetent fat-cat executives, nefarious bankers or politicians, or a cheerleading media for your losses. You might be spot on, 100 percent correct, but getting angry is just a distraction. It won't bring your money back. Leave the anger to the professionals, like me. Believe me, if someone is to blame, they will be taken to task for it. There's a reason why we do an "Outrage of the Day" segment on my television show, *Mad Money,* and have a Wall of Shame where I hold up the mistakes of the very worst CEOs, true destroyers of value ranging from the criminally incompetent to the simply criminal. I believe calling out these people shames executives into better, more shareholder-friendly behavior, and much less of an executives-win, shareholders-lose attitude. Believe me, no one wants to be on that Wall of Shame, and many of the executives I have enshrined have begged me privately to take them down. I tell them, "Do better for shareholders, and I will."

Stage three is bargaining. This is a bad one. You wait and wait for the stock to come back to even so you won't have to sell it at a loss. Trust me, this isn't how you'll get there. In thirty years of investing I would say there's about a 75 percent chance that the stocks you think are going to get back to even never do; that's been my ratio, and I have invested in a lot of stocks during that period. I have maintained a great laboratory for successes as well as mistakes that you can learn from.

Next comes depression. Of course you're depressed, you just lost a lot of money. But at best self-pity is a waste of your time, and at worst you can feel like you don't have any control over what's happening. As I say on the show, stop sipping that cheap stock and get off the dirty linoleum floor! In every big downturn I have seen, huge swathes of losses could have been avoided as you suffered through each stage, to the point where, when you get to depression, you think that there's not much worth preserving and you stop looking entirely, which then produces another whole round of losses that you simply did not believe could still occur. Remember the lessons of Fannie Mae or General Motors: depression set in for many when the stocks went under $10, but the losses were humongous, cataclysmic even—think declines of 80 percent or more—after those two stocks crossed into the once unfashionable single-digit territory.

You do have control. You just have to take it. So skip the drama of stages one through four and move immediately to stage five: acceptance.

Go through your portfolio, assess the damage, and figure out which stocks should be jettisoned and which ones you can circle the wagons around as they go lower. Don't worry, I'll help you figure out what's worth saving and what should be dumped. I will give you the tools to help you tell damaged merchandise apart from damaged stocks. During the crash all stocks went down, but some had bad balance sheets while others were pristine. Some had outsized dividends that weren't real, and others had accidentally high dividends because their share prices had fallen so low, and they turned out to be home runs. In fact, they were so good that in the next chapter I'll explain to you how to identify these magnificent "accidental high-yielders," and how to tell the difference between safe and precarious dividends so that you can put my dividend strategy, one that proved to be incredibly effective, short and long term, to work for yourself.

RULE 4: To stop the bleeding, shun stocks that are "cheap." One of the most difficult things to grasp during a downturn when the economy is in the dumps is that cheap stocks just get cheaper. If you own a bunch of inexpensive names that keep getting hammered, let me explain why. And if you don't own any but you're tempted, understand that when the Dow has dropped thousands of points in a matter of months, listening to some guy on the TV screen telling you that this or that stock is cheap is going to get you killed. What the heck is cheap anyway? Do we want to own stocks that look cheap, or stocks that can go higher? When the market is taking a beating, lots of stocks can appear cheap using traditional metrics, but that doesn't mean they're worth owning. How cheap was GM at $5, Lehman at $7, Washington Mutual at $3, or AIG at $2 (before it declared a twenty-to-one reverse split to make it seem like it was worth more)? No stock is cheap if it's going lower.

The absolute worst reason to buy a stock during a big downturn is valuation. The analysts love to throw this one around—"we think this or that stock is a buy based on valuation. We like it because its price-to-earnings multiple is historically very low." You know what? In a market where stocks can get crushed almost indiscriminately, you need a much better reason than that for keeping something in your portfolio. Many people, including a lot of professionals, are fooled by this. I remember one of the best managers of the 1990s taking me aside in the summer of 2007 and telling me that the cheapest stocks in the market were Bear Stearns, Lehman Brothers, Fannie Mae, and Freddie Mac. Ultimately, Bear was rescued in what I called a takeunder, rather than a takeover, by JP Morgan, Lehman was allowed to collapse, and Fannie and Freddie were seized by the government. (In a takeover, the acquirer pays a premium. In a takeunder, the acquirer pays a discount.) How did this guy get it so wrong? Because he was looking at where these stocks had been versus where they were at the time, and said they were cheap. But all four of these stocks were cheap only if you were comparing them to their past stock prices. None of them was truly cheap when you looked at its underlying businesses, which were in endless, indeed catastrophic, decline. They were damaged merchandise, not just damaged stocks. But by certain metrics they "looked cheap" and offered a great temptation to a lot of investors. A company that's hemorrhaging money, that might not even be viable, isn't cheap, no matter how low its share price goes.

Valuing stocks in an environment where the economy is crumbling can be incredibly difficult. To understand how all the usual tools we use to figure out what a stock is worth can go haywire when the market is crazy or crashing, you need to know the way things ordinarily work. In normal times we try to value stocks by figuring out what their future profits will be, and then determining how much other investors will pay for those profits. In true Wall Street gibberish fashion, we call what we're willing to pay for those future profits the "multiple." On Wall Street, looking at the share price tells you nothing about a stock's valuation. General Mills (GIS) at $60 a share might actually be cheaper than Kellogg (K) at $40. The price is just the price, it's not the value, and I don't mean that in the sense of the old proverb "a fool knows the price of everything and the value of nothing." You simply can't compare share prices on an apples-to-apples basis. Different companies have different numbers of shares and they have different earnings per share, which is the most important fact for determining whether or not a stock is cheap. So we use the price-to-earnings multiple as the real apples-to-apples comparison, and most of the time it works.

The multiple is actually pretty simple when someone bothers to explain it to you, but many of the professionals on Wall Street have a vested interest in keeping you ignorant, either in order to collect your commissions or take a cut of the money you have under management. To value stocks and find the multiple we take the share price, P, and divide it by the earnings per share, E, and that gives you M, the price-to-earnings multiple. $P/E = M$. Or you can flip things around and say that the price equals the earnings times the multiple, $E \times M = P$. It's not even real math, just arithmetic, and normally it's what you want to look at to determine a stock's relative cheapness. Once you find the multiple, then you have to take other factors into account. The most important is a company's growth rate. Companies with higher, faster growth tend to be awarded higher multiples by investors. The reason? Because the multiple is a way of valuing stocks based on their future earnings, and companies with better earnings growth have more profits in the future. That's why a company like Apple trading at 20 times earnings might not necessarily be more expensive than Kellogg, which trades at 10 times earnings. The multiples are different, but the companies are different, too. Apple is a fast grower with proprietary products known for innovation, while Kellogg is a slow, consistent grower, with good brands but lots of competition, including private label store brands. The first kind of stock typically gets a higher multiple than the latter one. You also need to take into account a company's growth rate to value it properly. On *Mad Money* we use a stock's PEG, its price-to-earnings-to-growth rate. You arrive at that number by dividing a stock's multiple by its growth rate, and voilà, normally you get a number that ranges between 1 and 2. In ordinary circumstances, the stock of a healthy company that trades at less than 1 time its growth rate—meaning a stock with a PEG of less than 1—is cheap, and one that trades at more than twice its growth rate—meaning its PEG is over 2—is expensive.

You can value the entire market by slapping a multiple on the S&P 500. When stocks got incredibly cheap at the end of the bear market in 1973, they were trading at 7 times earnings—historically inexpensive. Right before the crash of 1987, multiples got really high. We were trading at 29 times earnings before that crash, and afterward the average stock in the S&P 500 was trading at just 14 times earnings. But these are just rules of thumb in the best of times. By itself, the multiple doesn't necessarily tell you much of anything. You can't just say, "The market's at such and such a multiple, and therefore you should buy or sell stocks." That's unhelpful reasoning, but we hear it all the time on television anyway. In November 2008, we heard endlessly that the market was at 14 times earnings, and that was supposed to entice us to buy because the multiple was so low or "cheap" historically. But future earnings collapsed so it didn't matter. The "cheap" market turned out to be plenty expensive. In a hideous bear market coupled with a miserable economy, the logic that normally governs valuations—all the stuff about price-to-earnings multiples—pretty much goes out the window for a lot of stocks. Investing in these times can make you feel like you're a pilot flying an airplane without any instruments, or driving a car with the dashboard ripped out. All the ordinary ways of judging a stock's relative cheapness—particularly the future earnings projections—become much less useful. An economy that declines relentlessly tends to play havoc with all companies' future earnings forecasts, even companies thought to be as recession proof as a Heinz (HNZ) or a Kraft (KFT), where consumers turned to the cheaper private-label supermarket brands or cut back in usage entirely. Just as you can keep staring at the place where your dashboard used to be and not be a better driver—in fact, you'll be worse because you're taking your eyes off the road—you can keep buying and selling stocks based on their valuation, as determined by their multiples, when those things no longer count, but it will make you a worse investor.

When the economy is deteriorating, for many companies the multiple becomes in fact one of the least reliable ways to measure value. Why? It all goes back to that original equation: the multiple times the earnings equals the price. For the multiple to have real meaning as a tool to value stocks, you have to know what the earnings will be in the future. And when the economy's rolling over but the analysts have yet to cut their earnings estimates aggressively, we have no idea about what the future earnings will be. So the multiple on earnings is not all that valuable if *future* earnings can't be predicted in any sound way. Instead of E times M equals P, it's X—as in, unknown, times M equals P—and you can't do anything with that equation except scratch your head. Good for an algebra lesson, but no good for picking stocks in a difficult earnings environment where most of the gains come from firing people.

This is especially true for cyclical stocks, companies that need a strong economy to make money, that maybe only break even when the economy's bad, or worse, swing to a loss, like U.S. Steel (X) or Ford. I say this as grizzled veteran of more than one recession. You'll see cyclical stocks trading at one or two times earnings, and you'll think that's cheap as can be—but in fact, that's when these stocks are at their most expensive. The multiple looks small only because the earnings estimates are too high, and when those estimates come down—and who knows how far they could fall—you'll know how wrong you were to think you'd found something inexpensive. I've seen all this happen before. Back in the 1980s, Bethlehem Steel went from trading at two times earnings—looks cheap—to huge losses in about a year, and it was a sell all the way down. Of course the two times earnings represented past earnings. In reality, Bethlehem Steel was selling at what turned out to be 25 times the next year's earnings as its profits fell off a cliff, and more than 50 times the year after that's earnings, until Bethlehem Steel's earnings and then ultimately Bethlehem Steel itself, once the second-largest steel company in the world, disappeared. Buy-and-forget wisdom surely let you down hard in that vicious example.

If you think estimate cuts are coming, you simply cannot rely on the price-to-earnings multiple. And even if you're looking at a more secular growth stock, meaning one that's less vulnerable to the slings and arrows of an outrageous economic downturn, don't think that a historically low multiple on that growth will be enough to save it. When everyone's selling everything, a low valuation won't stop the stock from going even lower. So if you own stocks purely because you think they're cheap based on earnings, and they're not working out, it might be time to cut your losses.

When the economy is going into a recession or is getting worse by the month, the crowd is often right, and the companies with the most consistent earnings make the best stocks, even as they will often seem to have astronomically high multiples relative to their growth rates. These safe stocks with consistent earnings, secular growth stocks, stocks of companies that grow independently of the economy, names like General Mills (GIS), Kellogg (K), Procter & Gamble (PG), Colgate (CL), Johnson & Johnson (JNJ), and Kimberly-Clark (KMB)—think Kleenex—held their value much better than the stocks of companies with less reliable profits, profits that varied wildly depending on the health of the economy, even as the economically sensitive or "cyclical" stocks, to use the authentic Wall Street jargon, had much lower multiples. That's not to say that, like the examples of Heinz and Kraft, these companies had no economic sensitivity; it is simply to remind you that they are harder to do without in tough times, or actually do better as people go out less and save money by eating at home. The multiple didn't mean anything for the cyclicals—the stocks that swing wildly in price depending on whether the economy is growing or contracting—because we had no idea what their earnings would be. For the stocks of companies that ply their trade in the aisles of your local supermarket or pharmacy, on the other hand, the secular growth companies, the multiple still meant something because we could much more accurately predict what their earnings would be. Their multiples just happened to be very high by historical standards because they represented safe havens in an unsafe market. Investors are willing to pay much more for consistent earners like General Mills or Colgate when the economy takes a turn for the worse because these stocks let them sleep soundly at night. You rarely have to worry about them pre-announcing much worse than expected earnings because of the weak economy—although their raw costs can cause problems for earnings, as was the case when oil skyrocketed in 2007 and in the first part of 2008—and investors are willing to pay up for that kind of safety. There are still plenty of ways for consistent earners to screw things up, and at times these stocks just go down less than more economically sensitive stocks, but a slowing economy doesn't tend to crush their earnings, and that makes them more predictable. And when the economy is stabilizing or getting better, as occurred after the March lows, these kinds of safety stocks fall out of favor and the market gravitates to recovery plays. I will spend much more time on those stocks later in this book.

RULE 5: Remember to look at the balance sheet. While credit conditions have improved greatly, thanks to the swift actions by Fed Chairman Ben Bernanke and Treasury Secretary Tim Geithner, we still need to be careful not to buy common stocks of companies with too much debt, especially if the debt comes due within the next eighteen months to two years. How do you spot a company with a lot of debt? Take a look at its balance sheet, something you can find on just about any stock website. If you want to, you can get the balance sheet, along with all the filings of every publicly traded American company, straight from the Securities and Exchange Commission by going to its website: www.sec.gov/edgar.shtml. This should be your source for all kinds of great information that's necessary to do your homework. A company's annual statements, the 10-K; its quarterly statements, the 10-Q—you must read these if you're going to invest in individual stocks. But for our purposes, right now, we're concerned with balance sheets because they can help us find the businesses that are in the most danger, which will allow you to sell their stocks before their situations get even worse. Look up any company's balance sheet. On the left hand side you'll see a list of its assets, and on the right hand side are its liabilities. We're interested in the liabilities, and specifically, the total current liabilities line. This tells you how much money a business has to pay out in the near future, to everyone from employees to the IRS to the holders of its debt. If this number is greater than the cash flow the company is expected to earn over the next year, then it's in big trouble.

Think about it like this—would you invest in a person who owes $3,000 a month on his MasterCard bill and has an income of only $5,000 a year? Of course not. Those interest payments add up to just about all of the person's after-tax income. And we're not even taking into account all of the ordinary expenses a person has, like feeding himself and paying the rent. Companies have bills, too, lots of them. Normally it's dangerous to get involved with a company that's heavily in debt, but when banks aren't lending, or are lending only to people and companies that don't need the money, these stocks become even more dangerous. Consider these companies like people who can't make their mortgage payments. In good times, a person might be able to refinance and get a new mortgage with a lower, more affordable interest rate. But when credit isn't flowing, when banks are raising their standards about whom they lend to, then good luck trying to refinance that mortgage. A publicly traded company with loads of debt has the exact same problems. You might lose your home and have to declare bankruptcy. A stock? Its prospects are even worse, because the stock you own is essentially the collateral for a company's debts. The stock, in this analogy, is the same as the homeowner's house. That's right, so if the business goes bankrupt, then the bondholders who own the company's debt take over, and you'll be lucky if they don't totally wipe out the value of its common stock, sending your shares straight to $0. You don't own a car that's been repossessed by the lender, and you don't own stock in a company that's been repossessed, because the company is now owned by the lenders. That's why you have to stay away from companies that need to borrow or simply have unsustainable amounts of debt when the credit spigot has been turned off and they will have a lot of trouble refinancing. Sometimes the only real hope to avoid bankruptcy for these companies is to issue a ton of new stock to pay down debt coming due. If you like this kind of company, please wait for the offering to buy, do not buy in the open market. You will end up paying too much money!

RULE 6: Investing is all about augmenting your paycheck. If you don't have a paycheck because you don't have a job, you've got bigger things to worry about than your portfolio. Our unemployment rate is the highest it has been in twenty-five years. Without a steady source of income, you're going to have to eat into the money that you want to be investing. Take a job, even one that pays poorly and you're massively overqualified for, even if only to keep up another source of income if you can. We can try to plug the holes in your portfolio all day, but if you have to spend that money to survive, you won't have time to reap serious gains.

And of course, there's the usual necessities. You need health and disability insurance before you need to own stocks. If you support a family, you'd better have a life insurance policy from an insurer that seems solvent before you start to worry about your investments. You shouldn't be investing in the stock market if you haven't covered the essentials. Your money can be put to better use.

Once you've made sure that you're protected and what's left of your portfolio is safe, we can focus on getting you back to even.

3

PUTTING THE PIECES BACK TOGETHER

If you have a portfolio that's been torn to shreds over the last two years, like most people there's no way you are going to make that money back overnight. Younger investors have a terrific opportunity to buy low, but that doesn't help if you intended to retire in a couple of years, or need the money now to pay for your kid's college education, as I do. I cannot promise you any quick and easy results. I don't have a simple gimmick that will allow you to make money without thinking, like the guys who spent years telling you to flip houses—oops—right into the teeth of the housing bust. I refuse to follow in the footsteps of other so-called experts who either tell you that investing can be boiled down to five easy steps or repeat endlessly that index funds are your only hope, and they're not much of one. How do those people live with themselves? Investing is messy and it's labor intensive. It takes hard work—homework, at least an hour a week spent researching every stock you own to make sure the fundamentals, meaning the facts about the underlying company and the economic backdrop, are still favorable. My methods, particularly in this book, aren't simple to execute. That doesn't mean you can't have fun doing it. There's a reason everyone on Wall Street calls it "the game," and I'll give you a hint: it's not because they don't take it seriously. No, it's because it can be "gamed." But I know how to win it, no matter what the odds, which is why I am confident I can get you back to even. I've been preaching this one-hour-per-position gospel for four years now on *Mad Money* and invariably people grouse that it is too much time to spend to be worth it. I come back and tell them that if you want to do better than everyone else, if you want to make investing a game of calculated risk instead of a gamble, take the time out to do it and do it right.

I am wary about making the process of rebuilding your lost wealth sound too easy. That will only cause you to be discouraged and maybe blow you out entirely when you're faced with any serious difficulties, and every investor will have to deal with those at some point or another, especially because the chaos of the world's economies will take years, not months, to sort out. So know that making enough money in the market to get your finances back to even is going to take a lot of effort and a good bit of time. Do not be impatient; we will get there.

I've told you what to steer clear of, the common mistakes investors make when they're down that you can now avoid, and what you need to do to stop the bleeding in your portfolio if it's still hemorrhaging money. Now we get to the real work: how to actively start making money again. That means confronting a question that all investors deal with, but which poses less of a problem when your portfolio hasn't been hammered and you don't desperately need to make money, and make it fast, in order to maintain your standard of living and continue to be able to afford dozens of other things of importance to you and your family, to say nothing of pure necessities. What's the issue? There are two basic orientations—I wouldn't even go so far as to call them goals—that investors can have toward their money: capital preservation or capital appreciation, capital being a fancy-schmancy word for money. You invest your capital to create even more money. When you're in capital preservation mode, you take few risks and try simply to hang on to the money you have, perhaps investing it so that it grows faster than inflation, perhaps just being content that it doesn't go down! The idea behind capital preservation is to let your money live to fight another day. Capital appreciation mode, on the other hand, is all about investing aggressively, taking chances and making as much money as you possibly can. Our goal is to help get you back to even, and to do it well before you'd get there by owning an index fund, if you would get there at all, given that method of investment's lackluster performance over the last decade (if you call making no money at all an investment). You might think we should err on the side of capital appreciation, right? Maybe not. It takes money to make money, and if you've already lost quite a bit courtesy of the crash, then you need to be extra careful with the money you have left, to invest in stocks. You'll have to strike a balance between taking the necessary risks to get back to even—capital appreciation—and keeping enough of your capital out of harm's way—capital preservation—so that you don't destroy the best tool you have for making more money, the cash you can currently spare for stocks.

I still firmly believe that the best way for you to rebuild your wealth, the thing you should focus most of your efforts on, is building a diversified portfolio of the best stocks for you, using all of the important disciplines and tricks that make someone a good investor and a good trader. That's not the only thing, not by a long shot, but it gives you the best chance of restoring what you've lost and then raking in even more. Of course, stocks are what I know best, so it's possible that I'm a little biased, but they worked for me and I've seen them work for countless others, and I know how to make them work for you. After the experience of the crash, I'm sure that can be pretty hard for many of you to believe. I get it. Even though picking the right stocks can get you back to even and hopefully, make you incredibly wealthy, actually pulling that off seems far more difficult today than it did just a couple of years ago. So let me give you what may be the best argument for spending your time picking stocks, figuring out which ones will work in the new environment, and using the right strategies to buy and sell them.

Remember, I am not talking about buying an index fund filled with stocks that do and don't pay dividends, selected by a group of anonymous people who aren't picking them for their attractive growth and dividend characteristics but because they are "representative" of the "weightings" of stocks, meaning how many publicly traded stocks there are in different industries. A buy-and-hold strategy of the five hundred stocks in the Standard & Poor's index no longer can claim the title of long-term winner of all asset classes. U.S. Treasury bonds owned for twenty-five years have taken that title away. That's another reason why we don't believe in buy and hold, and instead believe in buy and homework, in buying as low as we can and selling as high as we can, even if that smacks of the dirtiest word in the investment lexicon, *trading*! Still, after a decade where stocks did nothing, a lost decade for investors, the theoretical long-term superiority of stocks over other asset classes is pretty cold comfort. But you *can* control your own portfolio. The real magic of stocks is that while you may make mistakes, and you may lose some money, you will always be in the driver's seat. When it comes to your finances, how many things can you really say that about? If the crash of 2008–2009 coupled with the most crippling economic slowdown since the Great Depression has shown us anything, it's that we're all a lot less financially secure than we'd ever imagined. Jobs lost, pensions slashed, home values eviscerated, 401(k) plans and IRAs cut in half if you weren't careful, out-of-control credit-card bills, the list goes on. Outside of the stock market, you can do only so much to take control of your money. You have to pay your bills. You may be great at your job, but the chances of getting a huge raise are slim, especially in this lousy job market, and even if you get a big one it still wouldn't match what you can make in stocks if you know what you're doing, especially after the new tax increases that are coming. You'd be crazy not to be worried about your or your family's economic security at a time like this.

Investing in stocks gives you the chance to actually make a difference, to truly manage your financial destiny. You can be proactive. You don't have to sit around feeling powerless as you get hit with one financial misfortune after another. I'm not going to tell you that it's more important to own stocks than it is to have health and disability insurance. That would be reckless of me. Making sure you rein in your spending and are able to save a chunk of your paycheck every week is crucial, too. But after you've found the best insurance policy and put together a reasonable budget, what else can you really do on those fronts? When you invest, the time and effort you put into researching your stocks pays off. That's been demonstrated countless times by great investors who have the time and inclination to stay with winners and prune losers. You will hear it from callers to *Mad Money* every night, and those callers are unscreened. They have taken control of their finances and getting back to even by the day. You'll hear their unprompted testimonials nightly. You want to get back to even? Well the stock market gives you a chance to really work at it and succeed.

And I do mean work. There are different ways for you to invest, different levels of intensity depending on how much time a person has to dedicate to stocks. And they are not all equal. Some are a whole lot more equal than others, to paraphrase George Orwell's *Animal Farm*. How much time and effort you put into investing will directly impact how long it takes for you to get back to even. As with any other endeavor in life, the more work you put in, the more you'll get out of it. Yet somehow this completely commonsense observation is totally alien to most of the investing community and the majority of the media pundits, who liked to poke fun, endlessly, about your and my ability to make more money than a passive strategy, that is, an index fund. There are the buy-and-hold ideologues who believe the best money manager is the person who does the least active actual managing of money. They are wrong, as we now know from the last decade of buy-and-hold investing.

Pay Attention to Price

When I talk about buy-and-homework, I mean a whole lot more than just doing the research to identify some stocks that are worth owning, and then following that up every week to make sure the thesis behind each of those stocks, the reason you liked it in the first place, is still intact. Most people, and most professionals, will then tell you to take a hands-off approach once you've made your purchase. As long as a stock's long-term prospects are still sound, then, according to them, you don't have to worry about any short-term gyrations in the market that propel your stocks higher or lower. In fact, and this is the part that makes absolutely no sense to me, they say that the way to make the most money is precisely by ignoring any short-term fluctuations in stock prices. These "seers" are willing to let you take any amount of pain, any beating the market can deliver, even if it means no gain. They are terrible dentists who don't use Novocaine; they drill and drill and accomplish nothing, then tell you that you deserve your punishment. We would never tolerate their logic in any other endeavor save investing, and in Cramerica we don't tolerate it at all.

This pain-but-no-realized-gain strategy seems insane to me because my investing philosophy is all about taking advantage of those short-term fluctuations to buy the stocks I like at cheaper prices than I should have any right to be able to get, and to sell them when they are driven quickly to unrealistically higher prices than I expect or deserve to get. It's one of the basic strategies that allowed me to make fortunes for myself and my already rich clients at my old hedge fund, but somehow it, too, is heretical, as if the bank you put your winnings in knows the difference between short- and long-term gains and only lets you deposit those taken over years, not months or days. I am constantly berated by critics of my television show and readers of my numerous daily postings on TheStreet.com for telling people to ring the register on a stock, meaning sell some of it, that I had previously recommended or said positive things about. What these bizarrely angry critics don't understand, along with most of the people who are trying to give you investment advice, is the notion that price matters. If I like Visa (V) at $50, and then it goes to $65, should I still feel the same way about it? How does that make any sense? My hate mail correspondents truly do not understand that the risk profile of an investment in Visa changes when its stock jumps 15 points. They are only seeing Visa the well-run, well-oiled machine of a company, not a stock that just spiked too high too quickly to be sustainable, and they're not alone in making this kind of mistake. The Internet is practically filled to bursting with countless websites that exist solely to tell the world how I am a terrible person who gives criminally bad financial advice. I have to believe, if only to preserve my sanity, that a lot of the hate springs from the fact that I often do things like praise Visa's fundamentals and recommend its stock at $50, only to tell people to sell shortly thereafter when the stock hits $65. That leads too many people to think I'm turning my back on Visa the company when I say to sell the stock, but the stock and the company are not the same thing. (Some viewers despise that register-ringing button I have, third in on the top row of my soundboard next to the bull and the bear on *Mad Money*. I keep it third from the left, in the most prominent position on my board, because I want to remind myself to hit it as often as we have big profits together, so as never to get greedy. That's why the pig-squeal button is right below it and the guillotine sound right below that. The sequence must be obeyed at all times!)

Stocks are no different from any other kind of merchandise, yet somehow the expectation is that once you like a stock, you should like it regardless of price. I'm always prepared to get off the bandwagon when a stock has become too expensive for my taste, particularly if it's been carried away by a moment of reckless market enthusiasm.

Instead of thinking of Visa as a stock, let's think of it as a nice sweater that catches your eye at the mall. You go to the store, look at the $50 price tag, decide that's a fair price to pay, and take it home with you. But what if you went back the next day, and all of a sudden that same sweater was selling for $65? Would you still pay for it?

Maybe, but you would have to think about it, because no one likes paying more money for the same piece of merchandise. That's the logic we apply to clothing, houses, cars, television sets, widgets, but stocks we're supposed to like the same at any price? Wrong. There is one big difference between shopping for shares of Visa in the stock market and shopping for a sweater in the mall: in the market you get a different price every day, allowing you to buy Visa when it's a bargain and sell it much higher, as long as you're patient and you pay attention. The market is Macy's on steroids; sale today, regular price tomorrow, basement price the day after, and then severe markup the day after that. At Macy's we would know to stay away from the markup days and buy on the basement days, saving tens of dollars. Why shouldn't we do the same thing with stocks?

There are two ways you can approach your portfolio. You can listen to the experts who tell you to ignore short-term changes in price, or you can listen to me. Before the crash, I would have told you that the first strategy, while nowhere near as good as the second, would still allow you to make money, although you might have trouble beating the market. But now? If you're struggling to get back to even, I don't see how you can justify holding a stock through a short-term swing lower that you saw coming after a huge and unjustified leap up. When you desperately need to preserve every penny of capital you have left, any loss that can be avoided should *and must* be avoided, even if we're only talking about sidestepping a relatively minor 5–7 percent decline. Then you can buy back the stock at a lower price. Making quick trades in and out of some of a stock that you consider a long-term investment may not feel like it's your style, but style shouldn't matter when you're at the financial equivalent of DEFCON 2, if not DEFCON 1.

In practical terms this means that you always have to keep an eye on the prices of stocks you own or might want to own so that you can actively buy and sell them as they become cheaper or more expensive. You don't have to be some sort of furious day-trader, or any kind of trader at all, even though many supposed experts who don't truly understand the market would call this rapid-fire trading. I see this as active, intelligent investing. What's the point of keeping your money in stocks if you aren't trying to take advantage of the regular opportunities the market always throws your way? Standing pat through a beating that takes you from big gains to big losses is simply no longer a tolerable regime. You can't do it and get back to even, regardless of the taxman or the possibility of momentarily higher prices.

I am simply talking about the level of personal investment you need to make your stock market investments pay off. I will show you how to put together what we can call your "getting back to even" portfolio. How to find the right stocks, how to know when to hold 'em and know when to fold 'em, how to understand the many things that have changed about the market, and how to recognize those things that have stayed the same. And believe me, it is a vastly changed market from the days before the crash.

Go Back to Portfolio Basics to Get Back to Even

You have to find the right stocks and analyze them before you can take advantage of prices that are too low or too high. And you have to understand how a portfolio of stocks is supposed to fit together before you can run off and start buying things. Good stock picking never happens in a vacuum. There's the purely historical context to keep in mind, and a lot has changed on that front in the wake of the most calamitous crash since 1929. The market has now stabilized and I have no doubt that the worst is behind us, but the trauma of the crash will undoubtedly change the way stocks trade for years, if not decades to come, so we must adapt accordingly. The essence of investing is flexibility. Losses are your enemy. The enemy must be avoided or beaten. The market is more dynamic and fluid than ever, so we have to be as well. How should you approach stock picking and portfolio building in this new environment?

First off, it almost goes without saying that your situation in life— your age, your family, how much money you have, how much longer you plan on working—will dictate your goals and your risk profile (how much you are willing to lose) and depending on your circumstances you'll want to adopt different strategies and favor different kinds of stocks. But there are some basic principles for managing your money that, no matter where you are in your life, you'll have to use if you want to stand a chance of getting back to even. I'll explain how to strategize depending on where you are personally later in the book. Right now I just want to give you the basic implements, tools, and tactics that you're going to need.

Some things don't change no matter how crazy or horrible the market becomes. Those of you who are familiar with my earlier books or my television show have heard some of this before, but it bears repeating here. If you're going to manage your own money, then you must maintain a diversified portfolio of stocks. I will shout this point because *diversification is the single most important key to staying in the game*. You violate it, and you will not be able to take advantage of the good times that will inevitably occur again. Why not? Either because you will have lost so much of your remaining capital by making undiversified bets, or, more likely, because even the Dalai Lama lacks the inner peace and emotional fortitude to stay in the game after taking the kind of losses that are practically inevitable when you invest in an undiversified portfolio of stocks. In your eyes diversification may prolong the time it takes to get back to even, a ball and chain to your leg as you race to rebuild capital. But believe me, without diversification, just throw the book away. It ain't going to happen. You are not getting back to even with that attitude.

All of your stock picks, every purchase or sale you make, should be evaluated through the lens of diversification. You'll hear this term thrown around a lot because it is so important, but sadly, not many people truly seem to understand it. Diversification is one of those things that sounds simple in theory but can be hard to implement in practice. At bottom it's about not putting all of your eggs in one basket. It's a cliché—what could be simpler than that? You'd be surprised. Keeping your portfolio diversified is not as uncomplicated as it looks, and the financial consequences of getting it wrong could be catastrophic. That's why every Wednesday night on *Mad Money* I play a game called "Am I Diversified," in which viewers call in and tell me their five largest holdings, so I can tell them whether their portfolios are diversified, and if not, which stocks to sell and what to replace them with in order to get there. I keep playing it because people keep flunking it, including longtime viewers. They keep confusing the sectors the companies they own are in; they keep missing that some sectors trade with others, like the drillers and the oils, or the foods and the beverages. They often don't even seem to understand what a company does. An aerospace company *is* a defense company. A software company and a hardware company are *both* tech companies and trade together. Drugs and hospitals may not *seem* to be the same, but it doesn't matter. They trade the *same* way. When everyone gets hallelujah and not the buzzer button, I will quit this game. But I have been playing it ever since my radio show *Real Money* started in 2001 and callers still regularly flunk the diversification test.

At the most basic level, having a diversified portfolio means owning stocks that don't overlap, so that if something happens to cause one of them to go down hard the rest will remain relatively unscathed or even go higher. You want to own the stocks of companies that belong to unrelated segments of the economy, or sectors. What's a sector? Health care, real estate, energy, technology, raw materials, industrial manufacturing, and finance all fit the bill. So do aerospace, infrastructure, oils and oil drilling, retail, and restaurants. Look at how each company in your portfolio makes its money and make sure there's no close overlap. (The annual report will break down the end markets, the customers, for you in a very easy and readable fashion. Make sure you read the annual report, or 10K, before pulling the trigger.) Look at how each stock has performed historically and try to find ones that tend not to go up or down at the same time. My rule is that you should never have more than 20 percent of your portfolio in any single sector, because if you concentrate any more of your money in the same area then all it will take to knock you out of the game is for a single calamity to befall that one sector, and believe me, you do not want to take those odds. What qualifies as a calamity? How about government cutbacks for health care or defense, higher gasoline prices that cause a slowing in retail, soaring foreclosure rates ruining real estate and banking, or a cessation of Chinese buying that devastates the raw materials companies. All of these plagues visited the stock market in 2007, 2008, or 2009, and if you had too much money invested in the afflicted sectors because you scorned diversification, you could have lost a fortune. These days we don't have fortunes to lose anymore, so you have to be especially careful.

Protect Your Portfolio with Gold and Humility

For those of you who have taken enormous losses, diversification goes a long way toward protecting the capital you have left without creating a situation where it's harder for you to make money. For example, I think it's a good idea for everyone's portfolio to have some exposure to gold. Why? Because gold prices tend to rise in times of chaos, uncertainty, and inflation, all things that usually cause other stocks to go lower. You can think of your gold position as a kind of insurance for your portfolio, something that will pay off in case everything else you own gets shredded. You might not want to ever bet against yourself, but what do you think you are doing with health insurance or homeowner's insurance or car insurance? Gold performs the same function for the rest of your portfolio; it pays off when those others fail you. It provides some protection for your limited and oh-so-precious capital. Of course, there are better places to invest your money than gold. I can think of numerous sectors that I would rather concentrate on because I think the potential upside is much greater, sectors that would probably make you much more money than you'd get from buying gold. Still, those others insure nothing; gold insures against everything from world chaos and calamity—the true accidents of history—to inflation, something that everyone expects will happen ultimately with all of these trillions of dollars in stimulus spending issued by governments worldwide. You don't necessarily make money from insurance; it just preserves what you have.

So what exactly does this precious metal have going for it, specifically when it comes to your holdings, other than being a shiny form of theoretical insurance? Bizarrely enough, gold is a necessity, at least when it comes to putting together a portfolio after losing a great deal of money. It helps you deal with the central difficulty of trying to get back to even by investing: the precarious balance between the need to risk your capital so you can rebuild your wealth—capital appreciation—and the need to protect your capital from an overabundance of risk that could wipe it out entirely so you don't lose your most effective tool for generating wealth—capital preservation. Having some gold in your portfolio takes care of some of the capital preservation side by acting as a hedge against your stocks falling. Think hedge as in "hedging your bets"; it is an investment that reduces your risk of losing money if the price of a given asset or group of assets, such as stocks, declines. Gold offsets losses in the rest of your portfolio because the same things that drive most stocks down tend to send gold prices up. Using gold as a hedge makes it relatively safer for you to be more aggressive with the rest of your stock picks. This doesn't solve the getting-back-to-even problem, but it's a big step in the right direction.

What's the best way to own gold? I like an exchange-traded fund, or ETF, called SPDR Gold Shares but mostly known by its symbol GLD, that owns the metal and does a terrific job of tracking its price. You could conceivably contact your broker and buy bullion, the actual physical bars of gold (not to be confused with the bouillon cubes I like in my soup). When I worked at Goldman Sachs as a broker, I sold a lot of this stuff and even sent it right to a depository bank for you, so you didn't have to worry about things like storage, insurance, or transportation. Buying bullion only makes sense for investors who have lots of money and can afford to buy gold in bulk and pay to store it. If you want something in a different price range, you can buy gold coins, but be sure you're only paying for the metal, not some kind of collector's item. The safest and smartest way to go would be with the American Gold Eagle coin issued by the United States Mint. Not only is the market for this particular coin very liquid, making it easy to sell for the full value of the metal it contains, but you can also use these coins to fund your IRA. These physical methods all have security issues that the gold ETF, the GLD, doesn't have, which is why I am partial to GLD, but the really paranoid among you, the ones who worry about the security of securities, should go the actual bullion route.

You could also own the stocks of gold miners like Agnico-Eagle (AEM) or Eldorado Gold (EGO), my two favorites in the group. As stocks, I think the best gold miners can make a lot of sense, but as hedges against global turmoil or inflation to offset the risk in your portfolio, you're better off with the GLD or the actual metal. Remember, we like that gold prices go up when many other stocks go down, but the stocks of gold miners are controlled by more than just the price of the commodity. They have debts, they have exploration costs, they have management teams that can mess up their companies in countless different ways. In short, they're public companies, and that's how they trade, not like mirror images of the commodity, which is what we want in our diversified getting-back-to-even portfolio. Why Agnico-Eagle? Because it has long-lived assets; the company is sitting on enough gold in the ground to last for twenty years without running out. Those same assets are also geographically stable, since its mines are located either in countries that are friendly with the United States and Canada, where Agnico-Eagle is headquartered, or in the United States and Canada themselves. You have no reason to fear that any of this company's properties will be expropriated by some tin-pot dictator or aspiring latter-day Salvador Allende, which is more than can be said for a number of other gold miners. Agnico-Eagle also has among the lowest extraction costs—which dictate how much profit is left after they mine the gold—save Eldorado, $300 an ounce for AEM versus roughly $280 an ounce for EGO, making them the lowest-cost producers by a mile. And finally, Agnico-Eagle is the rare gold miner that has repeatedly paid a dividend, and it's committed to raising that dividend every year, which gives it an added kicker over the bullion. Agnico-Eagle will pay you to own its stock. Try getting that deal from a lump of metal. What about Eldorado? It's a cheap producer, but it lacks Agnico-Eagle's stability, its dividend, and its philosophy of returning profits to shareholders, which is why I prefer Agnico-Eagle as my second choice after GLD to provide insurance for all of the other stocks in your diversified, getting-back-to-even portfolio.

People are always asking me how many stocks they should own. It's a question that's all about diversification, whether the people asking know it or not. I tell them between five to ten stocks will do the trick. Five is the absolute minimum number of stocks you can own and still be diversified. I think it's a bad idea for an ordinary individual investor to own more than ten stocks, because my method requires that you spend at least one hour a week per stock doing homework. Keeping track of more than ten stocks is like having a part-time job, and there's absolutely no reason for that. After you get to nine or ten stocks, owning more does very little to improve your chances of making money. Professionals can and should do it, but investing is what they do for a living. It's their job to do hours of homework every day. For you, it doesn't make sense. When you have more bets on the table it's much harder for you to keep track of them. And the added benefit, in terms of diversification, of owning five or ten more stocks that might turn out to be winners is more than canceled out by the detrimental effect of having to divide your attention among too many companies. With every additional stock you buy, you have less time and energy to focus on all the others. At that point you're practically a mutual fund without the exorbitant fees. Better to stick with five to ten names that you know very well and take the time to keep track of them.

The need for diversification is about as conventional as the conventional wisdom gets, but it still rankles many people's sensibilities. After all, if you believe that one sector is about to go on a tear, a real ripsnorter of a rally, then why on earth would you try to avoid having too much exposure to it? How can you have too much of something that's on fire? Shouldn't you be more worried about having too little exposure and missing the move? Take the oil stocks, for example, as they went on their tremendous multiyear run thanks to the soaring price of crude. You could have racked up truly colossal gains for years if you threw diversification to the wind and invested half or even all of your money in a big integrated oil company such as Chevron (CVX) or Conoco (COP), an oil service name like Schlumberger (SLB), and a driller like Transocean (RIG). And then you would have gotten smashed to pieces when oil prices took a nosedive in the second half of 2008. A lot of big, sophisticated hedge funds made exactly this bet, and some of them even went under because the losses were so bad. I know—I was too heavily invested in oil and gas and drilling during the summer of 2008 for ActionAlertsPlus.com, my charitable trust. While I preach diversification from the rooftops, I failed to see that not only would oil and oil service and natural gas companies trade together, but so too would the stocks of solar, infrastructure, agriculture, coal, and nuclear power companies. For this transgression against true diversification, I got hit worse than I care to talk about, although my charitable trust still outperformed the averages because I recognized what is known as "overexposure" to one sector before it was too late. I guess Mae West was wrong—too much of a good thing doesn't sound particularly wonderful.

There's always the temptation to invest heavily in what's hot, and that's especially the case when you're down big and hoping to recover your losses quickly. I won't say it's impossible. Maybe you'll get lucky. But it's more likely that your stocks will blow up in your face. You won't get back to even by taking unnecessary risks. Just imagine the shellacking you would have taken if you had concentrated your money in the financials in 2007 and 2008, betting that they represented "extreme value." All you got were extreme losses! Nobody really believes they're dumb enough to do something that boneheaded, but we all get things wrong, sometimes spectacularly wrong, and some of the so-called smartest investors in the world got this group really wrong, ignoring all diversification warnings to buy something that seemed so historically cheap at the time. Many of them and their firms are no longer in business simply because they didn't heed this simple rule of diversification. Believe me, I have debriefed enough of them; all they can talk about is how could they have been so silly to think they could buck the most imperative principle of investing?

One of the most important determinants to getting back to even is whether or not you prepare ahead of time to control the inevitable damage that will come even as or perhaps because the world's leaders are trying to put an end to the globe's economic decline. The best way to do that is through diversification.

I am not saying that you have to *equal-weight* every sector you own, a little piece of Wall Street argot meaning each sector takes up the same percentage of your portfolio. That's just silly. If you think technology stocks will outperform the rest of the market, then by all means, own more tech than any other sector. Just don't make it more than 20 percent of the money you have invested in stocks.

There is really no excuse for not being diversified, and that's even truer after your investments have taken huge losses. The money you can spare to invest in the stock market is a precious and scarce resource. It's the best tool you have to get your feet back on the path to prosperity so it must be protected carefully. It's cash that you worked hard to earn. Then you sacrificed near-term material comfort in order to save it so you could have some capital with which to invest. Odds are you've already lost plenty in the crash, and it would be a tragedy if you lost even more because you put your stock eggs in too few baskets and they cracked.

Think about it like this: diversification is all about humility. And despite the cartoonish, if often justified, portrayal of Wall Street money managers as arrogant know-it-alls, humility is one of the most important characteristics of a successful investor. Even the best money managers will make a lot of bad calls. You don't need to bat anywhere near 1,000 to do really well in the market. In fact, as long as you limit your losses by selling your bad picks quickly and the gains from your good picks are substantial, then you can be wrong more often than you're right and still make plenty of money. Letting your winners run, cutting your losses, and keeping your portfolio diversified are the ways of compensating for the fact that you're fallible—that you're human—by taking the vicissitudes of the market into account in advance. The case for taking a humble approach to stocks has never been stronger, especially given how few people actually foresaw the crash of 2008 and 2009, the biggest stock market event of the last eighty years. Or think about the even smaller percentage of investors who got the timing of the crash right—the doomsayers who were calling for a stock market collapse since 2005 or 2006 and consequently missed out on one of the greatest bull markets in history don't really count. In this game it's easy to be wrong, which is why preparing for when you're wrong is nearly as important as being right.

Say you believe that the economy is on the verge of a turnaround and the demand for cars will soon pick up, so you buy an automaker like Ford (F) or Toyota (TM). Since you know the rules and keep your portfolio diversified, you also own General Mills (GIS), the kind of consistent secular growth name that goes higher during a recession as investors flee to it for safety and consistency but underperforms when the economy is in better shape because then the big money is more interested in owning sexier cyclical stocks with torrid earnings growth. If your automaker thesis turns out to be right, then you rack up a big gain in Ford or Toyota, and General Mills languishes, while you pick up its nice dividend, which it boosts pretty much every year, by the way. But what happens if you're wrong and instead of a turn the economy nosedives into an even worse recession? Then you're getting killed in Ford or Toyota, but that pain is lessened by the fact that you could be making money in, or not getting hurt badly in, General Mills. That's what diversification does for you. If you had instead doubled down on the automakers without owning any defensive, recession-resistant stocks, any secular growers, then your losses would have been even larger and your gains nonexistent. Trying to be right with your stock picks is not enough to get you back to even; again, you also have to be prepared for when you're wrong, even if it means your winners make you less money. The amount of money you save by containing your losses will more than make up for it in the long run, and probably well before then. And you'll stay in the game for the inevitable better times to come. As the great Mark Twain said, it always *does* stop raining.

Now I would be remiss if I didn't mention that diversification is about a whole lot more than stocks. And in fact, one of the most important reminders from the crash was that it's important to be diversified among different asset classes as well, which is why I advocate the purchase of gold or the GLD ETF. Simply owning stocks and diversifying by sector did you little good when the market fell apart in 2008 and the beginning of 2009. When hordes of investors are selling stocks as an asset class, pretty much every sector is in trouble. I may be a total stock junkie, but that's one problem for which stocks are clearly not the solution. Where else can you invest to diversify across asset classes? There's always real estate, and while housing has been the bane of our economic existence for more than two years, I now feel that some of the best opportunities out there are in residential real estate thanks to the enormous declines in home prices across the country. Bonds of all kinds are very important—Treasurys, corporates, including the high-yielding variety, especially for your retirement portfolio, two things I'll discuss in more detail later. (Municipal bonds, as long as they are backed by government obligations to raise taxes, and not private entities' abilities to raise money, are great for non-tax-exempt accounts that you might have for retirement; I own them because my contract with CNBC does not allow me to own stocks, a restriction partially stemming from *Mad Money*'s market-moving abilities.)

For now, though, we're just focused on the fundamental principles, ideas, and tools you'll need to know in order to put together a portfolio that can help you make back what you've lost. Don't think of your portfolio as a collection of individual stocks, each one independent of all the others. To paraphrase the excruciatingly boring poet John Donne—and I hope get the attention of any of you who might be English teachers—no stock is an island. At least, not when it's part of your portfolio. Oh, and for the more pop-cultured among you, stocks don't feel pain like islands, but you cry if they lose you money, to stretch Simon & Garfunkel's lyrics. While you may want to own different kinds of stocks depending on your age and tolerance for risk, each stock should play a role in your portfolio. Many will simply give you exposure to industries that are in favor and going higher. But others, like the GLD for gold, will provide insurance, the stocks that go up when the rest of your portfolio goes down.

What about the actual process of picking stocks to fill out your portfolio? In later chapters I'll go over various types of stocks that I find appealing in the postcrash environment, and the unique types of homework each requires. First we should concentrate on the more general aspects of stock selection to help get you back to even, such as what determines stock prices, and how you can take advantage of big money, the guys who run the mutual funds and the hedge funds, either by running circles around the stocks they want to buy or taking a longer approach and looking for bargains among the stocks they crush and leave by the wayside. Before I can teach you how to do any of this the right way, you may need to unlearn a lot of what you believe about stocks. There is nothing wrong with being ignorant about the market or confused by it, but being misinformed can be quite perilous to your financial health.

The Wrong Way to Look at Companies and Their Stocks

Perhaps the most widespread misconception about picking your own stocks is that it primarily concerns making predictions about the future. Most people, including a lot of professionals, think the process looks something like this: You make a prediction about what's going to happen in the world; it could be regarding what the economic environment will look like or something more company-specific, such as a good earnings report. Then you buy some stock or group of stocks based on that prediction, and if you're right, you will make money. Good investors, in this misguided view, are the people who can best anticipate the future. Just about everybody assumes that this is how investing works. But this conception of stock picking represents only one component, really a fraction of the work that needs to be done, and it's a bad way to think about even this particular component of investing. To me this prediction method smacks of gambling, and we are about taking calculated risks in getting back to even, not gambling.

Making predictions about the future is not synonymous with picking stocks. There are many more considerations than just "what's going to happen?" Think about what we're trying to accomplish. We want to design a portfolio that can help you recover from serious losses and then keep on making more money so that you can, at the very least, maintain the standard of living you always expected for yourself and your family, until the crash so rudely interrupted your plans. To do that, you have to think less in terms of predictions and more in terms of probabilities and patterns. We diversify, for example, because we recognize the fairly strong probability that any given sector could implode and the inevitable fact that some of our stock picks will be wrong. When we pick individual stocks we also want to do that with an eye toward minimizing how much money we could lose if the stock turns out to be a dud.

Don't try to be an oracle. The whole notion of accurately deducing what companies will do in the future as the key to making money is based on a faulty premise: that a stock is the same as the underlying company, and that a stock's performance is inextricably linked to and indeed largely determined by that company's fundamentals. That's not true, even if intuitively it seems as though it should be. I cannot stress this point enough: stock prices at times, particularly at times of stress for the stock market and the economy, can disconnect radically from the underlying fundamentals. When you see a stock rallying, don't assume that it must be because of something good that happened at the company. And when a company comes out with good or bad news, don't expect the stock will react the way you think. You can see stocks soar off terrible earnings reports, while others founder despite putting up magnificent results. There are plenty of good companies with bad stocks out there, not to mention bad companies with stocks that are better than they have any right to be. Don't get me wrong, over the long term the fundamentals can matter, which is why I insist that you spend so much time studying them in your homework. But "long term" could mean decades, and many of you don't have decades to get back to even.

If the Fundamentals Aren't Everything, What Are They?

The fact that virtually every stock will come unglued from the underlying company's fundamentals should be taken as a given, especially in light of the fact that so many stocks, representing companies good and bad, hit multiyear lows in October 2008 because of the garden-variety depression brought about by the collapse of Lehman Brothers. How can I tell you that stocks can trade separately from companies' fortunes and also tell you that it's essential to study the fundamentals, mandating one hour of homework per stock per week? If the fundamentals don't determine a stock's short-term performance—*short-term* in this case meaning between a year and eighteen months—if they're just one of many factors, why spend so much time reading conference-call transcripts and quarterly filings to keep current with the company? How does that help you at all when there are other, more important determinants of where a stock is going? Shouldn't you be studying those things instead?

Sure, to the extent it's possible. I'll explain the main driving force behind stock movements in a moment, but we need to work through these ideas first so you understand not just how to research and analyze a company's fundamentals, but also why you're doing it. The homework will bore many of you; there's no getting around that. I've spent years trying to make it more interesting and I think I've shown

I will do anything to keep investors engaged, especially on *Mad Money*. I have come out onto the set while wearing a diaper to get you to buy Kimberly-Clark. I've eaten Frosted Flakes doused with beer to get you to buy Anheuser Busch. I've dressed in farmer outfits to intrigue you to look into Archer Daniels Midland or Monsanto, the seed company. I can't even put a figure on how many dollars' worth of expensive gizmos I've wrecked or how many pyramids of merchandise I have destroyed. I invoke has-been, one-hit-wonder rappers, as well as virtuosos like Biggie Smalls. So I am not concerned that too many of you will skip the homework because you lack the proper motivation, interest, or enthusiasm. Believe me, I will make this stuff entertaining for you. We have ways of making you motivated . . .

No, what worries me is something new, that after nearly two years of massive, gut-wrenching losses, you'll either be tempted to cut corners in order to make it feel like you're speeding up the process of rebuilding your lost wealth, even as that feeling is totally illusory, or you'll be so disillusioned and fatalistic about your ability to make your investments work that the homework will seem pointless. When you lose so much money in such a short period of time and know that millions of others are in the same boat with you, it would be a little unnatural if you didn't have one of those reactions. But if you want to get back all the money that's been lost, dealing with emotional liabilities that put you off your game is every bit as much a part of the process as listening to a company's quarterly conference call. Everyone who manages their own money is constantly bombarded by emotionally driven instincts, which are almost always incredibly harmful. Panic? Euphoria? Fear? Greed? Not helpful. Good investors learn how to repress their feelings.

Homework is by far the most onerous and for most folks the least interesting part of the process of investing. Most of the people who write books on investing make the mistake I mentioned earlier of assuming that a company's fundamentals control its stock, so they teach you only how to make sense of that information and declare you good to go. Learning more about stocks is not an all-or-nothing, make-money-or-bust proposition. I don't think familiarizing yourself with a company should ever be dismissed as less than useful just because it doesn't translate into immediate profit. Ultimately, stocks do tend to drift into line with where they "deserve" to trade given how the underlying companies are doing. On top of that, as long as you keep up with the homework, you have a good, clean way of deciding whether to cut your losses in a stock that isn't working, which is an incredibly valuable tool, especially when you're trying to claw your way back to even after the market vaporized a good third or half of the money you had in stocks. The better you are at avoiding stocks with a risk reward that is changing from good to bad—perhaps because they are oil-related stocks and oil just plummeted, or housing-related stocks and housing starts have fallen off a cliff—the better positioned you are to take more calculated, intelligent risks and be more aggressive with your investments in order to rebuild your capital more swiftly. These skills are useful no matter what, but they are of paramount importance when it comes to dealing with the central problem of getting back to even by investing in stocks: the tension between protecting your already diminished capital (preservation) and needing to risk that capital in order to make more money (appreciation).

Investors are always looking for an edge, some kind of leg up that provides them with an advantage over everybody else. That will never change. Not all advantages are of the same scale, but just by following my standard homework regimen, you should have an edge over most of the other people who trade the stocks you follow. How is that possible? Your homework involves looking at publicly available information. Anyone can check it out. According to some economists and most armchair investors, the very fact that the information is out there means it should already be factored into the stock, meaning the share price should reflect what you know from your research. Of course, we know that's not how stocks really work. And I can also tell you that if you're really following through with the homework, reading all the filings, the articles, and especially the conference-call transcripts, then you know more about the company than most of the people trading its stock, and that includes many of the professionals. Now, some of the pros will have their own insights as well as access to sell-side analyst research reports—*sell-side* is just Wall Street slang for the banks and brokers—that you might have some trouble getting your hands on as a retail investor. In my opinion, as long as you've been thorough in your analysis, you still have an edge on these guys, too, as they often rely too heavily on the work of the outside analysts rather than doing all of their own research and coming to their own conclusions. And while there's plenty of great work being done by the analysts, it's almost always better to depend on your research. Besides, quite a few of the excellent veteran researchers have left the major New York investment houses because of government restrictions on pay for those companies that have taken government money or set up their own hedge funds. Put simply, they aren't as good as they used to be! You can do better.

Since the fundamentals of the underlying companies often aren't even the main force controlling short-term stock prices, it doesn't matter if someone else has done an analysis that's superior to yours. What's imperative is for you to remember the facts and have confidence in your interpretation. Why? Because one of the most important reasons for familiarizing yourself with a company's fundamentals is so that you'll know what to do when that company's stock violently diverges from what you expect it to do if we lived in a world of perfectly efficient markets where the fundamentals actually did totally determine stock prices. I have always been partial, for example, to the stock of Panera Bread, the restaurant chain, because my eldest likes their classic Caesar salad and I like the chili bread bowl. I've done a ton of work on the chain's management, its growth prospects, and its ability to make more money out of its servings than just about any other food chain. Let's say I think the stock, which may be at $55, is worth $65 a share before it becomes as expensive as say, Darden, which owns the slower-growing Red Lobster and Olive Garden, or Brinker, which owns the less well-run chain Chili's. Then Panera reports a solid quarter, but only meets the Street's expectations instead of beating them, causing the stock to dive down to $45. Think about the professional money manager who's been buying Panera, not on his own work, but on the work of a bullish analyst who told him that his expectations would be beaten by the chain. While you might think that you would be hard-pressed to find someone who is actually that lazy, there are plenty of managers who are too often willing to substitute an analyst's judgment for their own. The money manager has a big problem in this scenario: not only does he lack the background knowledge necessary to make a snap decision on Panera, he can't even be sure whether he was right to like it in the first place because he took his cue from someone else.

Individual investors generally have far more conviction about conclusions they reach on their own than ideas they borrow from another person. In this example our hypothetical money manager might view Panera's decline as a refutation of the research that initially led him to buy the stock, and end up selling it down at $45. Many others will simply view the decline in the stock as a sign that something is wrong with the fundamentals and sell out of panic. But if you've done the homework, then you not only have the knowledge necessary to judge whether Panera's stock has come unglued from the fundamentals of the company; you should also have the conviction to follow through on that judgment and buy Panera at a discount, especially if you, like me, started your research because you liked going to the restaurant to eat. I bet many of the "pros" selling Panera have never even been to one! That's the time when you can make the most money—the momentary, violent disconnect between the true longer-term fundamentals and the short-term action in the stock.

What Really Controls Stock Prices

Now that we've made peace with the notion that the fundamentals are important even though they don't set stock prices in the short term, let's talk about what else actually does move stocks. The notion that a company's stock can and will rise or fall irrespective of how that company is doing seems profoundly unfair, completely illogical, and totally alien compared to the way we expect the world to work. Empirically, this is what happens all of the time, but that doesn't stop people from forcing an interpretation on the market that makes sense to them, however inaccurate it might be in reality. Many people, for example, view a company's stock as being analogous to a high school student's report card or GPA, a way of grading companies that also allows investors to make some money as long as they pick the straight-A businesses. Unfortunately, when people try to make sense of the market by assuming it operates according to familiar rules, they make everything much more confusing. It's bad enough for most people to be confused and angry when a company reports an across-the-board terrific quarter but its stock plummets anyway. But it's much worse if they turn around and say, "Oh, well, the quarter must not have been any good at all because the stock got hammered." The stock's instant action often produces an incorrect conclusion about the longer-term value of the underlying company.

And every time a newspaper reporter crafts an explanation for the market's action we take another big collective step backward. Financial misinformation is dispensed almost every single day with countless reporters desperately trying to please their editors by drawing out a shallow, meaningless connection between the performance of the averages and a newsworthy event that happened on the same day. I know that's how it works because the reporters would call me all the time at my old hedge fund hoping I would throw them a reason or two for the day's action. I also know it from having worked at newspapers where editors demanded I make sense of the short-term senselessness, even if I found the exercise misleading. When you can get headlines like "Stocks sell off on higher oil prices," and then a week or even just a day later, "Stocks rally on higher oil," you should realize that the whole endeavor is intellectually bankrupt. I'm telling you it obfuscates far more than it reveals about the market.

So what's the whole truth? What mighty forces decide share prices? In the near term, meaning a year to eighteen months, you might say there's a perpetual conspiracy afoot to control the movement of stocks, a nefarious group of people with the economic heft of the Bavarian Illuminati and the international reach of the Trilateral Commission. Some people call them . . . Big Investors. It's not quite like leaving the inmates in charge of the asylum, but sometimes it comes pretty close. Don't overlook the obvious here: the stock market is, first and foremost, a market, no different from any other, although one with an enormous variety of goods for sale and millions of participants. Markets are easy to understand: lots of buyers and sellers haggle over their wares and the end result of that process determines the price. It's the same whether we're talking about fresh fruit or equities. Of course with stocks, there's no actual negotiation as there are far too many people involved, but you get a kind of aggregate negotiation, mediated by brokers and market makers, that results in trade after trade. What causes stocks to go down? I hate to let you down, but it's the simple Economics 101 answer: when there are more sellers than buyers, regardless of which side is actually "right" in the longer term. Stocks go up when there are more buyers than sellers, again, regardless of the actual truth of the company's growth prospects and balance sheet. It's all about supply and demand. I'd like to think that people assume all of this when they talk about what moves stocks but consider the explanation too simple. They want to know what causes there to be more sellers or more buyers on any given day or for a longer period of time. Nevertheless, you can't just jump to asking those questions unless you first consider and continue to factor in the simple mechanics of the stock market.

We also can't ignore what some might consider the market's dirty little secret when you're searching for explanations. Even though every investor plays a role in the market process that moves stocks, some investors have a whole lot more clout than others because they manage a whole lot more money. Mutual funds, hedge funds, even university endowments and state pension funds account for so much of the action and manage such massive quantities of cash that it wouldn't be an exaggeration to say that the people in charge of these funds are the ones who decide where stocks go. What gives them that power? A fund that's managing billions of dollars will have trouble buying or selling meaningful positions in stocks without moving them multiple points—even the largest and most liquid of stocks, the Intels and the Microsofts and the AT&Ts and the Pfizers—but if each of these big money guys went off on his own direction, if they pursued different strategies, then the big money wouldn't matter that much. Luckily for us, money managers tend to be herd animals, less like bulls and bears than like wildebeests. There are a few important distinctions between different camps, but a large enough majority of the big-money guys operate using pretty much the same playbook.

This is why the fundamentals tend not to matter that much in the near term: you have mountains of money, think K2 if not quite Everest-sized, coming from various different money managers who are all pretty much buying and selling the same things at the same times. Sometimes you'll find the hedge funds squared off against the mutual funds since the incentive structure for most mutual fund managers encourages them to buy relentlessly if they're at all bullish, while hedge funds will often find themselves with a more negative outlook, at least in part because they have the ability to sell stocks short, which is a complicated practice of profiting from stock declines that boils down to something simple: in a short sale you bet against a stock by borrowing shares from a large institution that's just sitting on them, then you sell those shares immediately, and at some future date you buy back the same amount of shares—this is called "covering" your short position—and return them to whomever they were borrowed from, hopefully at a much lower price. Hedge funds can make money easily when the market stinks, while mutual funds are generally prohibited from short-selling, so they're always looking for the light at the end of the tunnel when the market and the economy are in bad shape, even if it turns out to be the light from an oncoming train. But even when the hedge funds and mutual funds are at odds, they still adhere to and agree on the playbook; they just disagree about what stage of the business cycle we're in, and thus which sectors and stocks to buy and sell. They are lumbering big-money giants, and you can dance circles around them and profit from their mistakes.

Getting ahead of the big-money playbook can be a terrific way to make a lot of money quickly, no question. And to help you pick out the patterns that will matter, not to mention help you get back to even, in chapter 5 after I describe how a recovery will look, I include a list of twelve stocks that these money managers will buy aggressively once they believe in the recovery, and which you can get in on right now.

This brings me back to the idea of investing based on probabilities and patterns rather than predictions about the future. You have no need to try to determine what the future is going to look like thanks to all of the help the big-money investors give the rest of us, even though it's certainly inadvertent help. This gamesmanship was actually a fundamental method of profit for my hedge fund. We would divine what the big-money guys would pick, not what was going to happen. Specifically, we would figure out which stocks the big-money funds were most likely to reach for when they were presented with a certain set of facts. How? Because we knew what they reached for in the past with a similar set of facts as inputs. This strategy is something you can execute now, and I can teach you to do it, because this kind of investing is all based on what are known as "cycles," overarching macroeconomic cycles of increasing and declining employment, and gross domestic products of this country and all countries worldwide. All of these cycles have probabilities attached to them that are easily discernable. But do be careful when you're treading under the feet of the big boys, because when the big-money hedge funds and mutual funds have piled into their sectors and stocks of choice and marched them to extremes that far exceed the values of the fundamentals of the companies underneath them, you want to be out. That's another pattern, another part of the cycle. Just as their mass buying can take stocks much higher, their mass selling, as we saw throughout 2008, can destroy just about any sector, and even the entire asset class of stocks for a brief period, taking stocks well below their breakup values and even their liquidation values. Try to strike a balance until you've made back enough money that you can start feeling comfortable taking big risks again. In the next chapter I've got some terrific strategies and stocks to help get you there.

4

DIVIDENDS
The Best Offense Is a Good Defense

Is it naïve to think investing is about more than just gaming out where the big money is going and getting there first? Is it foolishly idealistic to believe that stocks are more than just pieces of paper? Are we fooling ourselves when we act as though Wall Street is anything other than a casino with better odds, but where the house, or in this case the brokerage houses, still take home fortunes? If, as I've indicated, stock prices are controlled in the short term not by the fundamentals of their underlying companies but by the decisions of fat cats who manage huge sums of money, why do I still believe so strongly that stocks are the best and fastest way for you to get back to even? These aren't questions I normally care about. Casino or not, I know how to rake in the dough by investing in the stock market. My job is to help you become financially stable, then try to make you rich, and if I thought I could do that by running through the streets of every major city in the country naked or something even more embarrassing, I would do it. That said, it would be a big mistake for you to become too cynical about investing. How could you sleep at night if you believed your money was being kept in a supersophisticated lottery ticket? How could you have any confidence in your investments if you thought they could be crushed at the whim of an important money manager? There has to be something else that gives these pieces of paper their value, right?

Yes, if you take a longer-term view, then stocks do start to reflect the health of their underlying companies. Even in the short term, the fundamentals—again this means all of the relevant facts about a business—matter because the big-money players are making their decisions based, somewhat at least, on that information. Small-time investors are more than just ants scurrying around the feet of the masters of the universe, and stocks are, in fact, more than just pieces of paper that we buy and sell. Although I find that description very useful in practice, it's not true in fact or in theory. It's not often that you'll need to know the real definition of a stock—it just isn't the kind of thing that pops up when you're trying to figure out what you should buy or sell—but I'd be remiss if I didn't explain it to you. When you buy a company's stock, you're buying an ownership stake in that company along with a claim on its assets and future profits. The reason these things tend not to matter (unless you're incredibly wealthy) is that your stake in that company and your claim on its assets and earnings are both proportional to the size of your investment, which means that for all intents and purposes, they're infinitesimal. You could buy 100,000 shares in a company like Home Depot (HD), which at $25 a share would come to $2.5 million, and your ownership stake would be just as meaningless as it would have been if you'd bought only a single share. Home Depot doesn't care. Home Depot has 1.7 billion shares outstanding. That's the total number of shares of common stock held by investors, including restricted shares belonging to corporate officers that don't trade. Its float, which is the nonrestricted shares, the ones that are free to trade and not owned by insiders with trading restrictions, still comes to 1.65 billion. There's just no way you will ever make a dent in that, and if you do, well, you should be the one giving the advice to me. No publicly traded company will ever give you special treatment just because you're a shareholder, unless you have the money to buy enough stock to get on the board of directors. And if you want to try to use your paltry few votes to influence the company's direction, all I can say is don't hold your breath while you try.

While stocks regularly disassociate from their underlying fundamentals, there are important factors that reconnect the two that can make you a whole lot of money. There is always the potential for a publicly traded company to be acquired by another business, because it's more valuable to the acquirer than it is to the big-money investors who own most of the shares. Anticipating potential acquisitions is a terrific way to make money, as long as you get out when the deal is approved rather than waiting for it to close, because they often don't. And that's especially true when the economy is in tatters and companies are having a hard time borrowing money to finance takeovers.

The other key way companies remain connected with their stocks? They pay their shareholders dividends. And boy, do those dividends matter. If I had to pick one attribute that I most like to see in a stock, it's a safe, sizable dividend. When you're putting together a getting-back-to-even portfolio, no matter what your age or purpose, you cannot afford to pass up the tremendous moneymaking opportunities offered by dividend-paying stocks. I know that companies that pay large dividends have traditionally been seen as the dullest of the dull, with totally unsexy, boring stocks that only senior citizens and the incredibly risk-averse have any interest in owning. The truth is a whole lot different.

There are many different kinds of stocks that pay dividends, and they can play different roles in your portfolio. The important thing is that you be aware of everything dividends can do and that you take full advantage of what they have to offer. In the previous chapter I talked about the problem faced by anyone who's lost a lot of money and is trying to invest in order to get back to even: to make back what you lost, you have to risk losing even more, and because you're already down big, more losses could wipe out your ability to make money in stocks at all. In other words, you can't just stick your money somewhere safe, shove it in the First National Bank of Sealy, for example, or maybe a Serta or a Duxiana if you are a big hitter, because you need to use that money to invest. Meanwhile, you can't put all your cash in the kind of high-risk speculative stocks, or even fast-growing, fast-moving momentum stocks, not that there are many of those around these days, which often generate big returns at the risk of potential big losses.

Stocks with moderate-to-large dividends help you get around that problem. Many of them embody the kind of balance that you need in your portfolio, although for a variety of reasons, dividend-paying stocks are regarded as the kind you buy when you're focused on capital preservation, not capital appreciation. I think that's a mistake. These stocks do provide tremendous benefits for investors looking to protect their money, no question, but for that very reason they tend to be ignored by investors who are looking to take on more risk and make more money. That makes no sense to me. Just because dividend stocks work great in an individual retirement account, or as a source of income for jobless retirees doesn't mean more aggressive investors can't use them to good effect.

I'll admit that even I did not appreciate the full potential of stocks that pay dividends until we got hit with the crash. Stocks with big dividends become more attractive in a down market because everyone is trying to be more defensive and dividend payers are seen as stocks that will let you sleep at night, even when the sky is falling. The crash caused everything to go down because people were pulling money out of stocks as an asset class, and even if investors were buying more stocks with safe and large dividends, that buying was overpowered by the mass selling. I expect people to hide in these stocks during tough economic times; what I did not see coming was just how hard these stocks would spring back as the market gradually began to recover from the crash. In some cases the snapbacks were almost unbelievable. Forget capital preservation—there are plenty of dividend stocks that know how to go on the offensive, but hardly anyone ever talks about them or how you can use them. You've probably heard plenty of traditional advice about dividends, advice that I agree with and will explain momentarily, but there are also new ways to trade dividend stocks, ways that I pioneered on *Mad Money*. I believe they are downright essential for anyone who wants to get back to even, and go a whole lot further.

That's why I'm devoting this entire chapter to dividend investing, and don't worry, the subject is anything but boring. If the crash has taught us any lesson, it's that stocks with dividends that are big, reliable, and safe—I'll show you how to determine what's safe and what isn't—are by far the best game in town, some of the most powerful weapons in your moneymaking arsenal. You just need to know how to spot them, how to evaluate them, and how to trade them, which is what you've got me for. Once you know what to look for, even some of the stodgiest dividend-paying stocks can be some of the best names in your portfolio. That's why at the end of this chapter I've made a list of five of my favorite high-yielding stocks and why I like each of them. Also, you can use dividends as instruments, indicators that help you figure out where a stock is going. A dividend can act as a kind of thermometer, telling you a great deal about the health of a stock and the company underneath it. And of course, they provide a source of income, a cushion that keeps stocks from falling too far during a sell-off, another terrific way of valuing stocks in a world where, as I told you before, it can be difficult to try to value stocks with more traditional methods, such as price-to-earnings multiples where the future earnings are in flux. That is a mighty long list of things, so before we go over how dividends can protect and make you money, I should teach you some of the vocabulary and the mechanics you'll need to know to invest in these stocks.

Know the Dividend Language

For the uninitiated, let's take a moment to explain exactly what dividends are, how they work, and why they have become so important. What kinds of companies pay dividends? Stocks in certain sectors are more likely to pay dividends than those in others—for example, tech stocks hardly ever pay dividends but the banks love to, at least when they can afford to do so. Typically when a company is young and fast growing, it won't pay a dividend but will instead try to create share-holder value by reinvesting all of its profits in continuing to expand the business. Then as the company gets larger and more mature and its growth slows, it will often start returning a portion of its profits to you and all the other shareholders. That's been the experience for two aging tech titans, Intel (INTC) and Microsoft (MSFT). During the 1980s and 1990s, when they were experiencing extraordinary growth, they plowed back all of their earnings into plant, equipment, and re-search to bolster that growth. Eventually—and this is the ultimate fate of almost every high-growth company—the cash built up but the growth slowed. There was only so much more growth they could gen-erate by reinvesting that money in the business, so they initiated div-idends and, over time as they made more money, they raised them.

They didn't have the go-go excitement anymore, but ever since they started paying those dividends, Microsoft and Intel have put money right in your pocket, quarter after quarter. They are literally paying you to own the stock. Tell me if you can find a better deal than that anywhere else. Plus, thanks to favorable tax laws, you only pay a 15 percent tax on dividends, much lower than taxes on ordinary income.

Now, unfortunately, you're going to have to be subjected to a little bit of Wall Street slang to understand how dividends work. You'll hear terms like the *payout* when people are talking about dividends, and a lot of the time I'll talk about a stock's dividend yield. So just to make sure we're all on the same page, the payout is simply the annual amount of dividends per share that a company returns to its inves-tors. Take Altria (MO), one of the best dividend stocks out there, one that I like to buy for my own charitable trust when the yield exceeds 8 percent, as those who subscribe to ActionAlertsPlus.com, an online newsletter that describes what moves I am going to make before I pull the trigger, know so well. As I write this, Altria pays out four quar-terly dividends of $0.32 a year, so its annual payout is $1.28. This payout might be higher in the future because the company is a serial dividend raiser. How about the yield? That is just the percentage of a

stock's share price that you get back every year from dividend payments. To figure out the yield, you simply divide the stock's annual
dividend payout by its share price. This is something you can and
should do whenever you think about owning something with a fixed
return, like a bond, not just a stock with a juicy dividend. Let's say
Altria is trading at $16 a share right now. So $1.28 / $16 = 8 percent.
That means Altria's dividend yield is 8 percent, the annual return you
would get from simply collecting the dividend if the stock price did
nothing. If Altria's share price moved up to $20, then the equation
would be $1.28 / $20, and Altria would have a much lower 6.4 percent
yield. If the stock were to fall to $14, then we would do the same
equation: $1.28/ $14, and the yield would increase to 9.1 percent.
What a screaming buy that would be, given the company's consistently steady business—like it or not—and its commitment to the
dividend as well as its ability to pay it. This arithmetic is very important, and it is nothing more than that, arithmetic, not even mathemat-
ics and certainly not calculus. As a stock's price rises, its yield becomes
smaller. As the stock price goes lower, its yield becomes larger, making it a much more attractive investment.

What about the nitty-gritty details of how you actually go about
collecting a dividend payment? You'll have to sift through a lot more
Wall Street jargon, but it should be worth it when that cash hits your
bank account. Even though you might own a dividend-paying stock
for months or years, the actual capture of a dividend payment happens in a matter of minutes. It's finding out when those minutes occur
that can be difficult. Whenever a company announces a new dividend
payment, it throws around a lot of numbers and dates, but the two
most important terms, the ones you'll hear most often and the only
ones you have to remember, are the *ex-date* and the *record date*. The
ex-date is not a less important version of an ex-boyfriend or girlfriend;
it stands for ex-dividend date and it's the first day a stock trades without the right to the upcoming quarterly dividend. If you buy a dividend stock on or after the ex-date, you don't collect the next dividend
payment, period. How about the record date? That comes two trading

days later, when the trade actually settles and shows up in your brokerage account.

Now that we've gotten those dull, confusing textbook definitions out of the way, I want you to forget them and focus on a different, much more important term that's actually useful. It's something I call the *must-own date*, the last day when you have to buy a stock to be able to claim its next dividend payout. The must-own date is the day before the ex-date. Because of the way trades settle into your account, in order to be one of the shareholders on the record date you have to have bought the stock three trading sessions before, on the must-own date. When they tell you the ex-date, remember that the must-own date is the day before, and if they confuse you by telling you the record date instead, the must-own date is three trading days before that. It's really the only important date in the whole process.

So how does snagging that dividend payment actually work in practice? Let's revisit our example Altria. As I'm writing, Altria's most recent quarterly dividend payout, 32 cents a share, happened on July 10, 2009. The ex-date was June 11, so we know the must-own date was June 10. In order to collect that 32-cent dividend you would have had to be an Altria shareholder at the close of trading on June 10. As soon as Altria started to trade on the ex-date, the day after the must-own date, you could have sold it and you would still have gotten the dividend check in the mail. Investors who buy when the stock goes ex-dividend do not get to collect that dividend, but for those who feel ripped off that they missed the deadline and won't get the dividend, the stock usually gets knocked down enough to compensate for the missed payout. (All of these dates are available on a company's website or on Yahoo finance or TheStreet.com's stock pages.)

Traditional Reasons to Like Dividends and the Stocks That Pay Them

Now that you know the language and the mechanics of dividend payments, let's get down to business, the business of using dividend-paying stocks to protect your money and make more of it. In the wake of the 2008–2009 crash, I started using dividends to assess and value stocks, even though ordinarily they're taken into consideration only as part of a more holistic assessment by most money managers and analysts and never used as the basis for valuing a stock, as I was doing. I also endorsed a group of stocks that I call the accidentally high yielders, a group of mostly cyclical companies that had paid out small dividends and had low yields before the crash. Because their share prices were crushed courtesy of the market's savage decline, those once-low yields became high, even though the companies did not raise the actual size of their dividend payouts and probably would have much preferred that their stock prices had stayed high and their yields low. By the way, I consider a high yield to be anything above 4 percent, which after the terrific tax treatment of dividends, is superior to what you would get from even long-term U.S. Treasurys, where the interest you receive is subject to much higher ordinary income tax rates. These accidentally high yielders, though they can be difficult to find at the right price, are a fantastic and novel way to invest because they give you the safety of a high yielder with the risk and potential upside of a cyclical stock with earnings that swing wildly depending on the strength of the economy. These dividend payers were some of the best-performing stocks as the market rebounded from its March 2009 bottom. While the accidentally high yielders make for great trades and great investments, there are more important reasons to own different kinds of dividend-paying stocks that deserve to be addressed first. After all, if the accidentally high yielders work as well as I expect, then they're headed for extinction when higher stock prices eventually shrink those yields back down to size.

I'll go into more detail on each facet of dividend investing that I've mentioned, and I will explain how you can do the homework to make sure a company's dividend is safe, so I want to stress that different types of investors will prefer different angles. While everyone should own at least one stock with a high dividend, the particular kind of stock and the reason for owning it will vary from person to person depending on their investment style, risk tolerance, age, and all the other things that make us different from each other financially. Especially after a huge decline, dividends are something like the investing equivalent of a Swiss army knife. They have all kinds of neat, useful features if you just bother to unfold them and learn what all the different pieces do. Most investors still see dividends only as a source of income for those who need it to supplement their Social Security, and that silly prejudice has discouraged a lot of people, especially younger investors, from buying and profiting from terrific dividend-paying companies. Do not fool yourself into thinking that you have to live at Sunrise Senior Living to own these stocks (and certainly don't buy the stock of Sunrise Senior Living, which has been and will remain a nightmare because of its awful balance sheet). Do not shun bountiful dividend payers because they often lack the ultrahigh growth that Wall Street so loves. Dividend-paying stocks should be the foundation of your getting-back-to-even portfolio, no matter how old you are. They are too good to pass up, and essential not just for your retirement portfolio, which is inherently more conservative, but also for your nonretirement, discretionary investments, where the benefits from owning a good dividend name are tremendous.

That's why I want to begin by explaining standard, good old-fashioned reasons why people have always liked to own stocks with nice, juicy yields, reasons that made as much sense two or even four years ago as they do now. First, the main reason why stocks with substantial dividends allow investors to sleep more soundly at night, not to mention tear out less of their hair in the morning and drink less cheap whiskey on the dirty linoleum floor in the afternoon, is something called "yield support." This support is inherent to the way dividends work; they create a cushion, and at times a trampoline, if not necessarily a floor, underneath dividend-paying stocks. As the share price falls, the yield increases. Naturally, a stock with a higher yield is a better stock to own simply because you get a better payoff from your investment.

Consider Verizon (VZ), which at $30.50 yields an impressive 6 percent dividend. Now suppose something triggered a sell-off in Verizon's stock that sent it tumbling down about $4 to $26.28, where its yield would be 7 percent. There will be more value-oriented investors who are willing to buy Verizon at that level, and when they come in, their buying will offset the selling pressure and might even reverse it entirely, sending the stock higher. This is an example of yield support. Yield support is one of the reasons why stocks with large-enough dividends have an easier time standing up to the kind of heavy selling we saw in 2008. The lower price draws in more investors seeking stocks that generate consistent income. As I said, though, yield support is a cushion or a parachute, it's not a floor. In an economic environment where dividends are less attractive, say when we have high inflation and high interest rates, there will be fewer investors looking for high yielders, so stocks like Verizon won't get the same kind of yield support. And of course, none of this matters if the company cuts its dividend while it's being pushed down, reducing the yield and turning off investors, who generally dislike seeing dividend cuts. But during a downturn those companies with safe dividends will find themselves protected relative to the market as a whole. Yield support is one of the reasons why high yielders make such terrific places to hide when you're thinking mostly of capital preservation. The high dividend also protects you from short-sellers. When someone sells a stock short, he has to borrow it from an investor who actually owns the stock. The person who owns the stock expects to receive that dividend, and it is the short-seller's responsibility to pay it out of his own pocket to the person he borrowed the stock from, even as he typically has no idea who that person is. The fear of having to pay someone else a dividend with my money often kept me from shorting high-yielding stocks when I was a hedge fund manager. That same fear is what makes stocks with high yields much less likely to be targeted by the shorts than those stocks with no dividends. You can see how valuable this protection would be whenever short-sellers were sowing fear, wreaking havoc, and using bear raids to push down stocks left and right. A high yielder is a kind of fortress protecting you·from the shorts, although with enough pressure it can still be overrun; it's just a lot harder to do.

The second old-fashioned case for dividends is simply that the income you can get from a stock with a decent yield can be pretty significant. These are great stocks to own for retirement, and by that I mean both when you're retired and when you're saving for retirement. When you're retired—and I have a lot later to help retirees who are in dire financial straits because of the crash and the collapse of property values—your paycheck gets replaced by a smaller Social Security check. And that's assuming the program is still around, which seems likely for baby boomers like me (although it's possible we'll see benefit cuts), but unlikely for members of generation Y, or as they are called now, the millennial generation, like my daughters. I still believe in owning stocks while you're retired, but not if you may need that money to cover the costs of any major purchases over the next few years. Retirees should own stocks, even as most of their investments should be in much safer bonds, because people are living longer and longer, and they will need the additional upside from good stocks to cover those extra costs incurred by living longer. Not owning stocks in retirement, or at least early retirement, is a bet against your own longevity, and there's no way to win when you make that kind of bet against yourself. Since some of a retiree's money, perhaps as much as a third, should be in stocks rather than bonds, it helps a lot to have those stocks producing income by paying dividends with yields that are similar to or better than what you would get from owning U.S. Treasurys. That's a pretty good setup. Younger investors should favor owning dividends, especially when investing for retirement, because of their ability to compound over time as long as you reinvest the dividend in the stock that paid it, something I'll explain in a moment.

The best argument for making sure you get your quarterly dose of dividend payments is one of the oldest and most conventional: dividends represent long-term streams of income. I could not care less that it's the conventional wisdom; I'm writing this book to help you get back to even, not to be a shibboleth-smashing iconoclast. If you want to know why I'm so hung up on dividends, just consider the fact that going back to January 1926, about 40 percent of the total return from the S&P 500 has come through reinvested dividends. That's right—40 percent of the gains from stocks come from collecting your dividends and then using them to buy more dividend-paying stock so your profits can compound over time. Dividends have always been a terrific way to grow your money and to protect it, because the cushion effect of the yield going higher as the share price goes lower tends to bring in new money from the sidelines to push the stock up if it goes down too far. But in light of the market's performance over the last decade—or lack thereof, as it's essentially gone nowhere—you can see how much more important dividends get. In the aggregate, they were the only way people were making any money from the market as a whole over the last ten years. Say you invested in a stock with a 5 percent yield in 1999 and you used those dividend payments to reinvest in the stock. Over the last decade that would have given you a 64 percent win, even if the stock price did nothing. That's pretty impressive for just sitting on your hands. The S&P 500 is down about 32 percent over the same period, so that 5 percent yielder would have kept you in the green, even if the stock's performance tracked the market's—in fact you would have done even better because you'd have been buying more shares at a higher yield when you reinvested your dividends in the stock. But you get the point. You know better than to simply expect stocks to go higher. A lot of them deserve to, and some of them even will, but putting your money in a stock with a serious yield is a way to take control of your own financial destiny, to make sure you have income, and to allow yourself to sleep soundly at night without having to worry about the destruction of your wealth. Your stocks may go down, but as long as you're sure their dividends are safe—and I've got a checklist to help you do just that— then you can count on that income. And sooner or later the dividend cushion, or perhaps you could think of it as a parachute, kicks in and helps these dividend stocks go up if they've been beaten down too much.

It's very important that you reinvest your dividends, unless you're retired and more concerned about income than about growing your wealth. Reinvesting, as much as anything else, is really the key to making money in high-yielding stocks. If you use the dividend payout to buy more shares, you're going to benefit from what everyone likes to call the magic of compound interest—basically, earning interest on the previous interest you've collected, or in this case, getting paid a dividend for shares bought with money from a past dividend. Look at a stock's yield the same way you'd look at the interest rate you get in a savings account, except with more risk and hopefully greater returns. As long as you reinvest those dividends, they'll compound, and that means serious money over the long term.

There's a quick rule of thumb that I find very useful when thinking about compound reinvested dividends or compound interest in general: the rule of 72, a concept I often try to bring up on *Mad Money*. It is difficult to explain on television, and not just because talking about compounding dividends is the kind of thing that puts viewers to sleep. The rule of 72 allows us to figure out how long it will take to double our money for any given return, as long as we reinvest our gains. You simply take the number 72 and divide it by whatever your return—or in this case yield—is. So if we're talking about a stock that yields 5 percent, then $72/5 = 14.4$ years. If you reinvest your dividends in a 5 percent yielder, you'll double your money in fourteen and a half years, even if the stock doesn't move the slightest bit higher. That's not an outlying possibility anymore, and after what we've been through these last five years, I find it very comforting.

Dividend Signals

While we like dividend-paying stocks for the income they provide, why choose them over U.S. Treasurys, the bonds issued by the United States government, regarded as the gold standard for safety, in order to get a nice 4 percent yield (presuming longer term Treasurys are above that level)? Stocks, as a rule, are never as safe as bonds, and they're far less safe than Treasurys. In fact, long-term Treasurys were just about the only asset class that allowed you to make real money over the last two decades if you simply held them, something that's pretty astonishing when you consider how low their returns are. But Treasurys with these low yields will not get you back to even, at least not anytime soon. With high-yielding stocks, the income component and the safety component are perks. The great thing about a high yielder is that you're being paid to own a stock *that can also make you money by going higher.* The dividend, while important, won't get you back to even on its own, unless we're talking about some of the extremely high yielders, such as oil tanker stocks or energy trusts, which can have double-digit yields if you buy them correctly, but also frequently cut or lower their payouts depending upon fluctuating shipping rates or oil prices. We are counting on the dividend to help, but not to get us all the way to the finish line. A stock with a 5 percent yield, and that's a pretty darned high one, will take fourteen years to double your money *if the stock price goes nowhere.* Many of you lost half of your money in the crash, and you can't wait that long to get back to even, not even if you're very young and have decades to build up money for retirement or a home or anything else that's expensive and important to you. This is why we're looking for dividend-paying stocks that will go higher instead of nowhere. The great thing about high-quality dividend stocks—*high-quality* meaning that we have confidence in the underlying companies and believe those stocks will make us money—is that you get both the income you would from a bond, and, as always, the potential upside from stocks. Plus, bond issuers never raise their payouts, but companies do this all the time!

There are a couple of different ways you can use a company's dividend to determine what kind of shape it's in. When a company can raise its dividend, especially in the midst of a terrible economy, that's a sign of strength and health that you cannot ignore. It signals that you're looking at a business with steady, reliable growth, which is exactly what you want when the economy is doing poorly. I have to warn you, though, that that is not usually what big Wall Street investors like once there is any evidence at all that the economy is improving. Serial dividend raisers, companies that have increased their dividends every year for ten, twenty, thirty, or in some cases more than fifty years, are another consistent and stable group to keep your eye on, even if their yields aren't that high. Those dividend raises mean that the stock's yield keeps pace with its increasing price—as long as the stock has an increasing price. Think about a company like Procter & Gamble (PG), which has raised its dividend for fifty-three consecutive years, upping it an average of 11 percent annually over the last decade, and by 10 percent on April 14, 2009, the best record of any company on the New York Stock Exchange. At $50 a share, about where Procter has been trading as I write this, and with an annual payout of $1.76, the company has a 3.5 percent yield. That's not exactly huge, especially given that so many industrial stocks with inconsistent earnings now have accidentally high yields that dwarf Procter's. But to someone who first bought the stock years and years ago at much lower prices and has been reinvesting past dividends, the new $1.76 payout looks a lot better, although you have to go back pretty far to see the beauty of that payout, given that the crash knocked Procter's share price back to where it was almost a decade ago.

Let's move on to a new way of using dividends to assess a stock's health. So far I've told you about all the traditionally important benefits you get from owning dividend-paying stocks. Now I want to show you how dividends can help us identify which stocks have the juice to go higher and make us money, and which ones don't. This method is something that became increasingly important during and immediately after the crash, when everything went haywire and the old ways of grading and valuing stocks just weren't working. You could find stock after stock that looked cheap on a price-to-earnings multiple basis, but they would only go lower. The standard ways of looking at stocks were telling us nothing so we had to come up with different ways to assess their value. And as it turned out, using a stock's historical dividend yield as a way of measuring valuation worked incredibly well in some cases. Though learned during the crash, this is a lesson that could be applied any time a company's yield soars and there are questions about its value. Now that things have started returning to normal, it's still an extra tool in our kit, one that helps highlight potential long-term winners.

Here's how to use it. When you're trying to value a high yielder, regardless of how it came to have a high yield, take a look back at the course of its dividend yield over the last two, three, or even four decades. You want to compare where the dividend is now with where it's been. If, for example, you find that the current yield is only slightly higher than the historical average, you don't learn much, except that the stock has room to go lower based on its historical yield. But when you find a case where the stock's dividend has reached the current level only two or three times in the last twenty years, you could have the beginning of a great stock pick. I don't think you will find many of these stocks in a stable, healthy market, but when you do, they are home runs.

Take Emerson Electric (EMR), a classic smokestack industrial manufacturer, and not the kind you think of as a high yielder. Back on November 11, 2008, Emerson, which along with the rest of the market had been brutalized for months, fell to a price where its $1.32 annual dividend payout yielded 4.1 percent. I had never expected to see such a large yield from an industrial like Emerson. So I went back and found that the last time Emerson had yielded over 4 percent was on August 14, 2003, and if you bought it then you caught a 25 percent gain over the next six months. I took the fact that Emerson's yield had broken through 4 percent for the first time in over five years as a sign that it had become too cheap and so recommended it on *Mad Money*. How has Emerson done? The stock closed at $31.79 on November 11, 2008, down 45 percent from its fifty-two-week high, and by the beginning of the first week of May, it had clawed its way back to $37.35, a nice 18 percent gain in six months. Any time it retreats back to 4 percent I'd do more buying.

I used the same exact method with Honeywell (HON) when its yield broke through 4 percent at about the same time. Looking back, the last time the stock had such a high yield was on October 10, 2002, near the bottom of that nasty bear market. Over the next year Honeywell's total return was 44.6 percent, and since its yield first crossed the 4 percent line in early November 2008, it has managed to stage rallies of 20 percent or more in a matter of weeks. That kind of swift snapback is exactly the sort of move you want to catch if you're trying to get back to even and willing to scale in and out of stocks quickly, as I discussed in the previous chapter.

This method would not be my first choice for valuing a stock, but sometimes it's the only thing in the toolbox that works. Why not look at how close the stocks were to their multiyear lows? That seems very similar to using the yield, but you have to remember that these stocks were hitting brand-new lows practically every day. Also, when you use the dividend, it gives you something to hang your hat on. As long as the dividend is safe, you know you can rely on it in a way that you couldn't rely on price. The share price can go down further and further, but a dividend is much more secure.

Accidentally High Yielders

As it happens, most of the stocks where it made sense to use the historical yield as a valuation tool belonged to an interesting and incredibly profitable cohort that first popped up during the recent crash. These are the accidentally high yielders, and they have given us a whole new way to trade and a new basis for dividend investing that focuses less on capital preservation and more on using that yield to attract investors and leapfrog higher. I say that they're accidentally high yielders because the companies had always paid fairly meager, safe dividends that cost them very little and gave you a small yield. The size of their dividends didn't change dramatically. What changed was that their share prices got hammered to the point where those once-paltry dividend yields became impressively high. Take Nucor (NUE), the largest steel maker in America by production, and also the lowest cost producer—unquestionably the best of breed steel maker. In the big decline Nucor saw its yield rocket to 5 percent, and even higher if you count the special dividend that it often pays out. You should never have been able to get Nucor with this high a yield. It simply should not have been priced that low. I mentioned previously Honeywell and Emerson as classic accidental high yielders, but high yielders are not just limited to industrials. Anything that got pan-caked and had a modest dividend could make the cut. You had oil companies like Chevron (CVX), which yielded 2.6 percent at its peak and 4.7 percent when it bottomed, and BP (BP) with its accidentally superhigh dividend that at times has yielded as much as 8 percent. How should you handle these stocks? If you can pick them off when they yield more than 4 percent, then count your blessings and back up the truck to start buying.

Over time one of two things will happen to the accidentally high yielders. Either they'll work out as investments, their stock price will move much higher, and they will go back to having relatively small yields, or they will cut their dividends because they lack the money to pay for them. With the right timing, buying one of today's acci-dentally high yielders could turn out to be the investing decision of a lifetime. So keep your eyes peeled because you have to be pre-pared to sell if any of them dip back below 4 percent, and it's very possible they will, even if a recovery happens more swiftly than most people suspect. You still get pullbacks when the economy is im-proving. You would be getting the best of both worlds: the income from a high yielder and the upside from a stock that tends to do well when the economy improves. That's a great way to get back to even.

What about the possibility of a dividend cut? In general, the accidentally high yielders are more trustworthy on that front because their dividends were never very big relative to their earnings to begin with. Normally a very large yield is a big red flag telling you something is wrong and it's time to get out, or at least give the situation a much closer look, because the dividend could be cut—and that might be the least of your worries. Keep reading and I'll teach you to tell the difference between high yields that are opportunities and ones that are simply dangerous. For now, just know that superhigh yields that look too good to be true usually are.

The accidentally high yielders are special because they don't fit that profile. For the most part, every one of these companies saw its earnings crimped thanks to the dire economic slowdown. That was hardly a surprise, though. A large part of the rationale behind my recommending these stocks so vocally on *Mad Money* was that even in the worst-case scenario, I thought that the earnings or at least the cash flow would cover the dividend because the dividends were always kept so small before the crash. A handful of accidental high yielders did have to cut their payouts and more still may. But the vast majority of the accidentally high yielders kept up their dividends, even in the first two quarters of 2009, probably the worst business climate since the Great Depression.

So how do you handle these stocks while they're still around? I like to buy them on the way down using wide scales based on the yield. What does that mean? Normally when I talk about buying with wide scales I mean that you should buy a stock at a particular price and then wait for it to decline a good bit before buying it again. Here I think you should use a scale based on the yield instead of the price. So you buy some when you catch one of these stocks with its yield at 4 percent or higher, then buy more when the yield increases. Take Eaton, the electronics company, for example. If you want to buy 200 shares total, then you start by buying 50 shares when the stock yields 4 percent, which for Eaton means at $50. You only put on 50 shares, a quarter of your position in one go, because buying or selling all at once is pure arrogance. The same goes for stocks with no dividends. If you buy in increments, then you won't want to smash your computer screen when a stock falls immediately after you make your purchase. Instead you can just buy some more and take advantage of the decline. For Eaton, you might hold out until it yields 4.5 percent at about $44.50 before buying another 50 shares. That's still just half of your position—you could buy the next 50 shares with Eaton yielding 5 percent at $40, and so on. Be patient. It's not the end of the world if the stock fails to go down, or even goes higher, and you end up owning a smaller position than you had hoped in a stock that's made you money. There will be other opportunities to invest.

The corollary to buying accidentally high yielders using wide scales based on yield is that if you have any kind of trading mentality—and I recommend adopting one if you hope to get back to even quickly—then you have to sell some of your position when the market rallies and the yield drops to well below 4 percent. Why? Because if you believe there will be another pullback, you can buy back the stock for less during the next swoon lower. If, in general, you think the market is headed higher, you don't want to sell too much, because you might not get the chance to buy it back at a decent price. On the other hand, when you think stocks are headed down and any rallies are ephemeral, then trading accidentally high yielders, buying them using wide scales when their yields rise above 4 percent and selling entire positions when the yields go below the same threshold, is a great way to make money when you're stuck with an otherwise stagnant or negative market. Consider the aforementioned cases of Emerson and Nucor. Each time they got to 4 percent you could begin buying them. But as they rallied to where the yields were no longer outsized, they had to be cut back. Then in the next decline you went right back to them, beginning at 4 percent. That's how trading these stocks can make you so much money.

What Moves Dividend Stocks

Despite all the positive examples of high-yielding stocks I've cited, not every stock with a high yield is worth owning at all times. There are a lot of companies that pay consistently high dividends with stocks that are going nowhere, especially as the market and the economy recover. Many of these are good companies that are simply in danger of going out of favor on what I call the Wall Street fashion show. Many of the defensive so-called secular growth stocks that I mentioned in the last chapter have especially good yields because their stock prices have been mutilated as well. I'm talking about stocks like Procter & Gamble (PG), Johnson & Johnson (JNJ), or Kellogg (K). They all have fairly generous dividends, but they are also all the kinds of stocks that investors, especially the big-money guys who run billions upon billions of dollars at mutual funds and hedge funds, love to sell when the economy improves. They are a terrible way to play the rebound. There is only so much money in the market at any given time, and money managers will use their least-favored stocks as ATMs to get the cash they need to buy what's hot. The point here is that while a high-yield does offer that cushion I mentioned, keeping the stock from going too low, the dividend cannot protect you from the business cycle, the pattern of booms and busts in the economy. A high, safe yield will not make a stock invulnerable. If we're talking about a defensive stock like Procter & Gamble, which at the moment has a 3.5 percent yield, there are a lot of things that the dividend won't save it from. When the big mutual funds think the economy is turning around, they will sell stocks like Procter nonstop. The selling by those mutual funds, which want to dump safe, consistent stocks in favor of those that will improve with the economy, is like an oncoming train. In this situation, you would want to wait for Procter's stock to get crushed before you bought it for a longer-term time frame, as long as you believed in the company's underlying fundamentals.

Just remember that a strong dividend doesn't turn a stock into Superman. When people become too enthusiastic they make mistakes, and given how much money has been lost in the market over the last two years, it really pays to be careful. The other dividend-paying stocks you should avoid are those with unsafe dividends that are likely to be cut, and you can read my checklist for identifying these stocks later in the chapter.

You should also know that the market likes dividends more in certain circumstances than it does in others. A stock with the same yield might be more attractive to investors in one situation than in another. How can that be? A 4 percent yield is a 4 percent yield, right? Well, not exactly. When you're dealing with dividend-paying stocks, or any other investment that pays you income, the context is very important. Investors who are looking for income aren't just looking at stocks. In fact, stocks are often the last things they look at because there are so many other, safer sources of income. So what makes a dividend more or less attractive to these investors? Two things: interest rates and the competition.

That's right, interest rates matter, and here I'm talking about the short-term rates that banks are willing to give you for your deposits, which are ultimately controlled in many ways by the Federal Reserve. This makes a lot of sense when you think about it. Stocks with high dividends are being compared to things like savings accounts and certificates of deposit, as well as bonds. In a world where interest rates are low and you cannot get a good return from cash, dividends are more attractive. If you go to the bank and the best rate they'll give you on a one-year CD is 2.75 percent, which will be taxed at a higher rate than dividend income thanks to that terrific dividend tax break, then a stock with a 4 percent or 5 percent yield looks pretty darned good. On the other hand, when interest rates are higher and you can get a risk-free CD that gives you a 4 percent or even 5 percent interest rate, then the very same dividend-paying stock becomes a lot less sexy. Investors looking for income will look to stocks when interest rates are low and they cannot get a decent return from cash, but when interest rates increase, they'll leave stocks and head back to the bank to get the same level of yield with much less risk. Interest rates are always important for myriad reasons; one of those reasons is as a benchmark to compare to dividend-paying stocks to help get you back to even.

What else makes dividends more or less attractive in the Wall Street fashion show? In addition to interest rates, the overall level of economic growth, as measured by GDP, gross domestic product, is also important. In periods where economic growth is either slow or nonexistent—think recession—big dividends are much more attractive than in times when the economy is growing at a healthy rate. Why? Because in a low-growth world, investors are attracted to the stability and consistency of stocks with high, sustainable dividends. Some investors always find those things attractive, but when the economy grinds to a halt, the vast majority of players in the market are not looking to hit home runs with fast growing stocks—there just aren't that many of those when we're in the midst of a recession. They just want to get on base, and the high yielders let them do that. When we're in a world of higher growth, then those same investors tend to move away from dividend-paying stocks and toward companies that are more risky and grow faster. Again, economic growth is something you always want to keep an eye on for a variety of reasons, particularly when you're trying to figure out if a stock with a decent dividend makes more sense than one with better earnings growth that does not have a good yield. Low interest rates and low growth together cause investors to covet dividend-paying stocks. This is not a situation we find ourselves in all that often, as low interest rates tend to spur economic growth and high rates tend to strangle it. This is the scenario that's prevailed since the 2008–2009 crash, and I doubt it can last forever. As the economy recovers, investors will like consumer staple stocks such as foods and drugs less, despite their safe dividends. As deflation ends and inflation rears its somewhat less ugly head, the Federal Reserve will raise interest rates, making cash more attractive relative to dividend-paying stocks. Sometimes we're in the dividend sweet spot, but you have to recognize it will end someday. Keep in mind, though, that low interest rates and low growth make dividends *relatively* more attractive to investors. When that situation shifts, as it inevitably will, dividends become relatively less attractive. The case for owning some stocks that pay them is still strong, however, as long as you like the stocks themselves.

Is It Safe?

Over and over again I have told you that dividend-paying stocks are the key to getting back to even, as long as those dividends are safe. What does *safe* mean? How do you tell the difference between a dividend you can count on and a dividend that's on a countdown to explode right in your lap? On the one hand you want a stock with a high yield so the company keeps handing you more money; on the other hand extremely high yields are a red flag, a sign that the company probably cannot maintain its dividend and will have to cut it. And this is not the greatest time to be picking stocks just for the size of their dividends. There have not been as many unsafe dividends in decades. The dividend declaration page in the paper has turned into the corporate sudden-death obituary section, with companies slashing their dividends left and right, like a bad remake of *Friday the 13th* on Wall Street.

We don't want to take any chances when it comes to dividend safety. There are three tests, three criteria we look at above and beyond everything else to determine whether a dividend is secure. There's the earnings test, the free cash-flow test, and finally the balance-sheet test. After those three you can take other factors into consideration, such as how many years a company has consecutively raised its dividend payout, but you don't want that kind of thing to be the crucial factor in your decision about a dividend's safety. The three main factors, earnings, free cash flow, and the balance sheet, are the best places to spot any evidence that a dividend cut could be on the horizon. First we look at a company's earnings or net income, the bottom line on a company's income statement because it is, well, the bottom line. This is all of the money that's actually available to shareholders, and it's very important for our purposes because it's the pile of cash where our dividends come from.

To make this illustration easier, let's assume we're running our dividend safety test on Pitney Bowes (PBI), a postage meter maker I like that sports a stunning 6.4 percent yield (rule of 72: with Pitney Bowes's yield, as long as you reinvested your dividends, you would double your money in eleven years). In the earnings test we want to know if Pitney Bowes can afford its dividend, so we divide the company's expected earnings per share for 2010 by its dividend pay-out per share, and get something called the coverage ratio, as in, can Pitney Bowes's earnings cover its dividend, and if so, by how much? We like to see earnings that are at least twice the size of a dividend, a coverage ratio of 2 or greater. Why is that the bar? Because histori-cally companies in the S&P 500 have paid out about 50 percent of their earnings in dividends, so if something terrible were to happen and the earnings were cut in half, a company with a high coverage ratio would still be able to afford its dividend. So how does Pitney Bowes stack up? The consensus estimate is for Pitney Bowes to earn $2.63 a share in 2010, and it will pay $1.44 a share in dividends. It's not quite there, with a coverage ratio of 1.83. Paying that dividend will eat up 55 percent of the company's expected 2010 earnings. Does that disqualify Pitney Bowes? No. If we actually wrote off every com-pany with a coverage ratio of less than 2 we would end up excluding many, even most, of the safe, high-quality dividend-paying stocks we're trying so hard to find. Pitney Bowes did not fail the earnings test. I would say it passed, just not with an A—more of a solid B. A coverage ratio of 1.83 should not cause alarm unless there are red flags in the next two steps. Barring catastrophe, PBI should have very little trouble covering the dividend, and catastrophe isn't all that likely for a boring postage meter business.

Because Pitney Bowes can't quite cover its dividend twice over with its earnings, we have to pay special attention to test number two, the free-cash-flow exam. Think of this step as the place where compa-nies with not-quite-adequate earnings coverage can prove they have what it takes to maintain their dividends even when business gets very difficult. So what is free cash flow and how does it relate to the safety of your dividends? Free cash flow is the actual cash—no phantom money created by accountants—that a company has left after it pays all its bills and spends money on new investments as well as ongoing improvements. The main difference between a company's cash flow and its earnings is that while accounting rules require that a company take all kinds of noncash hits to its earnings, reducing its income even though no money ever changes hands, cash flow deals with only the amount of actual money that a company spends and receives over the course of a quarter or a year. Over the past four quarters, Pitney Bowes's free cash flow was 79 percent greater than its posted net income, so if necessary its free cash flow could cover the dividend three times over. There's no question that Pitney Bowes passes this part of the dividend security test with flying colors. You can worry that Pitney Bowes spends slightly more than 50 percent of its income on dividends, but ultimately it's the company's free cash flow that determines its ability to raise and maintain those dividends. If Pitney Bowes somehow calamitously lost half of its earnings, it could still use its free cash flow to make good on its promised dividend payments. It wouldn't have to, but it would be able to. That would be a far from ideal situation, and ultimately the dividend would disintegrate if nothing improved, but Pitney Bowes could tide itself over long enough either for you to sell before the dividend implodes, or for its earnings to come back. None of these situations seems likely, but after the speed and severity of the recent crash, it pays to be careful.

Finally, to round out your dividend safety inspection, you always have to check out the company's balance sheet. For whatever it's worth, Pitney Bowes has an A-rated balance sheet according to the ratings agencies. While the ratings agencies are almost universally loathed and their opinions considered by some to be punch lines to mediocre jokes, amazingly they are still very important because potential moneylenders listen to what they have to say. So an A-rated balance sheet, whether it's deserved or not, is a plus simply because the rating makes it much easier to borrow money. However, a company's credit rating is not generally key to the survival of its dividend. We need to check out the balance sheet in order to be sure of a company's dividend because if it has a great deal of debt in general, or worse, a great deal of debt coming due over the next few years, then it may be sorely tempted to slash the dividend in order to pay off angry bondholders. Fortunately, Pitney Bowes has very little debt coming due over the next few years, so we can consider its dividend safe. On *Mad Money* we've been hurt recommending some stocks where debt was coming due. We thought they would be able to roll over their debt to the out years, but that hasn't always been the case. Some companies have been unable to do so, including one of my utility favorites, Great Plains Energy (GXP), which cut its dividend even though business was really good, because the credit markets were closed to just about everyone when GXP needed new debt.

What about other factors, such as consistency? Doesn't a company get any points for raising its dividend year after year and decade after decade? Shouldn't we be more inclined to trust a company with a long history of dividend boosts? As I said earlier, I think dividend boosts are a terrific sign of strength in a company, but they don't necessarily show that the company doing the boosting will be able to maintain its higher dividend. Consider the case of Masco (MAS), a company that makes cabinets, faucets, and other fixtures for kitchens and bathrooms. Masco had a long history of dividend boosts. For fifty consecutive years this company increased the size of its dividend. For fifty years the company had no need to cut its dividend. Then Masco raised its annual payout to 94 cents a share on October 28, 2008. Masco's dividend was the very opposite of safe; it ran roughshod over all three rules, and when its business tanked in 2009, it had to slash its dividend severely. To this day I still cannot fathom what was going through the heads of the people running this company when they approved a dividend increase. Probably not very much.

You need to know what an unsafe dividend looks like so you can avoid them. The sad truth is that the people running many companies are often too out of touch or overconfident to know what's happening and what needs to be done until it hits them right in the face, and by then it's too late. Masco's dividend was extremely unsafe even before the October 2008 increase from a 92-cent annual payout to a 94-cent annual payout. No one who understood how to do this kind of basic homework—the dividend safety test that you just learned—would ever have permitted the company to raise its dividend at that time. First, we subject Masco to the earnings test. Since it's a much more cyclical company than Pitney Bowes, being heavily levered to housing, you would expect Masco's earnings to be much less consistent, swinging wildly with the gyrations of the economy. That would have been fine by itself if the company were either paying a much smaller dividend or making a whole lot more money, but the actual numbers were just plain absurd. For the four quarters leading up to Masco's dividend boost in October 2008, the company's earnings per share never once reached the level of the quarterly dividend payout. The estimates of how much Masco was expected to earn in 2009 and 2010 were all over the place, but even the most bullish analysts fell well short of predicting that Masco could earn 94 cents in either year, which would have meant three years in a row where Masco's dividend payout towered over its earnings per share. Masco even had an outrageously high yield of 9.4 percent, practically screaming to the world that it was too high to be maintained and would soon be slashed. That's practically a textbook case of a dangerous dividend.

Now, of course, you know exactly how Masco was capable of sustaining a dividend that cost more money than the company earned: by making the case that it had enough free cash flow to finance its dividend in the short run despite its lack of coverage. When Masco raised its dividend in October 2008, management was still talking about generating $600 million in free cash flow for the full year. In fact Masco's free cash flow came to only $560 million for 2008. Moreover, a little homework showed that Masco was generating much of its cash by taking longer to pay its own bills and demanding that its customers settle their tabs with Masco more quickly. That's just not a way to sustainably strengthen your business. How about Masco's balance sheet? After failing the dividend safety test based on earnings, then again on free cash flow, a clean balance sheet wouldn't change anything. In fact, Masco had about $4 billion of debt at the time, although management usually spent more time highlighting the billion dollars of cash on its balance sheet. On all three criteria, Masco's dividend looked about as unsafe as it could get, a dividend disaster area. So the very next day after doing this analysis, I went on my television show and predicted that this company would have to cut its dividend and its yield was totally illusory, and Masco did just that after the close on February 11, 2009, bringing its annual dividend payout down from 94 cents to 30 cents a share.

Every time you want to buy a high-yielding stock, you have to go through these three steps to make sure that dividend is safe. Consider them a checklist to help with your homework on dividend-paying stocks. Believe me, you aren't really protecting your investments from downside risk, or anything else for that matter—your future, your children's future, you name it—if you aren't careful about where you put your money. A company that looks unable to maintain a big dividend usually finds itself connected to a stock that loses you money. So be careful and be safe when you use stocks with big dividends to help preserve your capital or to grow it.

Diversified Dividend Portfolio

Given all the benefits you get from owning stocks with high dividend yields, is there anything stopping you from putting together an all-dividend portfolio? Would that high-yielding portfolio pass our standards of diversification as long as all of its stocks were in different sectors, or would relying on dividend income for such a large portion of your returns be too much like putting all of your eggs in one basket? Remember, there are certain factors, such as inflation and interest rates, that make dividend-paying stocks more or less attractive as sources of income relative to other investments. You could see how that might theoretically cause all high yielders to trade closely in line with each other, but compared to other factors, like whether a stock's sector is in or out of favor, the attractiveness of its dividend as a source of income is just not that important: not as inconsequential as a drop of water in the ocean, but more like a few buckets of water in a swimming pool. So here's what I would say about whether a portfolio of all high yielders could be diversified: it depends. You would be walking a fine line between diversification and nondiversification, but not because all your stocks would have big dividends. Bear in mind that when we talk about a diversified portfolio of stocks we mostly mean diversified by sector. Companies that pay consistently large dividends are hard to find in some sectors and plentiful in others. Even if you did make sure there was no overlap, you still would lack some important groups, including fast growers, and growth is precious on Wall Street. Still, it is difficult for me to imagine an event that made paying a dividend a huge liability and crushed every high yielder out there, especially since the companies could simply eliminate their dividends.

Dividend-yielding stocks make tons of sense for a discretionary portfolio. But the best place for them, at least for most of you, would be your individual retirement account, your IRA, where you could reinvest your prodigious payouts and let them compound tax-free for years, even decades. The dividend tax rate may be a paltry 15 percent, but I would rather keep that 15 percent for the purposes of growing my capital, as an IRA allows you to do—no taxes on anything inside the account until you pay income tax on the money you withdraw after you have retired. That's a subject I'll tell you more about later. For now let's concentrate on using high yielders to get your retirement portfolio and your nonretirement, account back to even, the milestone you need to reach with your money before you can get rich.

To that end I have put together a diversified portfolio of intentionally high yielders with the help of Dave Peltier, who knows all of this stuff cold as the writer of the *Dividend Stock Advisor* newsletter, part of the lineup of excellent services TheStreet.com offers to investors seeking knowledge about investing and rigorous analysis in this most critical area. With Dave's assistance I came up with five terrific stocks, or actually four stocks and one ETF, which you can choose from, as the template for a dividend portfolio, or simply view as examples of what to look for before you buy, not just a high yielder, but any stock.

What I am about to do is considered the height of insanity by anyone who writes about stocks. Many of these people are either afraid or unable to recommend a stock in a column, but a book? What the heck am I thinking? I could be wrong! And it would be in print forever! Anyone who picks stocks will be wrong sometimes; that's why I've spent so much time teaching how to minimize the damage from these inevitable mistakes. The real reason I feel like I'm putting my head on the chopping block is that you could pick up this book a year or two from now, and in that time just about anything could happen to ruin one of these stocks, or the fundamentals could change in a more subtle manner, making these stocks more dangerous. I can live with being embarrassed, but what I cannot handle is the idea that you might lose money—especially after all that's already been wiped out by the crash and the real estate collapse—because you bought one of these stocks after the fundamentals had changed and the story no longer made sense. You need to promise me something. It's the same thing I always demand from anyone who wants to own individual stocks: do some homework before you buy any of these stocks. Don't think you can be lazier with these stocks or any others in *Getting Back to Even* just because I put them in a book. Understood? Good, because I don't want you reading this list unless you're willing to research these stocks before you buy them. Here they are, the five stocks in my Dividend Defensive Line.

1. **Eli Lilly (LLY):** With a hefty 5.8 percent yield, the Indianapolis-based Lilly has one of the highest yields of any big pharma company, and it's the only member of that cohort still consistently

raising its dividend. Pfizer (PFE) cut its payout, while Wyeth (WYE), Merck (MRK), and Bristol-Myers Squibb (BMY) are just holding pat. Lilly's willingness to increase its payout is sign of strength that you will find nowhere else in big pharma. The company made some smart acquisitions in 2008, including buying ImClone for $6 billion.

The ImClone acquisition was worth every penny. Its strong biotech franchise provides immediate growth, the kind that companies like Lilly salivate over, thanks to the cancer drug Erbitux. The acquisition also helps bolster Lilly's drug pipeline before its current top seller, the antipsychotic Zyprexa, loses patent protection in 2011. Thanks to Erbitux, Lilly is now one of very few companies with a strong anticancer franchise, a category of drugs that governments around the world are still willing to reimburse insurers for. That matters at a time when almost every developed country faces ballooning budget deficits and the president of the United States is committed to cutting health-care costs.

How about that dividend? Eli Lilly has boosted its payout for forty-one consecutive years, most recently in December 2008, when it raised its quarterly dividend to 49 cents a share, which comes to $1.96 annually. How does Lilly stand up to the safety test? The company can cover its payout 2.2 times with expected 2009 earnings of $4.22 a share. Two thumbs up, way up. And since Lilly's profit is expected to grow another 7 percent in 2010, we will likely see more dividend boosts here. LLY has a fair amount of debt on its balance sheet, but it still garners an A rating from the major agencies. Part of this is because the company has only $400 million in debt coming due in 2009, and nothing else until 2012. No need to worry on that front, either. But not everything is smooth sailing in this stock.

Lilly's and the entire industry's biggest fear is the potential pressure that President Obama could exert on pricing with the group. That's why I picked the high yielder with the best earnings coverage in the industry, and a decent balance sheet to boot. As one of the largest employers in Indiana, a swing state, Lilly has strong support among the state's senators and congressmen, which has allowed it to get maximum reimbursement for its breakthrough mental health drugs. I also believe that no matter how committed Congress and the Obama administration are to health-care reform, Lilly's valuation reflects a worst-case scenario.

2. **Consolidated Edison (ED):** Better known as Con Ed, this Manhattan-based 6.4 percent yielder has the highest yield of all the regulated utilities whose debt gets an A rating from the major credit rating agencies. In January 2009, Con Ed boosted its dividend for the thirty-fourth consecutive year and now has a quarterly payout of 59 cents, adding up to $2.36 annually.

Unfortunately, covering that dividend will eat up 74 percent of the company's expected 2009 earnings of $3.21. Normally, to consider its dividend safe a company's earnings should be at least twice the size of the payout. Con Ed, however, is not a normal company. State regulators set the rates that Con Ed and other utilities can charge, as well as the return on equity that they can earn. In April 2009, Con Ed was granted a $721 million rate increase and demand for electricity should pick up once the economy begins to recover, two reasons to feel far more comfortable that Con Ed's long history of dividend boosts won't come to an ignominious end any time soon.

Part of the reason Con Ed got that rate hike is its terrific management. Its CEO, Kevin Burke, is a longtime utility executive who knows the in and outs of the regulatory regime. Unlike other utilities, Con Ed's earnings are far less vulnerable to the possibility of climate change legislation like cap-and-trade, since it stopped burning coal decades ago and has in fact sold most of its electric generation business. Rather, Con Ed is focused on the most basic of utility businesses, transmitting and distributing electricity, natural gas, and steam to its customers. I consider it one of a handful of utilities that can be considered "Obama-proof."

3. **AT&T (T):** Along with Verizon (VZ), which could just as easily have been on this list since it's just as good as a company and a stock, AT&T is dominating the wireless space and paying you a 6.4 percent yield to watch it happen. We all know the iPhone has been a big winner for the company, bringing over new customers, who are paying for a more expensive, high-speed data plan. AT&T's U-verse television offering has also quickly reached 1 million subscribers, though both of these growth drivers are somewhat offset by the loss of traditional landlines, once the company's bread and butter. This isn't your old Ma Bell, but rather a super high-tech company that is at the cutting edge of all things communications. Despite the losses in the plain old-fashioned telephone business, wireless customers are spending more per user than ever. And through cost cutting, the company's operating margin has been steadily climbing.

   In December 2008, AT&T raised its dividend for the twenty-fourth consecutive year, with a new quarterly payout of 41 cents a share, adding up to $1.64 for the full year. AT&T's dividend will eat up 78 percent of its expected 2009 earnings, which is nowhere near as safe as we would like. But AT&T deserves some leeway here because of its stable business, which also has room for price increases for its services. Even though the earnings don't come to twice the dividend, AT&T does pass the free-cash-flow test, since it generated 43 percent more free cash flow than reported net income over the past four quarters. Its debt is also rated in the A range by the major ratings agencies, and it has a terrific CEO in Randall Stephenson.

4. **PowerShares Financial Preferred Portfolio (PGF):** This is not a stock, but an exchange-traded fund, or ETF, that yields roughly 11.6 percent and follows thirty preferred stocks in the financial industry, allowing you to gain exposure to different companies without concentrating too heavily on any particular one. (I'll say more about ETFs in a later chapter.)

Preferred stocks are like a hybrid security that's half bond and half stock. The dividends are fixed, like a bond. And if there's not enough money to pay all of a company's dividends, preferred holders get their money before the common stock dividend can be paid, the same as if the business is liquidated—preferred shareholders come before the common when it comes to receiving any available proceeds from liquidation. In return, you usually give up voting rights and some potential upside if the common stock really takes off—as we saw in the financials after the bottom in early March 2009.

This ETF could come in handy, since banks will have to pay high preferred yields to survive in this difficult environment in order to raise capital. The underlying index that this ETF tracks is a market-capitalization-weighted portfolio from Wachovia, now a subsidiary of Wells Fargo, that is subject to its own selection methodology. It does include some international exposure.

The ETF has paid a monthly dividend since inception in 2006, lately ranging from 10 to 12 cents. Based on the most recent payout of 11.404 cents, the fund yields 11.6 percent. That's about four times the average yield of the benchmark S&P 500. I am including this ETF because I don't want to single out any particular bank preferred stock for fear that the bank might stumble, but taken collectively the yield here is simply too juicy to ignore now that it seems very unlikely that the government will nationalize the banks. I believe banks will rally strongly as the economy recovers, and this security should capture most of that move with a lot more safety and much better income.

5. **Kinder Morgan Energy Partners (KMP):** This company is what's called a master limited partnership, or MLP, and MLPs like this one are often referred to as energy trusts. These MLPs pay no corporate taxes and pass almost all of their earnings to shareholders in the form of a distribution, which is very similar to a dividend. The MLP structure may seem confusing to you, but Kinder

Morgan Energy Partners trades just like any other stock and you can look it up and track it under its KMP symbol. KMP yields about 8 percent as I write, although with this kind of company the yield tends to be volatile as the distribution changes every quarter, depending upon how much money the company makes. The company is a pipeline operator with 26,000 miles of lines and about 170 terminals. As opposed to other companies that bring oil and natural gas out of the ground or refine it into other products, Kinder is more like a toll collector that earns money by storing and transmitting the commodities from one place to another. The tolls never stop coming as the customers rely on KMP's pipes for their natural gas use. It has no exposure to the actual price of the natural gas it ships, making it far less risky than almost all other energy trusts, so don't fret if you see the fuel skyrocket or crash. It's all the same to KMP.

Kinder Morgan, currently trading at about $50, has steadily raised its payout every quarter or two since 1997. The company currently pays out $1.05 a quarter, which management can more than cover with internal cash flow. The company is not shying away from new potential growth projects (when backed by long-term contracts) that the competition is not in a position to undertake, which means it could be able to raise its payout for years and years to come.

Now that you know how to play defense with dividends, we can get more aggressive. In the next chapter we'll explore a bit further the stocks that might lead the recovery, and how you can get on them before the recovery happens.

5

HOW TO INVEST IN THE RECOVERY
Twelve Stocks to Watch

No matter how gloomy the economic environment may seem, no matter how grim the state of business may feel, both in America and across the globe, sooner or later the economy will recover. Believe it or not, I think sooner is actually a whole lot more likely than later. But regardless of when the economy recovers, it's important not to lose sight of the simple fact that it will recover. After the vicious financial thrashing the market has doled out to most of us over the last two years, it would be far too easy to convince ourselves that things will never get better, that we will be stuck in a permanent rut, or at the very least in one that will take years to get out of. As intuitively appealing as that notion might be, it is very unlikely. Given the losses many of you have taken, the idea of betting on an economic rebound may seem insane or worse. Investors, both professionals and amateurs alike, lost countless billions of dollars trying to anticipate a rebound as the global economy stalled and stocks collapsed throughout 2008 and early 2009. Every time you convinced yourself that the worst was over and put your money on the kind of stocks that do well during a recovery, the economy failed to rebound and you lost even more money.

Even if it was wrong to believe in a recovery as business activity slowed to a crawl across the globe, that doesn't mean that betting on a recovery will always be a sucker's move. And despite the negative pronouncements of numerous economists, including some Nobel Prize winners who claim that a quick a speedy recovery is impossible and we're in for a lengthy period of slow to nonexistent economic growth, you have to be willing to believe that things can and will get better. They always have. Sure, we have experienced the worst recession since the Great Depression, the worst stock market crash since the Depression, too. Our financial system came close to collapse. Few anticipated just how bad the situation would get—certainly not anyone in government—until it was too late. Does that mean a recovery could take longer than usual to arrive? That's a possibility. The idea that it will never arrive, on the other hand, is absurd. And not only that, it's a money loser.

You're probably willing to acknowledge that the economy will eventually recover. So what? Why not wait patiently for the signs of a recovery to arrive, signs such as improved GDP growth, decreasing unemployment, and rising corporate earnings, before sticking your neck out and betting on a rebound? Because if you do that, you will miss the easy money, the big money that's there for the taking in the stock market at the beginning of any turn in the economy. If you let yourself wait until the turn is obvious to everyone, then the stocks you would buy to play that turn will already have made serious moves higher. My goal in this book is to make back the money you've lost in the market or from losing your income or having to take a pay cut, so that you can have the life you always planned on living, and eventually make enough money to do even better than that. If you invest in the stocks that will snap back the hardest when the global economy starts to recover, if you buy them ahead of that turn, then once it hits, you can sit back and let the market make money for you. Just as owning stocks caused you to take enormous losses on the way down, buying stocks on sell-offs now, I believe, will give you terrific gains on the way back up. You will still have to do the homework, but it will be some of the easiest money you have ever made in the market.

It's easy, even reflexive, to be afraid and pessimistic after the awful times we've been through, but you cannot allow the recent past to cloud your judgment and blind you to opportunities. We always want to keep our eyes peeled and be open to any opportunity to make money, even if it goes against the prevailing sense that everything is horrible and will stay that way for years. I just can't buy into that forecast. I have managed money through multiple recessions, and there has always been light at the end of the tunnel. Seeing that light before anyone else, or simply banking on it being there even if you can't see it yet, by buying the stocks that soar during an economic recovery, has always been a sound strategy, as long as you don't come in too early. I now believe we are no longer too early. I think we are at the moment of greatest risk-reward to buy stock that perform well in an improving world economy.

There is already ample evidence of a turn starting in China, and I would not be at all surprised if the U.S. economy and the global economy recover fairly strongly in 2010. I think it would be extraordinarily unlikely if we are not the midst of a full-blown recovery by 2011. Remember that stocks typically forecast about six months into the future, meaning their prices reflect not the way the world is now, but what it will look like, or at least what investors think it will look like, in six months. As a prediction machine, the market is unequaled by just about anything else ever devised, intentionally or accidentally, by mankind. So if you expect the economy to begin recovering in six months, you don't wait half a year to start buying the recovery stocks, you do it immediately.

Given that a recovery could be that close by the time you read this, I want to do my absolute best to make sure you can capitalize on it. So, I am going to give you a list of twelve stocks that I consider to be some of the best plays on a turn in the global economy. These are the stocks that I would buy in order to profit from a recovery. In fact, I own many of these stocks for my charitable trust, which you can follow at ActionAlertsPlus.com, because even when the profits all go to charity, I still believe in putting my money where my mouth is. I opine on these stocks weekly, sometimes even daily, so remember that if you need to be kept up to date on them. (If one of these stocks develops a problem, you should be able to sidestep a big decline by reading ActionAlertsPlus.com or by watching *Mad Money* and hearing what I say about the stock.) One of the reasons I think it's safe to recommend these stocks, and safe for you to buy them, is that even if I turn out to be wrong and the recovery takes longer than expected to arrive, we've reached a point where the downside in these cyclical stocks is fairly limited. Their earnings estimates have already been slashed, severely, for 2010 so there's little danger that these companies will disappoint by reporting worse-than-expected numbers. Many of the stocks on the list have dividends that offer solid downside protection as I described earlier, and for the most part their valuations are low enough that there's only so far down their share prices can slide before opportunistic buyers will step in en masse, or, with some of the smaller companies, another business will launch a takeover bid.

I believe it is safe to start investing in cyclical companies, like the recovery plays on my list, because the economic situation has stopped deteriorating. We no longer need to fear massive, widespread bank failures. Countries all around the world are spending colossal sums of money on economic stimulus packages in order to jump-start their economies, immediately creating business for some of these stocks and making the conditions for a global recovery possible. And central banks the world over, especially the Federal Reserve here in the United States, have dramatically cut interest rates in order to spur economic growth. In any other recession, if the Fed effectively took rates to zero, as it did in December 2008, the economy would have immediately begun to rebound. Given the severity of the latest downturn, rate cuts alone were not enough to get us out of the morass. Nevertheless, I almost always think it's a bad idea to fight the Fed. What do I mean? When the Fed is raising interest rates, that slows economic growth and causes the big institutional investors who control stock prices in the short run to sell the stocks of economically sensitive, cyclical companies. In that situation, fighting the Fed would mean buying those cyclical stocks and selling the more consistent defensive stocks that do well during most slowdowns. When the Fed is cutting rates, or taking novel steps to dramatically increase the amount of money in the system, as it started to do after cutting rates to zero, fighting the Fed would mean buying the dull, defensive, consistent growers and selling the cyclicals. So when you buy any of the recovery stocks on my list, the Fed is on your side, and eventually the mutual funds that predictably move vast sums of money around based on factors like economic growth and interest rates should be on your side, too. Buying by mutual funds should move these stocks sharply higher. If anything, I think it might be more risky not to own any recovery stocks than to buy some of them and bet the economy will improve.

Beyond the specifics of the current situation, I also don't want to hold anything back. I don't mean to brag, but I've always been a good stock picker. So while I still firmly believe that regular people are just as capable of picking winners as professionals, so long as they're willing to put enough time and effort into the process, it would be disingenuous not to reveal the stocks that I think represent the best plays on an economic recovery, even if some of them end up being wrong. If you want to buy any of my twelve recovery stocks, you still need to do the homework yourself, since relying on someone else's judgment instead of your own is a sure way to lose money. That said, I'm willing to meet you halfway, to explain the reasons why I like each stock, and to show you how I do the homework and make decisions about buying and selling these stocks in my ActionAlertsPlus.com newsletter so that you can follow along.

Before you read through my twelve recovery stocks, you need to understand what this list is and what it is not. I am not giving you a diversified portfolio of stocks that are poised to make money when the global economy recovers. That would be a contradiction in terms. Even though the list covers more than five different sectors, you are not diversified if every stock in your portfolio is levered to the strength of the underlying economy. You cannot own only these stocks in your portfolio, even if, like me, you believe that a recovery could be imminent. At the same time, this is not just a list of stocks that I think are worth buying. These are examples of what you should look for in high-quality stocks, both generally speaking and in order to make money from an economic recovery. The analysis of each company and its stock that I am including mirrors the analysis that you should do whenever you are evaluating the stock of a company that's new to you. One more caveat: if the facts have changed by the time you read this and what I've written about any of the twelve companies below is no longer true, then take a pass. I think these stocks are great plays on a turn in the economy, and they could all make excellent long-term investments if bought at the right, low price, given what I know about them right now. But companies can change their stripes quickly, and as with any stock, if the thesis behind owning any of the stocks on this list falls apart, then you have to be willing to acknowledge that fact and sell the stock. Now let's get down to business with my twelve favorite stocks for playing the recovery, my very own not-so-dirty dozen.

RECOVERY STOCKS

Caterpillar (CAT)

When it comes to a global recovery, the most important and economically sensitive segment of worldwide business, the part of industry that will snap back the hardest and make you the most money when things get better, is machinery, particularly machinery that helps build infrastructure. That's why you should consider owning Caterpillar, the largest and best manufacturer of construction equipment around the world, a recognized machinery brand name like no other, and one of America's most important exporters. Although most people think of this company as a simple maker of earthmoving machinery, Caterpillar also makes all kinds of engines and turbines for industrial use. I like this Peoria, Illinois–based company now because many governments around the world want to put people to work building bridges and roads, and they can't really embark on those kinds of public works projects without buying Caterpillar's engines, tractors, and earthmovers.

Caterpillar has had a very tough time since the global economy peaked, but 2010 looks to be a big improvement over the last two years. In order to cope with the worldwide slowdown, the company has fired thousands of workers and slashed $3 billion in inventory to cut costs, so it will be a leaner, meaner, more profitable enterprise when things finally improve. Wall Street doesn't care how you get to a good bottom line; it will buy the stock of any company that is efficient and squeezes the most lemonade out of the fewest lemons. Caterpillar's aggressive workforce and inventory reductions will make its earnings explode once all of the stimulus orders hit its factories.

Caterpillar is a truly global company and it has substantial operations in the United States, Europe, the Middle East, Africa, Latin America, and Asia Pacific. It generates over 60 percent of its sales outside the United States, including a large China business, where it has already started to see a recovery, with record sales for its excavation equipment and solid diesel engine orders. The downturn has been anything but easy for Caterpillar, with engine sales falling 8 percent, machine sales dropping 29 percent, and operating margins, that is, how much money it makes from each dollar of sales before paying interest or taxes, plummeting from 11 percent to 2 percent in 2008 as lower revenues, sales volumes, and restructuring costs negatively impacted results. Yet, amazingly, as dire as those numbers were, the company's profits actually didn't fare much worse than the optimistic analyst community expected, largely because Caterpillar is among the best-run manufacturing corporations in the world. Even as business slowed down across the entire industry, Caterpillar has managed to take market share from all of its competitors during the downturn, while actually improving its balance sheet through aggressive sales of existing inventory and better cash management. Not many companies, particularly of the industrial, smokestack variety, can say they spent the recession taking market share *and* cleaning up their balance sheets. Once the recovery picks up, Caterpillar will truly be in better shape than ever.

At first glance, Caterpillar appears to be an expensive stock, at least at the moment. When we analyze a stock's valuation, the first, most basic step is to compare its price-to-earnings multiple with the price-to-earnings multiple of the average stock in the S&P 500, sometimes called the market multiple, because that's what every money manager uses as a benchmark. Caterpillar sells at 25 times earnings, while the average stock in the S&P 500 sells for about half of that. Even though this stock looks prohibitively expensive, its multiple is so high only because those earnings are extremely depressed. When the business bounces back, Caterpillar will end up looking very cheap on what is known as forward earnings, meaning what it's expected to earn in the future, such as 2010 or 2011. Once we get a turn in the economy, Caterpillar's earnings will rocket higher, and based on those numbers the stock's multiple will be much smaller. You have to buy these big cyclical companies when their price-to-earnings ratios are at their highest based on trailing earnings, meaning the earnings per share over the last four quarters. That is the metric normally used when you look up a company's price-to-earnings ratio, because those past earnings do not represent the future profits that a company like Caterpillar should generate in the kind of turnaround we are expecting. I know it's counterintuitive, the notion that you have to buy cyclical stocks like Caterpillar when they seem to be at their most expensive, but those seemingly expensive multiples only indicate that you're buying before the company's earnings have turned around and you are getting into the stock ahead of the crowd. That's exactly the way you want to approach Caterpillar and other companies like it.

On top of everything else, Caterpillar has reduced expectations to where I think almost any disappointment is already factored into the stock, including any potential damage to its dividend. So as you wait for the rebound, very little in the way of bad news could still crush the stock. I have owned or traded Caterpillar for thirty years, and I can never recall this highest-quality manufacturer trading as cheaply as it has in 2009.

3M (MMM)

Few companies stand to benefit more from a global economic resurgence than 3M, which manufactures perhaps the broadest product array of any American company. Its businesses are so diverse, so different, ranging from Post-its and glass computer screens, to health-care products and road signs, to Scotch tape and Thinsulate, that money managers tend to view 3M as the ideal proxy for any rebound. Believe me, this Dow stock will be the first thing most money managers reach for when they are confident that a strong recovery is at hand, and you want to be in it ahead of the stampede of big-money investors. You get well compensated for waiting, since 3M has a bountiful dividend. The company boosted its payout in early 2009, despite the harsh global economic environment. Based in St. Paul, the old Minnesota Mining and Manufacturing has more revenues from overseas than just about any other major American manufacturer, with only 36 percent of its sales coming from inside the United States. The one thing we can say for sure about the recovery is that it will start in China, which, with its massive and effective stimulus packages, will be the engine driving any global economic rebound. We don't know where it will take hold next, but given that 20 percent of 3M's business is in China, 25 percent in Asia Pacific, and 11 percent in Latin America and Canada, we can be confident that 3M will get its fair share of the recovery pie.

The company is a market leader: 72 percent of its sales are in businesses where 3M is growing faster and more profitably than its competitors. Over the past ten years 3M's margins have outpaced those of the industry by more than 10 percent, a pretty enviable record. It also has a fantastic balance sheet with over $2 a share in cash and has raised its dividend for fifty-one straight years and 370 straight quarters. That kind of consistent, dependable dividend raising is a pretty strong indication of 3M's consistent, long-term health.

What's more, 3M was one of the few companies that saw this huge downturn coming. It quickly set the bar extremely low, predicting a dramatic decrease in volume for all its businesses, which cratered the stock to levels not seen for decades. But now, because the company has managed to put through price increases on many of its product lines and has enjoyed a hefty decline in commodity costs, particularly those involving petroleum-based products such as plastic, 3M can easily meet or beat the Street's earnings expectations for several quarters, and given its record of inventing new products, perhaps for years to come. And that's without even factoring in much of a recovery. This is especially important, since there is no better recipe for a higher stock price than reporting a better-than-expected quarter. Like Caterpillar, 3M's stock trades as if the recession will never end, so the snapback could propel the stock substantially higher than its current price.

Emerson Electric (EMR)

Some companies quietly go about making parts and tools for other businesses, equipment that helps fluids and gases move swiftly and rapidly, or keeps engines humming or the power running evenly and cleanly. You don't ever buy their products as a consumer, but when big corporations want to build new plants and install better equipment or want to expand—both logical outgrowths of an economic rebound—you can bet that Emerson Electric will get a ton of business. Emerson's a diversified global industrial company with more than 75 percent of its businesses tied to infrastructure spending, so every time you hear the word *stimulus* from a world leader, you can bet this company's bottom line will benefit. Its products are offered across no fewer than eight diverse platforms: Process Management, Industrial Automation, Network Power, Climate Technologies, Appliances, Storage Solutions, Professional Tools, and Motor Embedded Systems, exactly the kind of gear that businesses invest in when the economy starts to expand again.

I believe that among the first markets to snap back to normal growth will be the so-called emerging markets, that is, the economies of less-developed but faster-growing countries that have ample room to build new plant and equipment. Emerson is such a great recovery stock because 55 percent of its businesses sell into those emerging markets. Despite being the envy of almost every other industrial company in the United States, with its legendarily run motor and flow control products (the gear you need to determine if you are getting enough fuel into your turbines, if you are wasting energy, or if your machines are overheating), Emerson has had to slash its earnings outlook several times to the point where I am at last confident that it can easily beat expectations for several years to come. This proud St. Louis–based corporation is an extremely conservative company, so it astonishes me to see that its stock yields 4 percent, absurdly high for such a solid growth enterprise. However, that's not because the company is being reckless and paying out a larger dividend than it can afford; Emerson is one of the accidentally high yielders I discussed earlier. It has a high yield only because its stock has come down much further than almost anyone had ever thought possible, so the low share price of the stock, divided by the dividend, produces large yield. Emerson is another company that will pay you to wait for the economy to rebound, and I think that's a pretty sweet deal.

I don't like recommending that anyone "buy and hold" a stock, because I believe in buying and doing homework, but ever since I got to spend some time with the top executives of Emerson back when I worked at Goldman Sachs, I have been enamored of this company's ability to stay ahead of all of the other traditional Midwest "metal benders" that compete to make the best tools and engines needed to meet plant and equipment expansion.

The company is not waiting for a turn; it has trimmed its workforce aggressively, figured out how to cut $400 million in costs out of its budget, and dramatically cut back its capital expenditures. It will be in fabulous shape to reap the benefits of this restructuring when business eventually rebounds. Emerson is the most expensive of the pure industrial companies I am recommending here, but that's because it has a long history of consistent growth even in the toughest of times and mutual fund managers like the comfort of that record when the world's economies turn as grim as they have over the last few years.

Union Pacific (UNP)

I have been a huge fan of the U.S. railroad business ever since the government allowed the many railroad companies across the country to merge into four nationwide enterprises that don't compete with each other in most markets. If I were a railroad customer I would certainly not have favored these mergers, since they have allowed the Big Four to raise rates substantially beyond what they used to be able to charge back when there was genuine competition. But that's precisely why we want to own one of them as a play on the recovery. Their only real competition now is from trucks, and the economics of shipping in a world where diesel prices are much higher than they used to be—a train runs about four hundred miles on a gallon of diesel—drastically favors the rails. It also helps that many of our exports to overseas, mostly coal, grain, timber, and fertilizer, can be shipped to ports effectively only by railroads, not trucks.

Which one to pick? Why not go with the largest, Union Pacific, with thirty-three thousand miles of track throughout twenty-three states. The company's revenues come from a diversified variety of industries—agriculture, coal, auto, chemicals, energy, and other industrial products—so, unlike several of its competitors, it is not dependent on one or two industries that could contract still further if the economy doesn't improve. Another advantage Union Pacific has over its peers is that it has the highest concentration of two of our largest exports to China, agricultural products and coal, which represent 37 percent of its revenues and tend to be more stable sources of earnings than other goods. Union Pacific is also a worst-to-first situation: it was an amalgam of the most poorly run and least economically rational railroads from before the mergers, and now it stands to gain the most as its integration, cost cutting, and higher contract prices start to hit the bottom line.

As the economy gradually recovers, railcar traffic will pick up, even as it's been in the doldrums for most of the year, with carloadings, the metric we use to measure how a railroad is doing year over year, down more than 20 percent in 2009 from 2008. I believe that railcar volume has started to bottom and that you want to get into this stock before it rallies back to the old, precrash levels. The stock has begun to move higher as the decline in shipping has leveled off, and I expect this rally to continue as the data begins to go positive. Despite the national economic weakness, Union Pacific should be able to increase prices by around 5–6 percent for the next several years (which is higher than the industry average) because many of its older contracts, negotiated when there was still serious competition, are up for renewal and are uniformly being renegotiated at higher prices. Union Pacific has a meaningful number of contracts that are five to ten years old with outdated prices that will increase even if the economy just muddles along, because much of the freight-forwarding competition has been eliminated in the time since these deals were inked. In addition, Union Pacific, unlike the other rails, still has substantial fat to cut, and its aggressive cost cutting during this severe recession could produce big upside earnings surprises down the road. In its most recent quarter, at the time of my writing, Union Pacific improved its operating efficiency ratio by 1.2 percent, to a record 80.3 percent, which matters when you are being paid hundreds of millions of dollars to move freight. I think Union Pacific's management can generate another 10 percent cut in costs and productivity improvements, which should add between 50 cents and $1 a share to its 2010 earnings, even in a worst-case scenario situation with no economic recovery.

But I don't think we're in for that scenario; I see a recovery coming. As the economy gradually rebounds and volumes slowly improve, I believe pricing will get even stronger and the cost cutting will balloon the company's bottom line. Combine all of these facts with a cheap valuation—Union Pacific is the cheapest of the rails, since the market has yet to grasp the positive changes that the company has made—and the stock should be able to work its way higher for several years to come. As I write, the shares remain attractive at 11.4 times 2010 earnings estimates, a valuation that's well below the company's historical average of 16 times earnings, and one that he might look back on in disbelief one or two years from now. Take a ride on the Union Pacific and prepare for multiyear gains.

PPG (PPG)

When you're putting together a list of stocks to take advantage of a recovery, you are going to need at least one chemical company, such as a DuPont (DD), a Dow Chemical (DOW), or a PPG, the old Pittsburgh Plate Glass. While DuPont is a venerable brand, it has too much exposure to housing and to pharmaceuticals that are coming off patent. Dow Chemical would have been my favorite in another era, because it had a fine balance sheet and a big dividend. But the company has hurt its finances by ludicrously overpaying for Rohm and Haas, another U.S.-based chemical company, and it has subsequently had to cut its dividend and, insult to injury, offer new stock at 50 percent below the price where it was buying it back just a year earlier to shore up its cash balances! (Participating in that offering made you a huge amount of money in a short time, a strategy we will discuss in a later chapter.) Dow management is suspect and its CEO at one point landed on *Mad Money*'s "Wall of Shame," a place I reserve for the most egregious *Titanic*-like captains of industry. That leaves PPG, the best of the lot, and a company that has reinvented itself without a bit of fanfare, making itself over from a company that just produced paint and commodity glass for car windows into a specialty chemical company in all sorts of great niches that will recover much faster than any of Dow Chemical or DuPont's businesses will.

PPG is a perfect way to play the recovery because of its vast exposure to many different end markets around the world, including manufacturing, construction, automotive, consumer products, and chemical-processing industries. Its geographic sales breakdown is a good mix as well: about 37 percent in North America, 37 percent in Europe, 11 percent in Latin America, and 15 percent in Asia, the last the fastest-growing region for its chemicals.

PPG has been relentlessly exiting businesses that have a huge amount of competition, including its namesake business, plate glass, and getting into specialty glasses that save energy or provide value added that you probably don't even know about. I recently bought a pair of "transitional" glasses that are clear indoors but turn into sunglasses outside and I was surprised to learn that they were made by PPG, a typical innovation that you can now expect from this once-sleepy company.

Management is not done paring back underperforming businesses, and I would not be surprised if PPG sold off some of its more uninspiring product lines, including flat glass, fiberglass, and chloralkali chemicals. The company also has a gigantic bill for natural gas, a key ingredient for all of its glass and coatings businesses, and it's just beginning to benefit from the dramatic decline in natural gas pricing from 2008 levels. That alone could make PPG more profitable than the Street expects as the downturn continues. In 2008 it spent $450 million more on fuel than it had anticipated, so its lower energy bill could be a key swing to big profits. The company should also have integration gains from its purchase in 2008 of SigmaKalon, a European chemical company, and the $70 million left in its restructuring program that should be realized by the beginning of 2010.

Most of PPG's businesses have been under pressure from weak global demand. But its optical business, 8 percent of sales, is growing at a double-digit clip and has just started penetrating some big retailers like Costco and Wal-Mart, and it hasn't even been introduced yet in India or China, although plans are under way for a dramatic expansion to those countries. In the old days, if you told me that we would build only half the number of cars in this country that we built a few years ago, I would have told you that PPG was a "short," meaning that I would bet against it, and I would think that its plus-4 percent dividend yield would be in big trouble because a huge percentage of its business was with American automakers. These days PPG's auto exposure is down to 15 percent of its business and most of its share is with the stronger foreign makers, especially Toyota and Nissan. Expectations remain low for its industrial coatings, glass, and construction divisions throughout the end of 2009, but I think the company is already beginning to see an uptick in worldwide business activity. Don't worry; you have time to get in. The people from PPG are among the least promotional in the world and they won't signal that things are better until they are absolutely sure an upswing is occurring—even though, when Charles Bunch, the PPG chief executive officer, appeared recently on *Mad Money*, he endorsed the notion of a 2010 recovery for his company. We have to anticipate that, which is why now is a great time to start accumulating this once-dowdy chemical maker. In the meantime, you can wait for the recovery in style as PPG's plus-4 percent yield is one of the most bountiful and safest on the New York Stock Exchange.

ConocoPhillips (COP)

Oil prices will remain elevated, maybe not going back to $140, but certainly staying in the high double digits with any recovery, and we should cash in on that move before it happens. But even more important than catching the increase I'm expecting in crude oil prices is cashing in on the coming increase in natural gas prices, as that commodity fell more than 70 percent in a single year! So we need to find a company that is levered, meaning it has exposure, to both oil and natural gas. That eliminates most of the majors, including Exxon (XOM), BP (BP), and Shell (RDS-B), because they are largely oil producers. But one major company ConocoPhillips, has its finger in both pies and could be the most balanced way to profit from the coming energy recovery. Not only does Conoco have a terrific natural gas business, it is also a large refiner and marketer, making it a safer, more diversified play on a recovery than just buying an oil driller or a wildcatter with big natural gas exposure like so many of the high-fliers favored by speculators. ConocoPhillips is the third-largest integrated oil company in the United States, the largest U.S. natural gas producer, and the second-largest refiner, making it a true energy titan, yet because it has gone about its acquisition strategy quietly, most people don't even regard it as a major player in the energy complex. That's to our advantage as the story gets told over time. Conoco is the biggest value in the oil and gas business, trading at 4 times cash flow as I write this, a historic low, and a huge 25 percent discount to its peers Chevron and Exxon. That's just crazy, as I think it is every bit as well run as those companies if not better. The disparity, I believe, will close during the coming recovery.

Among the large-capitalization integrated oil stocks, Conoco is considered a pure play on oil and gas, meaning that because it pumps everything it sells, and has no other real businesses outside of oil and gas, it rises and falls with the prices of those two commodities. That made Conoco the worst stock in the group to own when natural gas and oil were at their highs and going lower, but makes it by far the best to own when we are at a trough and headed higher, as I think we are now. As economies across the world begin to improve, oil and natural gas prices will naturally work their way higher over time, as a healthy, growing economy consumes more energy, and Conoco has the most upside in the group.

For several years I thought Conoco had lost its way. After virtually no new oil and gas finds in 2008 along with a disappointing 4.8 percent decline in production, this company looked like a pathetic also-ran compared to a Chevron or an Exxon or Occidental (OXY). But 2009 has seen the beginning of a recovery in Conoco's production and the momentum should improve right through 2010, driven by new projects in China, Canada (an oil sands venture), Indonesia, and Qatar (a natural gas partnership), as well as partnerships and joint ventures with EnCana (ECA) and with Russia's Lukoil. In fact, already in 2009 volumes rose an impressive 7 percent largely because of stronger international production growth, and I believe Conoco will deliver a greater increase in oil and gas production than almost all of its competitors in 2010.

Conoco is the second-largest refiner in the United States, with 25 percent of total production. This has been a challenging business to be in, but Conoco is performing much better than its peers because it has strong utilization rates, meaning it is using more of its refinery capacity than its peers. Conoco has a big advantage over its competitors thanks to its large-scale and efficient operations.

As for its natural gas business, Conoco is not content to simply wait for the price of the commodity to return to its old levels in order to make a lot of money off the fuel that heats 63 percent of American homes and is vital to the plastics and paper industries. It's been drilling like crazy for natural gas, but at the same time it has lowered its exploration and production costs—the amount of money it takes to locate and extract natural gas from the ground—by 12 percent and is now one of the lowest-cost producers in the industry.

Overall, Conoco has plans in place to reduce its expenses by $1.4 billion, which will help cushion its earnings if oil prices stay at the current price, about $70 a barrel as I'm writing. But I don't see that happening, especially since China has been buying crude voraciously as its economy roars back to life. On top of everything else, Conoco's another company that's paying you to wait for the global economy to rebound, with a safe 4.3 percent dividend yield, which is well above the industry average. Conoco is deeply committed to its shareholders and has always returned value through buybacks and dividend increases, and while the company stopped its share repurchase program in 2009 (as did all the other major oil companies), the dividend is not in doubt. I think it is only a matter of time before the company begins to boost it once again.

BHP Billiton (BHP)

If you want to play the coming economic recovery, you must invest in China. No country has done a better job of responding to the global economic downturn than the People's Republic of China. The Chinese government recognized early the worldwide decline in demand for just about everything and quickly implemented a huge $600 billion stimulus program in the fall of 2008 to deal with the slowdown. There are many reasons why I believe China will be the country that leads the rest of the world into the coming recovery, not least among them the fact that China was the engine of international economic growth before everything fell apart, but its smart and effective response to the slowdown ranks near the top. Unlike our stimulus plan in the United States, which took months to get passed and months more to get into the system, China's stimulus kicked in rapidly with an emphasis on building infrastructure throughout the country, again in stark contrast to our stimulus package, which was a hodgepodge of tax cuts, extensions of unemployment benefits, and handouts to the states. Not only did China's stock market surge on the news, handily outperforming nearly every other market in the world, but it also didn't take long for the Chinese economy to start seeing the positive effects of the plan.

The best way to take advantage of China's resurgence? You want a mining company, a supplier of metals, minerals, and other natural resources. In order to build out infrastructure, you don't just need bricks and mortar, you also have to get your hands on copper, steel, iron, and numerous other commodities for any serious construction. The one I like as an investment in China and a global economic rebound is BHP Billiton, the world's largest diversified resources company. Based in Australia, it is just a quick boat ride away from the People's Republic. BHP Billiton gets 30 percent of its revenues from China, which is a huge amount of exposure to the engine of the global economic recovery.

BHP Billiton produces large amounts of several different minerals, so it's not dependent on the strength of just one or two commodities. You could go with Freeport McMoRan (FCX), another miner that I really like, but it's more of a pure play on copper and lacks BHP's broad-based exposure. I prefer BHP since it's the second-largest producer of iron ore in the world, and half of its ore goes straight to China. It is the third-largest producer of copper, for which China makes up a third of the world's demand; the third-largest producer of nickel, which is needed for stainless steel; and the market leader in seaborne-traded metallurgical coal, the kind used to make steel. BHP Billiton is the lowest-cost mineral producer, giving it margins that are the best in the industry. The company also has a significant oil and gas exploration and production business, which accounts for 20 percent of its revenues and which should do very well if I'm right about the recovery.

The company's operations are spread all across the world, which gives it excellent geographical balance, reducing the risk of any particular government deciding to expropriate its assets. It dwarfs its competitors in size, scale, and scope and has a stellar balance sheet with an attractive and safe 3.1 percent dividend yield. As the environment improves, I expect BHP Billiton will raise its dividend again, something it has done consistently for decades. Thanks to industry-wide production cuts in iron ore, copper, and coal, we should ultimately see higher commodity prices that benefit BHP down the road. In addition, because BHP has such a strong balance sheet, it is in a real position of strength to acquire good assets from its competitors if they become available. That balance sheet has also allowed BHP to exploit the downturn and take market share. While other natural resource companies have been forced to cut production and defer capital spending on new projects, BHP Billiton has been taking advantage of falling capital costs to grow its business and prepare for the next upturn in demand. One last thing—BHP is an ideal hedge against inflation, something that many investors believe we will be saddled with when we come out of this worldwide recession. Although I think the inflation coming out of this morass will be a long time in coming, if it happens at all, you will profit even from the talk of inflation if you own BHP.

Hewlett-Packard (HPQ)

When mutual fund managers start to see signs that the economy is improving, do you know what they love to buy? Technology stocks. These funds control huge sums of money, and at the slightest hint of a turn they instinctively start pouring oodles of cash into tech. For that reason alone, you need a tech stock as a recovery play, a stock like Hewlett-Packard, because you do not want to miss out on the kind of move that heavy mutual fund buying can create. That's not the only reason for buying HPQ, though. As economies around the world begin to improve, more corporations will buy technology products to enhance productivity, control their supply chains, manage inventory, and simply expand their businesses. Corporate budgets have been cut to the bare bones, so pent-up demand from businesses combined with the increased demand from consumers that we see whenever the economy picks up should lead to substantial increases in tech spending. We need a technology name that can take advantage of this kind of rebound, and the one I would pick, a company that has emerged as a real leader throughout the downturn, is Hewlett-Packard.

Over the last several years this company, under the fantastic leadership of CEO Mark Hurd, has transformed itself from essentially a one-product business into a worldwide, diversified technology enterprise, all the while cutting costs along the way. Hewlett-Packard now offers a plethora of products and services for its customers across the globe, and in many markets this company is the one to beat. It's the number-one maker of PCs and printers, and also makes blade servers, storage, software, and workstations, with an overall revenue mix of 52 percent of its products tied to hardware and 48 percent in software, services, and storage. Hewlett-Packard has gone from being a hardware company that was predominantly consumer focused to a more balanced company, with a customer base now made up of 40 percent enterprise clients, 30 percent small and medium businesses, and just 30 percent consumer. In a relatively few years HPQ has caught and passed Dell, once the number one PC maker, and, in combination with its printer business, it now dominates the world's personal computer market.

Not only has Mark Hurd changed its products and customer mix, but he has also concentrated on growing Hewlett-Packard's services business. I like this because services, which now accounts for 30 percent of the company's total revenue, tends to be a more predictable business than hardware, given the multiyear contracts that go along with it. Plus, information technology budgets have held up much better than hardware during the slowdown. Corporations may not have the money to buy new computers but they need to have upgrades installed and to fix and maintain the computers they currently have.

The real game-changer for Hewlett-Packard was its acquisition of Electronic Data Systems, EDS, which gives the combined company major opportunities for growth in the services business—with EDS services should grow to 40 percent of the company over the next few years—and gives Mark Hurd more room to increase profits by cutting costs. The EDS acquisition should cause Hewlett-Packard's earnings to become more stable going forward as they'll be more concentrated in services almost always under long-term contracts, with recurring revenue streams, and on top of the new services business the company also gets new clients to sell to. Most importantly, with EDS, Hewlett-Packard can now offer its customers a total solution set of hardware, software, and services—think of it as a one-stop shop for corporate technology needs—something that gives Hewlett-Packard a huge advantage over its competitors that have only one out of these three offerings. In addition to expanding its services offerings, Hewlett-Packard also has initiatives to grow its software, storage, and server businesses, all areas with more growth than traditional hardware.

Thanks to the cost-cutting initiatives within EDS, Hewlett-Packard should have enough flexibility to deliver on its earnings targets even if the recovery takes longer to kick in than I expect. Longer term, the company's pursuit of faster-growing segments of the technology business, and its expansion into services, should lead to better earnings growth and more consistent earnings in the future. And a recovery should revitalize Hewlett-Packard's slower-growing PC and printer businesses, too. No question, this is the tech stock I want to own to play the coming economic rebound.

Home Depot (HD)

Housing is the linchpin of the recovery here in America, and with inventories down big, prices down even more, new supply diminished, and low mortgage rates, I think this market has finally bottomed. Once the recovery arrives, we should see even fewer foreclosures, thanks to the decline in unemployment and more people with the money and the confidence to buy homes. Traditionally, as we've come out of past recessions, most money managers have piled into the home builders and related stocks as classic recovery plays. I don't feel comfortable putting a home builder on this list, even as I think the housing turn has arrived, but I'm perfectly happy suggesting a home improvement retailer like Home Depot, the largest of its kind, with over two thousand stores in the United States, Canada, Mexico, and China. You need some stock to play the housing bottom, a major part of the recovery, and Home Depot is my favorite name with housing exposure. Lowe's (LOW) is also a good company, but I prefer Home Depot because it has undergone a gigantic internal restructuring to become a better company after years of neglect and mismanagement. Both companies benefit from a turn in housing, but Home Depot has more upside as these new restructuring initiatives lead to better operational performance and increased future earnings. And, let's put it bluntly, I think HD's starting to kick LOW's butt, a judgment that's been confirmed by many of the suppliers to the two companies that come on *Mad Money*.

Founded by Bernie Marcus and Arthur Blank in 1978, Home Depot revolutionized the home improvement industry by bringing the know-how and the tools to the consumer, allowing ordinary people to save money by doing the work themselves instead of paying a contractor. From the beginning the company aligned itself with industry manufacturers and provided a combination of brand-name products as well as less expensive private-label products in order to offer a wide selection to its customers, both the do-it-yourselfer and the professional contractor. After going public in 1981, the company enjoyed tremendous growth for two decades, expanding in the United States and abroad. But as the growth started to slow and competition from Lowe's and others increased, the founders decided to go outside and hire a new CEO, the dreaded Bob Nardelli, now of Chrysler infamy. Nardelli had no retail experience—he had an industrial background—and under his leadership the company lacked, among other things, serious growth initiatives, innovation, customer service, and a vision for expanding the company beyond the United States. After six long years of making Home Depot a toxic stock, Nardelli stepped down. His replacement, Frank Blake, stepped up and along with his new team announced a total restructuring and an overhaul of the company with the customer as its number-one priority. In a short time he undid much of the damage that Nardelli caused. Under the new plan, Home Depot shut down Expo, its home design chain, closed underperforming stores, implemented a productivity program emphasizing supply chain and inventory management, sold off a disastrous supply division, and improved its merchandising with a focus on making the in-store experience more enjoyable.

The results? Home Depot has dramatically improved its balance sheet and increased its cash flow, giving the company more flexibility either to pay down debt or grow the business and pay a nice dividend. Right now Home Depot is mainly a U.S. story, but management's focus on international expansion in China, Canada, and Mexico could lead to better growth and increased earnings in the future. When economies around the world begin to recover, say in 2010, Home Depot will have the cash to dramatically expand the number of stores it has in those regions.

Home Depot trades at 17 times depressed earnings as I write this, and remember, as with Caterpillar, the time to buy a stock like this is when it looks most expensive based on its price-to-earnings multiple because the earnings don't include the enormous potential growth that could be in the offing when the economy snaps back. And Home Depot is in a much better position to capitalize on the coming recovery now that it's been through its restructuring. Plus, the company is paying you a roughly 4 percent dividend yield just to wait for the turn, one of the highest-yielding retailers, which is not too shabby. I think the Street's estimates are still too conservative and don't factor in all the improvements that this company has made, let alone the idea that we could be in for a full-scale recovery.

VF Corporation (VFC)

When the economy rebounds, so will the consumer. Once people shake the recession mind-set and feel wealthier, they start shopping. For that reason, we know we need a good old-fashioned retail name, a company that makes more money as people spend more money on discretionary purchases like clothing. And when it comes to apparel, there's no question about which company is best of breed: it's VF Corporation.

Not only does VFC own some of the best-known, highest-quality brands, such as Wrangler, Lee, Riders, North Face, Vans, JanSport, Eastpak, Nautica, 7 For All Mankind, and Lucy, among others, it also has what I regard as the best strategy in the business, not to mention a visionary management team led by CEO Eric Wiseman. It's not too dependent on any one distribution channel. It sells its products through department stores, general merchandise chains, and athletic specialty stores, and operates 601 company-owned full-price and outlet stores. VFC isn't about stores, it's all about brands—they have the brands that people want to buy, regardless of where they're being sold. When the economy recovers, VFC's merchandise will be flying off the shelves. Plus, with its strong balance sheet, as well as the $750 million in cash flow from operations the company should generate this year, it will continue to use its strong cash position to buy topnotch brands at bargain basement prices from weaker competitors who have no choice but to sell if they want to survive.

VFC has worked the same way for ages: it creates value when it makes an acquisition, buying high-quality brands from vulnerable competitors. These brands have usually been underinvested in because their previous owners lacked the funds, so VFC can spend money on improving the product and use its global distribution to sell that product around the world. VFC has used this strategy to its advantage and picked up some of the best-known brands in the industry to garner huge returns. As an example, take the North Face story. The company bought the North Face brand in 2000 when it had $200 million in sales and was losing money. After investing in the brand and putting the product through its massive distribution channel, VFC managed to grow sales of North Face at a 27 percent compound annual rate. Now the brand does over $1 billion in sales. This environment is perfect for VFC: it can take advantage of its weaker competitors to buy more brands, and when the economy begins to recover VFC will be able to move more and more merchandise.

On top of its big-picture strategy, VFC also has an extensive cost-cutting program that could save the company 60 cents of earnings per share, or about 12 percent of its 2009 earnings. The company has set a very low bar for itself after missing the Street's estimates in the first quarter, so expectations for 2009 should be easy to beat, especially if the global economy improves and consumers start spending again.

Even if the recovery takes longer than I expect, VFC has a safe 4 percent dividend yield, and it's trading at just 11 times forward earnings as I write this, a pretty low multiple for a company that should be able to post double-digit growth for the foreseeable future. Management is paying you to wait for a turnaround that I think will happen shortly, given that much of the recent weakness was concentrated on their smaller brands and in European sales, both of which can be fixed rather easily.

JPMorgan Chase (JPM)

The financial crisis was an incredibly humbling experience for most investors, but imagine the level of shame the bankers who lost fortunes must have felt. As I look back, I can honestly think of only two companies in the financial sector that not only survived but became stronger because of the crisis, two companies that will lead the industry going forward. They are JP Morgan and Goldman Sachs (GS). Both have fantastic franchises and terrific leadership and you can't go wrong owning either one (which is why I own both for my charitable trust). But for the bank you should buy in order to capitalize on the coming recovery, I am going with JP Morgan because it is cheaper and because I expect its stock to increase over time as investors come to appreciate its diversified businesses, its $800 billion in deposits, and its global presence. The company has an extensive list of clients in institutional investors, hedge funds, governments, and wealthy individuals in over one hundred countries around the world with $2.1 trillion in assets. It provides investment banking, financial services for consumers, small and commercial banking, securities processing, asset management, and private equity.

Throughout the credit crisis, JP Morgan has been regarded, correctly, as one of very few financial services companies that could withstand the downturn on its own given its strong balance sheet, conservative risk management, and best-in-class management team, led by the great Jamie Dimon. In fact, it's awareness of JPM's strength that has resulted in a flight to quality, allowing JP Morgan to take market share in nearly all of its businesses, and specifically in M&A advisory, debt and equity origination, and commercial banking. Its strong capital position led the government to decide that even under the most draconian stress-test scenario, JP Morgan would not need to raise additional money.

Because of its strength, JP Morgan was able to take advantage of the weak environment to make two acquisitions in 2008, both additive to earnings, which have made the company stronger and better poised to benefit from a turn in the economy. When it took over Washington Mutual, it increased its retail deposits funding by $126 billion, added five thousand additional branches, strengthened its commercial banking franchise, and created the opportunity to generate $2 billion in cost savings over time. And the Bear Stearns take-under improved its prime brokerage, fixed-income, and commodities businesses. I think we will look back and realize that JP Morgan "stole" these two banks for next to nothing. JPM wrote down the value of these assets to levels that I think will produce hefty profits down the line.

JP Morgan's investment banking business is the biggest revenue driver at the firm, an area where it shouldn't have much trouble growing and taking share. The competition is either distracted or has simply disappeared. The core banking business, where the folks at JP Morgan turn on the lights every morning and make money because they can borrow from you at very low rates, pay very little for your deposits, and lend at much higher rates, is also doing very well and will hold up as long as the Fed keeps short-term rates low.

The challenges the company still faces in home equity, prime and subprime lending, and its credit card division should become much easier to handle once a real recovery is at hand, as a healthier economy means fewer people losing their jobs who can't pay back their home equity loans, mortgages, or credit card bills. Remember, these are recovery stocks I am recommending, ones that will do best in the turnup in worldwide business, and it is the leverage that will come from these underperforming businesses, the turn from loss to gain in these product lines, that makes JPM so attractive to me.

JP Morgan trades at a premium multiple to the group, totally justified given its product diversification, proactive management, and strong balance sheet and capital position. But at 1.5 times tangible book value—the key metric you use to value banks—the stock is trading at a discount to its historical average of 2.1 times tangible book value. Jamie Dimon has navigated this company through the most challenging period for the banks at least since the savings and loan crisis, and perhaps since the Great Depression. And he has used the downturn to build a better company. I have no doubt that once a recovery gets under way, JP Morgan's share price will reflect what we already know, that it has become one of the strongest banks in the world. One caveat: this company, unlike all of the others mentioned, is heavily dependent on one individual, Dimon himself. If he were to leave I would have to rethink this stock's placement in the best dozen equities to play in a rebound. (Speculators take note, if you are much more bullish on a rebound than I am here, consider buying Wells Fargo, a great company, but one that needs a big lift in the economy to rally substantially.)

Visa (V)

For our final recovery stock, I want to highlight one of the best secular growth stories in my charitable trust portfolio, ActionAlertsPlus.com. That stock is Visa, arguably one of the best-known brands in the world. But wait a second: Doesn't secular growth mean that this stock should be able to make us money whether the economy recovers or not? Absolutely. I'm not trying to give you a list of stocks that work only when the economy recovers. We want stocks that can make you a lot of money quickly once the big players in the market recognize that a recovery is at hand, without losing you money if the turn takes longer than I expect. And Visa definitely counts as part of that group.

How does Visa benefit from a recovery? First, understand that while Visa is a credit card company, it doesn't lend anyone money. The company makes its money from transactions, operating the world's largest retail electronic payments network. It provides processing services and products such as consumer credit, debit, prepaid, and commercial cards under the Visa name. Visa's customers include over sixteen thousand financial institutions around the world and it has the dominant market share in the industry. The more transactions Visa processes, the more money it makes. So as consumer confidence improves and spending increases, two things that go hand in hand with an economic recovery, volumes should rise, meaning consumers will swipe their credit cards more often because they're buying more things. That in turn will provide upside to Visa's earnings and potentially give it faster growth, too.

That's what makes Visa a recovery play. The reason I am so positive on the stock is that there is a huge transition happening in the United States and around the world that plays directly into Visa's hands, which will give this company double-digit earnings growth for some time. Consumers want a paperless society. They want plastic over checks or cash. Worldwide, Visa is the way to play it as it offers both credit and debit cards. It's simply more convenient and the Visa name is accepted just about everywhere. This shift has been taking place over the last several years but there is still plenty of growth potential, especially because nearly half the transactions in the United States are currently completed with cash or checks, and more than half internationally. As consumers change the way they pay for things and use more credit and debit cards, volumes will increase. That directly benefits Visa because it charges merchandisers a fee on each transaction. One of its advantages over the competition is that it has more debit market share. Since consumers tend to use debit for non-discretionary purchases, the recession has actually helped Visa's debit card business, which is growing much faster than I thought it would even a year ago. Also, given Visa's dominance in the industry, it has the ability to raise prices on a regular basis, which helps it maintain predictable and predictably good earnings regardless of the economy's strength. In addition, Visa has a strong balance sheet and it's engaged in a massive, larger-than-expected cost-cutting program that could boost earnings into 2010.

With a recovery, Visa earns more money. Without one, it's one of a small group of stocks with consistent, double-digit growth. Either way it works, but I think earnings could explode to the upside if economies around the world improve and consumers conduct far more transactions with their credit cards. Remember, Visa, unlike Capital One or JP Morgan or American Express, takes no credit risk. It is not a lender; it is a transaction processor. While it appears to be a "financial," it has all the earmarks of an emerging technology company where the technology is being adopted every year by millions of new people. That's worth cashing in on.

That's it, my twelve favorite stocks that you can buy ahead of a recovery to make a lot of easy money when everyone else figures out that things are getting better and buys these stocks hand over fist after you already own some of them. As I said before, this is not a portfolio, since it isn't really diversified. And there may be better recovery plays out there. But there aren't better recovery plays that I know more about. If, like me, you believe that a true recovery is not far off for the world's economies, then I suggest you go through the list and pick out two, even three stocks to add to your portfolio so that you can capture the huge snapback in them when it happens. If you agree with me, if you have total conviction that the rebound has arrived, you still don't want to load up your portfolio only with recovery stocks, as you can always be wrong. This market is rocky, it's a tug of war, and you have to own some stocks that go against even your strongest convictions at all times just in case you're wrong. If you think the recovery is still a long way off, go through this list, figure out what the downside is on these stocks if I'm wrong—it shouldn't be much—and then imagine the upside you could miss, the upside you cannot afford to miss in order to get back to even if I'm right. Even if you don't think we're anywhere near a true recovery, you can find a stock in that list that's worth owning for other reasons. Hold your nose and buy it just in case I turn out to be right. Because eventually the recovery will happen and the opportunities to make money will be immense. But this opportunity will be short-lived, so it's much better to be early than to be late.

6

THE NEXT BIG THING
Regional Banks Poised to Grow

Historically speaking, do you know which stocks have been the best ones to own coming out of a financial crisis? Would you care to hazard a guess? I'll give you one hint: you are not going to believe the answer. As we emerge from the financial crisis, I believe that the absolute best opportunities for you to make money are to be found among *the banks*. That's right, the banks. You did not suddenly start hallucinating. No need to break out the Lithium. I know it sounds crazy. Even now that the financials have bottomed, no group of companies has lost more people more money over the last few years than this one. None. I hardly even have to recount the litany of what's been wrong with these companies. It's all common knowledge, the stuff you've been reading on the front page of the newspaper. We came very close to seeing a full-scale collapse of the financial system, not just in America, but internationally. We've witnessed bank failure after bank failure, with more than fifty smaller banks, and some not-so-small ones, taken over by the FDIC since the beginning of 2008, and many other failing banks taken over by their healthier competitors at what I like to call "take-under" prices.

I expect many, many more failures before the crisis ends. After all, we closed more than 1,600 ailing institutions in the great savings and loan crisis of the late 1980s, so you could say we are just beginning the seizures. This is an industry that required a $700 billion federal bailout in the form of the Troubled Asset Relief Program, or TARP, to prevent a full-on banking apocalypse and even that wasn't enough. I doubt our financial system could have survived without numerous—and wise—interventions from the Federal Reserve, with more acronyms like the TALF, which stands for Term Asset-Backed Securities Loan Facility, a program created to make it safer and more profitable for banks to grant more student loans, auto loans, and credit card loans by allowing them to use securities backed by those loans (so-called asset-backed securities or ABS) as collateral for as much as a trillion dollars in generous loans from the Federal Reserve. This is the industry where I expect to find the stocks that will turn out to be the biggest winners over the next several years? Stocks that could go a very long way toward helping you get back to even? Have I lost my mind?

I know that many investors, and perhaps many of you, tried to buy the banks on the way down based on valuation, and until the sector started to rebound in March 2009, that play lost you money almost every time. On Wall Street we call that trying to catch a falling knife—unless you time it perfectly you're liable to end up in the stock market emergency room bleeding profusely. For well over a year so many alleged experts were telling you it was safe to buy the banks. Just watching them turn out to be wrong over and over again has got to make you very suspicious of anyone who says that investing in certain banks represents perhaps the best way to get back to even by investing in stocks. What makes me any different from the clowns who backed these stocks on the way down?

Remember, I come at this as someone who was literally screaming about the danger of the impending financial crisis in order to encourage some preemptive action to soften the blow as early as the summer of 2007. I know there are many troubled banks out there, from those that have had to eliminate their dividends in order to conserve capital, to those with no choice but to sell branches in order to raise capital, to the biggest losers of all, the ones that are simply insolvent, that cannot survive on their own. I know that a lot of the banks are still in awful shape. But, after sidestepping most of the bank losses of 2008 and early 2009, I think it's time to own the best ones, and not just JP Morgan, as I suggested in the previous chapter. And that's exactly the reason why I think you can make so much money by finding the banks no one knows about that are in good shape, the winners, the ones that at the very least will be able to take share away from their ailing competitors.

The crisis has created a new order in finance. It has opened the door for a total reshuffling of the banking system. In the new banking order, there will be winners as well as losers, and I can tell you that if you identify and own the winners, you should be able to make tremendous amounts of money. Right now the best way to understand the banks is through the lens of college basketball. The government is taking banks that are the equivalent of Division III schools and propelling them into Division I powerhouses because the current Division I schools did the banking equivalent of violating academic standards and have been stripped of their status. The trick is to find the right D-III banks that are in good shape and have the ability to expand. Do that, and you could own a stock that will produce mammoth profits for years to come. I'm certain of it.

How can I have so much conviction? Simple: because I am not describing a once-in-a-lifetime opportunity in banking. What we have here is a twice-in-a-lifetime opportunity. This is not the first time in my professional life that the American financial system has been brought to its knees. I was around for the savings and loan crisis, which, while smaller than our latest financial catastrophe, was also similar to it. The situation we're in right now is incredibly reminiscent of what happened at the end of the S&L crisis, the period from about 1989 to 1991, back in the early days of my hedge fund. The financial crisis of the late 1980s and early '90s was caused by a crash in commercial real estate, while today's was brought about by a crash in residential real estate, not much of a difference to get hung up on. The similarities, especially in terms of how the banks made out, are far more important.

What happened back at the end of the S&L crisis? Hobbled banks stopped lending or went under with their brands forever tarnished. Then new banks sprung up, or banks that you weren't familiar with, and they expanded in the chaos of the Hobbesian banking environment. Life was nasty, brutish, and short for the troubled banks, but some of the smaller regional banks that were in good shape managed to gobble up their competitors, often with an assist from the feds, and become massive regional leviathans of finance. That's why we want to search for banks that resemble the winners from the previous S&L crisis. Their modern-day analogues should be able to give you gigantic gains for years, that's right, *years* to come.

So what's the template here? What did the banks that came out ahead at the end of the S&L crisis look like? Many smaller regional banks advanced to become national powerhouses during that period, including PNC Financial, NationsBank (ultimately Bank of America), and Bank One, which later merged with JP Morgan for a huge gain for shareholders. The best of the best, however, was Fleet, a conservative bank based in Providence, Rhode Island, that, beginning in the late 1980s, took advantage of the depressed prices in the financial sector and started buying neighboring banks, like the very low-priced Norstar Bancorp in Albany, New York, which it acquired in 1988. At the same time as Fleet was expanding, most of the banks around it in New England were getting into trouble and blowing up, including the reigning banking king of Massachusetts, the Bank of New England. Because of its innate conservatism, Fleet, this little bank that no one was familiar with, was essentially granted most-favored-bank status by the regulators, an entirely unofficial designation that was nevertheless completely obvious to anyone who had eyes to see or ears to hear. So when the FDIC put Bank of New England up for sale after it failed in January 1991, Fleet was allowed to buy it. With that acquisition, Fleet became a regional powerhouse, one of the three largest banks in New England. Fleet went on to acquire another big, troubled New England bank, Shawmut, in 1995, making it the ninth-largest bank in the United States as well as the largest in New England, and then bought BankBoston in 1999, becoming the seventh-largest bank in the United States, with a large Latin American presence as well. Fleet transformed itself from a small regional player mainly based in Rhode Island into one of the largest and most important franchises in the country, something that was possible only because Bank of New England failed, courtesy of the S&L crisis, and Fleet was in the right position to impress the regulators. If Fleet hadn't been able to acquire Norstar on the cheap thanks to the depressed price of Norstar's stock, along with most other bank stocks at the time, those of us who don't live in Rhode Island might never have heard of Fleet Bank.

Financial crises, once it's clear that they are not going to annihilate the entire banking system, create opportunities for companies like Fleet. And, oh boy, are those opportunities fantastic, especially for the shareholders. Ultimately Fleet, having shaped itself into a fantastic takeover candidate, was acquired by Bank of America in 2004. So how did you do if you owned Fleet from the time of the Norstar acquisition until it was acquired by Bank of America? Including dividends, and you know how important those are, Fleet gave you a 500 percent return over that sixteen-year period. Owning this bank allowed you to sextuple your money. You hear about doubles, even triples, but increasing your investment sixfold is pretty darned impressive, even over sixteen years.

Once again we've reached a point where the nation is littered with unhealthy banks, and a handful of small survivors, the best regional banks in the areas where the competition is at its weakest, are poised to become the next Fleets. Every time you see a bank failure going forward, instead of bemoaning its sad fate you should be thinking, Who gets those juicy deposits? Because whoever does will have the ability to grow like crazy and go from zero to banking hero in practically no time at all.

We want to be looking for those banks, for the new regional banking superstars following in Fleet's footsteps, because this may very well turn out to be the strongest, most important, and most profitable trend in the U.S. economy over the next several years. Remember back when I told you that good investors don't try to make predictions about the future, they look for patterns and weigh probabilities? Well, what I want to help you do now is a great example of what that really means. People who discuss stocks, be they professionals or amateurs, often end up talking about cycles. There's the business cycle, the big picture of the economy as it speeds up and slows down, often because of intervention from the Federal Reserve. Then there are all kinds of different cycles based on spending that are worth investing in because they have worked before. When we're dealing with tech stocks, there are product cycles as companies develop new gadgets that become popular and cause the consumer to spend like crazy. We saw how well these cycles played out, for example, for Apple over the years with its iPod, iTunes, and iPhone cycles. Each one produced bountiful returns. You have semiconductor cycles, like all the new Intel models, from the '86s to the Pentiums, and you have telco equipment cycles, based on data, then text, then Internet, and then aerospace cycles based on new Boeing iterations like the Dreamliner. All of these are patterns that you can recognize if you watch stocks long enough, patterns that repeat themselves. So if you know what they look like and know when they're coming, you can make money simply because you know which stocks go up as each cycle unfolds. What, exactly, does this have to do with the banks? Well, even though this is just the second time I've seen a major financial crisis in my lifetime, you could almost say that there is a financial crisis cycle. It's a pattern I've seen before and can recognize now that it's happened again. We've been through the part where every bank gets taken down willy-nilly, and I believe we have now reached the phase where the winners sort themselves out from the losers and start taking advantage of their newfound strength.

Our goal, then, is to find the banks that fit the pattern. We want the ones that look like Fleet did in the late 1980s, healthy regional banks that can gobble up share from their tarnished competitors, or even better, buy them up for a pittance from the FDIC. This is where we start dealing in probabilities. I could find one bank and tell you it has the most in common with Fleet so you should buy it and it alone to play this huge trend. Unfortunately, if that bank turns out to be a dud, or simply not as good as some of the others, you will have missed out on a great move because you didn't acknowledge that I might be wrong, and so you failed to spread your money around multiple different banks. One bank is not the way to go, no matter how similar it might seem to Fleet. I have a better approach, one that's actually been field-tested. Remember, I wasn't just an observer of the S&L crisis, I was down in the trenches, running a hedge fund and making money off the same trends in banking that we see repeating themselves today. What did I do then? I found six healthy regional banks spread out all across the country, and I bought 9.9 percent of each of them, the maximum percentage of any publicly held company that a hedge fund is allowed to own. These banks eventually emerged from the morass better, stronger, and bigger than they had been going into it, or they got taken over. I was and am happy with either outcome.

Now I'm going to help you replicate the success I had in picking regional banks at the end of the S&L crisis by giving you my five favorite regional banks for playing the end of the current financial crisis. I'll explain why I consider each one healthy, what makes them well positioned to take advantage of the weakness of their competitors, why the FDIC would favor them when it has to sell off the assets of failed banks or when it's trying to put together a shotgun wedding style merger to avoid having to seize a bank, and why I believe they will thrive and expand. Or to put it another way, I'll explain how each bank resembles Fleet in the late 1980s. A twice-in-a-lifetime crisis produces, well, twice-in-a-lifetime opportunities to get back to even. As weaker banks fall by the wayside, my five regional banks should be there to strip the fallen banks of anything worth taking. Before I get into this list, there are a few things you need to keep in mind. As with the twelve recovery stocks I discussed in the last chapter, it really is halfway insane for me to be recommending individual stocks in a book. I don't believe in the philosophy of "buy and hold," so it's very possible that any of these banks could falter and no longer be worth owning. That's why, if you buy any of these regional banks, you absolutely must do the homework. Research them to make sure the facts I like about each bank as I write this chapter are still true as you're reading it. I think these banks could deliver stellar returns for years to come, but the fact that these are investments with potentially long time frames does not give you an excuse for avoiding the homework or shrugging off any losses you might take as "short-term fluctuations." If any of these banks stop working for any reason, do not simply assume that they will get back on track because Jim Cramer wrote that they were terrific long-term plays. Far too many investors use the idea of a "long-term" holding to regard any bad news about a company as irrelevant. These five banks will be long-term winners only if they do what I expect them to, but if something happens to derail those expectations, or if current managements, all of which are excellent, depart for other opportunities, you had better be ready to change your mind.

I'm sticking my neck out to recommend these five stocks not because I have a very strong masochistic streak but because I believe the expansion of the strongest regional banks with the weakest competition will very likely be the most important trend in the stock market over the next several years. I would be remiss if I didn't do everything in my power to bring this twice-in-a-lifetime opportunity to your attention and help you profit from it so that you can get back to even or do a whole lot better than that if the gains turn out to be Fleet-like in size.

What if I'm being too negative? So far I've tried to assuage the fears of those of you who might consider my outlook on the banks too upbeat, but I suppose the real threat to this twice-in-a-lifetime opportunity is the possibility that not enough banks go under. In that case, wouldn't we end up with a much smaller pool of spoils for the banking victors, and a dramatically decreased likelihood of any one healthy bank being able to buy the good assets of a failed bank from the FDIC? That's a legitimate concern, given that the government has essentially given a pass to most of the country's largest banks, with both the Obama administration and the Federal Reserve determined to prevent banks from failing. The worst of the worst, the banks with the most exposure to bad mortgages, including Washington Mutual, Wachovia, Countrywide, Downey Savings, and IndyMac, worked their way through the system and were either acquired or, in the case of IndyMac, placed into conservatorship by the FDIC, a long time ago. Will there be enough troubled banks left for my five favorite regional bank names to cannibalize? I think there will be plenty, but we should consider the positives. The so-called stress tests the government used to determine the solvency of the country's largest banks were just stressful enough to have credibility and force banks to raise capital without putting undue pressure on them, while setting things up so that the healthier large banks should have no trouble taking over the remaining unhealthy large banks, in case that proves necessary. But will that leave enough scraps for the regional banks, the new Fleets, to grow as I expect them to? I think so, because there are many banks, mostly regional institutions, that are just now getting into trouble with both residential and commercial loans.

There will still be plenty of weak banks that just don't have enough capital to make it through to the other side, and if the government concentrates hard on saving the large banks, then the losers will simply come from the ranks of the small- and medium-sized players.

The stocks I am about to recommend are the five regional banks that look most like the winners from the S&L crisis, the banks that fit the Fleet template that gave you a 500 percent return the last time many banks failed. There may be others out there that are similar to the stocks on the list below that I've missed. If you find one and it stacks up well compared to the regional banks on this list, more power to you. One of the reasons for going over each of these stocks is to explain what to look for in a regional bank, as I rarely recommend a stock solely for the purpose of telling people to buy it. If you don't come away from this list with a better idea of how to analyze a bank stock and what to look for when you buy one, then I'm not doing my job.

No more caveats: here we go!

Glacier Bancorp (GBCI)

Sometimes all it takes for a bank to thrive is a propensity *not* to loan and *not* to screw up. That's what I think of when I look at Glacier Bancorp, which is based in Montana but also operates in Idaho, eastern Washington, Wyoming, and Utah with 98 branches. In some ways Glacier is just plain lucky, an accidental geographical winner: its locus happens to be in the states with some of the most consistently low unemployment rates in the country: Montana, 5.4 percent; Idaho, 5.4 percent; Utah, 4.3 percent; and Wyoming, 3.4 percent, versus the rest of the country, which is almost at double digits as of when I'm writing. Plus, because the population in those states is increasing at a faster rate than the national average, it has innate, organic growth.

But Glacier wouldn't be in the great position it is today, with the ability to pick up assets on the cheap from the FDIC, if its terrific management hadn't made their bank an exemplary lender. On Wall Street, the profitability and success of banks is measured with several different yardsticks, known as key metrics, the most important information about the business that we can use to make apples-to-apples comparisons between different banks. We look at how much capital they have, and for most banks lately that capital has been knocked down by bad loans. We look at how many nonperforming loans they have, meaning loans that are in default or close to it, as a percentage of their total loans. On a bank's balance sheet, loans are considered assets and your deposits are actually "liabilities," which can be pretty confusing. Think of it this way: your deposits are considered liabilities because the bank has an obligation to pay them back to you whenever you decide to withdraw money. Technically you are lending the bank money whenever you make a deposit, and that means the bank is a borrower. When you're calculating your own finances, any money you owe to another person or entity is a liability, so your deposits are the bank's liabilities because it owes you that money. And just like your deposits, your loans from the bank, which you consider your liabilities, are its assets. So when we look at nonperforming loans as a percentage of total loans, we're basically measuring what percentage of the bank's assets have gone sour.

Don't feel bad if this is making your head spin. After all, it's accounting; it's making me a little dizzy and I'm the one writing it. All you really need to know about the percentage of nonperforming loans is that it's what I call the deadbeat ratio. It tells you whether a bank has lent money to a lot of deadbeats who can't pay it back (and yes, this is a completely unfair generalization, as many people who can't repay their loans are hardworking individuals who are down on their luck in the midst of a lousy economy, but "deadbeat ratio" makes the problem pretty clear). Too many deadbeats and the bank becomes insolvent and gets seized. Banks with low deadbeat ratios are the victors, and to the victors go the spoils. The third main measure of a bank's health and success is something called the net interest margin, which just means how much money they make on your money. It's the difference between the interest rate the banks pay you for your deposits and the rate you pay them on a loan. With the Federal Reserve, which controls short-term rates, determined to keep them low, meaning the banks have to pay you little on your passbook and checking accounts, banks make a ton of money between how much they are charging on mortgages or commercial loans and how much you earn on your deposits. The Fed does this because this allows the banks to rebuild capital, making them more profitable every day they turn the lights on. It's one of the reasons why I am drawn to the banking industry as a place to make money once the bad loans are disposed of or minimized.

How does Glacier stack up? On all three key metrics Glacier has it all over almost every other bank in the country. Its Tier One capital ratio, the main measure regulators use to determine if a bank has enough capital (that is, can it withstand losses in real estate and consumer loans), stands at 14 percent, more than 35 percent higher than the national average. And if you really want to get a feel for just how strong its capital position is, you should know that Glacier was one of the few banks that rejected TARP money, as it had no need for the extra cash, especially not with all the strings attached. Its deadbeat ratio, the nonperforming loans as a percentage of all loans, comes in at just 1.3 percent, much lower than the average for its cohort of 5.7 percent. And its net interest margin is 4.71 percent, while the average for its peers is just 4 percent. That may not look like a big difference, but when it comes to banking, a small-seeming difference in how much money a bank can make after paying you for your deposits and investing them can have huge consequences for the company's earnings. All three of those levels are simply extraordinary, which is why I believe Glacier will be a real darling of the bank regulators, who prefer to put the worthwhile pieces of broken banks in the hands of good operators whenever those pieces need to be sold.

Even without government intervention, Glacier is a shrewd acquirer of banks in its own right, and it knows how to integrate the banks it buys. That includes the brilliant takeover of First Company in Wyoming, the state with the most robust economy in the country thanks to an abundance of natural resources and very low unemployment. Glacier paid for the acquisition with a stock offering that worked out well for all involved. We know Glacier wants to expand, but we also know the company is chary with its money from its 52-cent annual dividend, which works out to just a 4 percent yield. That's fine with me, though, as Glacier was conserving capital while other banks threw it away on higher dividends than they could afford or ridiculous buybacks, and that prudent attitude was a major reason why it could reject TARP.

Still, despite all these positives, nobody cares for Glacier. The bank has hardly any sponsorship from the Street, just like little Fleet right when it was about to bust out of Providence. A disciplined lender, a prudent bank, Glacier will be handily rewarded by the regulators when the other banks in its region go kerflooey.

FirstMerit (FMER)

The small banks that will emerge from the current period of financial chaos as regional powerhouses won't necessarily be those with the best operations. They need something beyond that as well: fragile, to say nothing of desperate, competition. Fleet didn't succeed just because it was well run. It took the failure of Bank of New England, Fleet's main competitor, which it turned around and acquired from the FDIC, to give fleet its chance at greatness.

And that's why I think FirstMerit of Akron, Ohio, will triumph in the current environment, just as Fleet did at the end of the S&L crisis. FirstMerit, a well-managed bank with $11.1 billion in deposits and 160 branches, is the fourth-largest bank in Ohio, arguably the state with the worst set of banks in the union. While this bank has plenty of good qualities, the best reason to like it is the poor quality of its competitors. The major Ohio banks have been downright mutilated by losses. FirstMerit's branches are primarily in the counties around Cleveland, where PNC (PNC) is the number-one player and Key (KEY) holds the number-two spot. PNC has been distracted by its acquisition of National City, while Key is seriously troubled and might be in need of cash. FirstMerit, far from needing additional dough, was one of the first banks to repay the TARP money it took from the government. In Columbus, where FirstMerit hopes to expand, Huntington Bancshares (HBAN) is the market leader by deposits. It is another hobbled bank that needed new capital, although new management is doing its best to stay independent, and I think it is. Fifth Third (FITB), another troubled bank, rounds out the list of FirstMerit's less-than-fearsome foes in the Ohio area. Should any of these banks so much as stumble, FirstMerit can step into the void and fill their shoes, and even if only one of them falls, FirstMerit could take over many of their branches in the region with an assist from the FDIC, something management has expressed a clear interest in doing. This bank could very well come out of this period of financial reshuffling as a dominant player in Ohio. Even without government assistance, FirstMerit has been working successfully to attract commercial customers away from its competitors.

Unlike its rivals, FirstMerit is a superior performer with key metrics that are sure to impress the regulators. Its net charge-off–to–loan ratio, which gives us a good idea of how many bad loans it's being dragged down by, is a mere 0.68 percent compared to 1.11 percent for banks in its neighborhood. This company makes very few bad loans, with a very low deadbeat ratio. Its return on assets—how profitable the bank is relative to its total assets—comes in at 1.13 percent, much better than the 0.23 percent that its peers average, and its return on equity is 12.76 percent, compared to a puny 2.38 percent for its cohort. And when it comes to the main thing the regulators look at when they want to cordon off the healthy banks so they can acquire the weaker ones, how much capital the bank has, FirstMerit is in good shape with a Tier One capital ratio of 11.49 percent, nicely above the national average of 10 percent, along with a tangible-capital-to-assets ratio of 7.27 percent versus 5.5 percent for its peers. Tangible capital or tangible common equity is a more stringent way of assessing a bank's solvency than Tier One Capital, but on both measures First-Merit is in good shape, much better off than the competition, and much more likely to be allowed to gobble up any banks that fall by the wayside.

Why has FirstMerit done so well? One of the reasons is that the Cleveland housing market, while not especially vibrant, has held up much better than the United States as a whole. Prices there never really ran up in the first place, so they had less far to fall. And while people fret about auto-workers in Ohio who bank at FirstMerit getting laid off, only five auto plants owned by the not-so-big three are in areas where FirstMerit operates. The company also has a terrific CEO in Paul Greig, who came aboard in May 2006 and really turned the company around, and just in time, too. Prior to his arrival it had been an underperformer, but once Greig came in he hired a chief credit officer, rebuilt the company's underwriting and risk monitoring, and sold a portfolio of residential development credits, reducing FirstMerit's exposure to residential development loans to just 2 percent. Best of all, FirstMerit is paying you to wait until it gets an opportunity to expand at someone else's expense with a $1.16 annual dividend payout, which works out to a 4 percent yield at current levels. Be aware, though, that FirstMerit is paying some of that dividend in stock, rather than cash, in order to increase its already high levels of capital, which should make it easier for the company to make any acquisitions. I don't mind taking part of the dividend in stock since I think you should reinvest the entire payout in the stock so that your dividends will compound over time. Besides, it's very hard to find a decent dividend among any bank stock right now given that the government has pretty much demanded that dividends not be paid if you need or are thinking of getting government help to stay in business.

First Niagara Financial Group (FNFG)

There's more than one way for a regional bank to pick up new branches, new deposits, and new assets—remember, that's Wall Street jargon for loans—at ultralow prices. While other banks wait for their neighbors to fail so they can buy the decent parts of the fallen financial institution from the FDIC, First Niagara went through a different federal agency entirely, the Antitrust Division of the Justice Department.

First Niagara, a responsible Lockport, New York–based bank that you've probably never heard of before, managed to strike a deal that grew its deposits by over 70 percent and increased its branches by 50 percent in exchange for a mere pittance, and nobody seemed to notice. The bank took advantage of a situation that will become less and less unusual as we see more and more mergers in the industry. When PNC acquired National City, the Justice Department ordered them to sell off sixty-one National City branches in western Pennsylvania, a region that's both very close and demographically very similar to First Niagara's area of operations in upstate New York. When the federal government forces a company to sell, the buyer always gets a great price, no matter what industry we're talking about, and that's exactly what happened here. First Niagara agreed to buy fifty-seven of those branches, $4.2 billion in deposits, and $839 million in solid, performing middle-market commercial and small business loans—no subprime, no loans outside the geographic footprint, none of those awful home equity loans or residential construction loans, either. This acquisition marks a huge increase over the bank's 114 branches in upstate New York and $5.9 billion in deposits, and the company expects it to increase its earnings per share by 20 percent in 2010. Best of all, First Niagara paid only $54 million to take this merchandise off PNC's hands. How much of a steal is that? A bank with a $1.8 billion market capitalization paid $54 million to expand its deposits by 70 percent and grow its branches by 50 percent. If PNC hadn't been a forced seller and the financial world wasn't in crisis, then PNC probably could have charged closer to $420 million and found a buyer. When the deal closes First Niagara will be the third-largest bank in western Pennsylvania. If that's not taking advantage of the chaotic environment and the weakness of the competition to vastly expand the size of your bank, just as Fleet did at the end of the S&L crisis, then nothing is.

First Niagara is also expanding to Eastern Pennsylvania, with the recently announced agreement to acquire Harleysville National. After the close of the deal, FNFG will have almost 4 percent of Pennsylvania's banking business, a great move on management's part. At these levels the stock's bountiful 56-cent annual dividend yields 7 percent, paying you to wait until the market figures out that this bank is already well on its way to being one of the big regional bank winners from the crisis and until First Niagara gets still another shot at a large, inexpensive acquisition.

First Niagara has been one of the more responsible lenders. Its net charge-offs–to–loans ratio is around 0.28 percent, compared to

0.51 percent—nearly twice that—for its cohort. And its ratio of non-performing loans to total loans—the deadbeat ratio—is just 0.72 percent, versus 1.03 percent for its peers. The company has far fewer bad loans on the books than other, similar banks—that's another big reason why I have confidence that it will be a winner. Unfortunately, First Niagara expects the acquisitions to lower its tangible common equity ratio from 9 percent to 5 percent, which, while still on par with the capital levels at the top twenty banks, is considerably lower than I like to see, and more important, than I think the regulators like to see. But the company is taking action to quickly increase that figure to 5.5 percent and to 6.4 percent by the end of 2010 through some well-timed equity offerings that make the institution a better, stronger, player in the new banking world. Plus, First Niagara's Tier One capital ratio of 11.5 percent is significantly higher than the national average of 10 percent. And given that First Niagara plans on repaying the $184 million of TARP money it received from the feds, and may very well have already done so by the time you read this, it seems absurd to worry about the company's capital levels. This is a bank that can clearly stand on its own two feet, one that's already started expanding in the chaos and could grow much, much bigger before the financial sector gets back on an even footing. Again, do not be put off that you have never heard of it. Most of the biggest winners in my bank portfolio from the time of my hedge fund would have been unknown to you. The losers? All the famous banks that produced simply awful returns.

NewAlliance Bancshares (NAL)

What company would I say looks the most like Fleet in 1988? I think it might be NewAlliance Bank, a once-sleepy small-town Connecticut bank that could inherit a ton of new assets courtesy of faltering banks in the declining New England real estate market. Run by one of the most experienced East Coast bankers, Peyton Patterson, NewAlliance is famous for its incredibly low delinquency rate—the percentage of total loans that are thirty to sixty days past due with no payments being made—at around 1 percent, versus an average of 1.85 percent in its neighboring banks and 3.8 percent nationwide. That's about the same ratio that the best of banks would have in the best of times. This bank really knows how to spot deadbeats so as to avoid giving them loans, unlike so many others, which spent years falling all over themselves trying to give mortgages to the least creditworthy among us. Under Patterson, NewAlliance never went in for that sort of thing

It has a small but growing footprint now, with eighty-nine branches in Connecticut and as of fairly recently in Massachusetts as well, since it just finished a niche acquisition there. What I find most exciting about NewAlliance is that it has only 5 percent market share by deposits in Connecticut behind Bank of America, Webster Financial (which I used to own a gigantic chunk of when I was a hedge fund manager), People's United Financial (another winner you can see below), Wells Fargo, and TD Bank, so the regulators will most likely favor NewAlliance before giving out too much to the others, as they are all considerably larger and have more market share. After eight years of the Bush administration, it's a little shocking to see that the government is concerned about things like antitrust law, or simply too much concentration among a small group of oligopolistic businesses in any given market. I used to joke on *Mad Money* that Bush had leased the Antitrust Division of the Justice Department to the Commerce Department for the duration of his two terms in office, but with Obama in charge, you can bet that the feds will be eager to give smaller banks like NewAlliance the good assets from banks that fail in the area. The smaller but still healthy banks like this one will likely get favorable treatment. NewAlliance only has 0.23 percent market share by deposits in Massachusetts so it has a whole lot of room to expand there.

I have to like NewAlliance's conservative credit policies and all the room it has to take market share, but if there's one stock that's on this list because of terrific management it's this one. CEO Patterson is simply an amazing banker. While others are scrambling to raise capital,

NAL has 18.7 percent Tier One capital, the most of any bank I follow. And it's not like she got there by hoarding money. NewAlliance is making plenty of loans, and doing it well, with a portfolio of about 51 percent residential loans and the rest a mix among commercial, construction, and consumer loans. This bank is so well capitalized I have a hard time seeing how the regulators could refuse to sell New-Alliance any assets that the FDIC ends up having to sell in the New England area. This difference will become clear in the coming years, as New England was the last area to begin to collapse in house prices, so there's more ahead in opportunity for acquiring banks.

What really amazes me about this stock is how little support it has among the analyst community, with only one of the eleven analysts who follow NewAlliance rating it a buy. No matter how long you've been in the game, the analysts will always keep finding ways to surprise you with their cluelessness. But if I worked at NewAlliance, I would take the lack of sponsorship as a badge of honor, since this company certainly doesn't need Wall Street to grow, let alone encourage it to be reckless, as the analysts did with so many other banks before the real estate market started to tank. This bank maintained its conservative and responsible lending standards, and that's why NewAlliance didn't need any TARP money, making it one of very few banks that rejected the government's handout. This is a bank with $4.4 billion in deposits, and I bet the size of its deposits doubles by the time this crisis is over. I think NewAlliance will be a heck of a lot larger and worth a substantial amount more once the FDIC finishes dealing out its good banks, meaning the profitable, worthwhile operations of the failed institutions it seizes, and keeps the bad—the lousy assets that cause banks to fall into the FDIC's not-so-loving embrace. However, given its incredibly bountiful capital position I believe NAL will be hard-pressed to stay independent since it is worth more to a poorly capitalized large-cap bank than it is to its own shareholders. That's what I call a high-quality problem.

People's United Financial (PBCT)

The final regional bank that I believe will be able to benefit from the crisis by gobbling up chunks of failed banks that the FDIC puts on the auction block is another New England bank, People's United Financial, based in Bridgeport, Connecticut, which should share the spoils with New Alliance. Given the severity of the housing downturn just starting in this region, believe me, the FDIC will need more than one bank as a savior. With three hundred branches in Connecticut, Vermont, New Hampshire, Massachusetts, Maine, and Westchester County, New York, People's United operates in some of the wealthiest areas in the country, with much lower than average unemployment. Currently People's United has $20 billion in assets—remember, that means loans when we're talking about banks—$14 billion in deposits, and is among the top five banks by market share in Connecticut, Vermont, and New Hampshire. The company clearly recognizes the immense scale of the opportunities created by the financial crisis, as management plans to double or triple its assets over the next two to five years. There is more than enough room in the region for People's United to grow without butting up against New Alliance for dominance of New England.

But what makes me so confident that the regulators will take such a favorable view of People's United? The one thing the FDIC wants to avoid more than anything else is selling the good pieces of an insolvent bank to another bank that turns out to be troubled, or even insolvent itself. As I explained before, the regulators look for the healthiest, most disciplined banks when they make these sales, banks that can stand on their own two feet, and People's United fits the template almost too well. Let's run down the checklist of what the regulators look at, and I'll show you why People's United will never be defeated. The company has a net interest margin of 3.5 percent, so it's not tremendously more profitable than its neighbors, which have an average net interest margin of 3.25 percent. But People's United's nonperforming assets as a percentage of its total assets—its deadbeat ratio—is just 0.25 percent, versus 1.75 percent for its peers. That means similar banks have seven times as many bad loans as this one. Pretty impressive. That's the kind of conservative lending practices and effective management of credit risk that the regulators adore, and it also means People's United is quite simply a fantastic bank.

However, People's United does have one problem, albeit one that most banks in the country wish they had. The bank has been so conservative that it has way, way too much capital. That's right, as other banks struggle to raise money in order to stay solvent, People's United has a tangible-capital–to–assets ratio of 19.5 percent, while the other banks in its cohort average 6.1 percent. That is nothing short of amazing—People's United has three times the average. I doubt any other bank comes close. That ratio translates into $2.7 billion of excess capital that forms a very large buffer against any kind of catastrophe. This bank didn't take a cent from TARP, and not just because it already has so much capital. Unlike virtually every other bank in existence, People's United reported that its net charge-offs as a percentage of all loans—meaning the percentage of loans it wrote off as bad debt and assumed it would never collect—in 2008 was unchanged from 2007, in spite of the recession and the further collapse of home values. That's just incredible. In the event of a worldwide nuclear war, I wouldn't be surprised if People's United were to make it through and still be completely solvent, trying to find the most creditworthy cockroaches to lend to. Seriously, though, with that enormous level of capital, the FDIC is going to give this bank all the best pickings.

And in the meantime, People's United is on the prowl for plain old acquisitions, taking advantage of depressed prices in the stock market to get good deals. Last year it bought Chittenden, the largest full-service bank in Vermont, with a depressed valuation. People's United has plans to purchase a commercial bank in the Northeast, and of course, it's now ready for regulatory-assisted acquisitions, meaning People's United is eager to buy the worthwhile pieces of failed banks from the FDIC. As you can see, the similarities with Fleet are far more than geographic, and if People's United makes more fill-in acquisitions and gets to buy the best of what the FDIC will have to offer, then this midsized regional bank will soon be a regional banking titan. Oh, and People's United, like my other favorite regionals that I expect to go national, is paying you to wait until it expands over New England with a 61-cent annual dividend that it has raised for the last seventeen consecutive years, which at current levels yields about 4 percent.

There you have it, five banks in the mold of Fleet in the late 1980s that should be able to benefit from the current financial crisis the same way that the healthiest banks in the late 1980s and early '90s benefited from the savings-and-loan crisis. Glacier, FirstMerit, First Niagara, NewAlliance, and People's United should each be able to buy assets from neighboring banks that are in worse shape, for a pittance, thanks to the distressed stock prices of the weaker banks. Even better, all five of these regional banks have attributes that appeal to the regulators, which should encourage the FDIC to offer to sell them their pick of the worthwhile pieces of failed banks in their regions and make them logical acquirers in take-under situations when an almost-insolvent bank has to go to the regulators for help and the regulators set up a deal. I believe that all five of these banks could double within the next three years. That's an incredible opportunity, one you can't afford to pass up if you're trying to get back to even. I have seen all of this before, so I have conviction in the ability of these regional banks to grow through savvy, inexpensive acquisitions that would be possible only when the financial system is in tatters. Just as Fleet grew from a small bank in Providence to the dominant bank in New England, all five of these banks could expand rapidly at the expense of weaker banks. Even if you don't want to try to take advantage of this twice-in-a-lifetime opportunity, you should seriously consider buying a bank like JP Morgan, Wells Fargo, or Goldman Sachs, the best of the larger banks.

Let me pay these five the highest compliment I know. This beaten-down group is finally ready for a big move. The crash has already occurred, now it's time for the rebound if I were still running my hedge fund, I would buy 9.9 percent of every one of these banks, as I did when I made a fortune for my partners and myself off the last crisis. Just like it was back then, most analysts, pundits, and professors who opine on the industry see only the gloom and doom. I see the coming boom and I want you in before it becomes obvious to all that the next big thing is these survivor regional saplings that can grow up to be mighty oaks.

7

GETTING BACK TO EVEN LIKE A PRO
Using Options to Replace Stocks

What's the most conservative moneymaking strategy on Wall Street? What course of action allows you to take on the *least* risk with the largest percentage reward? What method gives you an opportunity to exploit big moves in the market's hottest stocks with a fraction of your money, while at the same time husbanding lots of your cash for the safest bonds or for high-yielding stocks? Are you sitting down? Because the answer is options. That's right, call options on common stocks. Shocking? Yes, probably to almost all of you because you've been schooled to think *Danger! Danger! Danger!* when you even hear the term *options,* let alone actually consider trading them. People are taught that options either give you a phenomenal return or they will lose you every penny you put in them. Most regular, nonprofessional investors usually don't touch these presumably radioctive instruments, and if they do, they find the lingo impenetrable: calls, strikes, spreads—might as well be talking about betting on a baseball game you know nothing about. Indeed, options *can* be dangerous and the worries for real if you do not use them correctly, especially given that the vast majority of all options expire worthless.

However, if you follow the method I am about to unveil for you, options are not only safe, they're actually among the most conservative ways to invest. In my method you are far less likely to lose money by buying call options on stocks than you would by owning those same stocks. Before I go into how these seemingly most risky investment instruments, common stock derivatives that profit from quick upward movements in price on the underlying stocks, can actually be safer than you think, I have to ask you to do something for me. I have to ask you to suspend all preconceptions, all worries, and all fears about a topic that is, I admit, sometimes mind-numbingly hard to understand. By the time I get through the usual "right but not the obligation to own common stock at a price predetermined" boilerplate caveat, I know you will be thinking: "Come on, Cramer, I am a stay-at-home mom, I can't do this," or "Jimmy, listen, I am a retired individual on a pension; how can you be so cavalier as to risk my hard-earned money on something that only a reckless, rich youth could afford?"

You know what? My method is too good, and—doggone it—I am going to teach it to you no matter how hard it might be to learn. There's just too much money to be made and saved using my system. I have thought for years about revealing one of the most important secrets behind how I made the most money at my hedge fund, what really brought me the big money, and how I finished up 36 percent in 2000, when almost everyone else got hammered. I was tempted to put it in *Real Money: Sane Investing in an Insane World,* but balked at the last minute because I feared the strategy would be too hard to explain and that it would be unreasonable to expect you to try it.

I now know those reservations were wrong. The moment is too dire, the sheer amount of money already lost too horrific. We've got to get serious here. We have got to get you back to even without risking the farm, so you must understand this strategy. I think it is incredibly conservative, but nevertheless, it offers gigantic upside on a percentage basis, just what you need to regain what you have lost or to rev up your portfolio's gains. Heaven knows, this system has gotten me back to even at times when I was well into the hole, and I've been in the hole many times over the course of my career, the same hole you might find yourself in. Now you can pull yourself back to even the same way I did, using my almost-oxymoronic conservative method with tremendous upside.

We're all taught that the definition of a conservative strategy is one with very little risk that offers equally minimal gains. Now I'm telling you there's a way to invest that's less risky than simply buying common stock, and at the same time vastly more rewarding, something most economics professors would say is downright impossible. Good thing you're reading this book and not some dry tome written by one of the zillions of academics who love nothing more than to tell you all the ways you can't make money. I'd much rather show you how to make boatloads of money without risking very much of your precious capital, which is doubly precious if it's been radically diminished in recent years.

Sound too good to be true? Believe me, it's for real, although there is one *very important* caveat: this method requires you to be hands-on. Most of the instruction I give you about stocks requires you to do some homework at least once a week, to stay current on the fundamentals of the companies you own stock in. But for this new strategy to work right, you need to be current on the actual trading of the stocks themselves, a more intensive, daytime chore, as well as the fundamentals of what you are trading. I know it is time-consuming, hard work. It might be best used by those who are able to look at quotes during the day, which, believe it or not, makes it ideal for stay-at-home parents and retired people who can watch over their stocks during the day. Those who can't follow the market relatively regularly might have a difficult time making the incremental money that this strategy can bring in, but I still want to encourage it, because it requires taking on less risk than buying most common stocks. Those who can check in a couple of times a session when the market is open stand to benefit the most from the style's possibilities.

I am so hell-bent on getting you to follow this strategy that I am going to dispense with all the arithmetic *for now,* and am not going to let you get bogged down in the idea that one option gives you the right but not the obligation to buy 100 shares and that you have to multiply the price of the call by 100. I will get to that. I am not an ir-responsible promoter of call options. I want you to think conceptually for a moment about what we are trying to accomplish when we use call options the responsible way, not the way most people use them. Only then will you know that my style is a conservative one that can save you more money on the downside than owning common stock, and only then will you be comfortable enough learning the difficult ropes to climb using options.

So let's take a step back and look at the big picture. What are we really after when we invest in stocks? We are basically trying to wring the largest possible return out of the least amount of capital, which is the very definition of a great risk/reward. We need to be able to capture as much upside as possible while we limit our downside. That's what classic professional investing is really about.

So, I am going to demonstrate to you the day-to-day dilemma of owning common stocks, even the best common stocks, and then, after I give you the tools, I will show you how to solve that dilemma. I promise to point you on a path that will give you the biggest reward for the fewest dollars.

I am going to start by using a stock you all know and I hope you like, Google. This is the perfect example because a share of this stock simply costs too much money to be worth buying in its current form. Unless you are already superrich, you can't own enough shares of this high-dollar amount stock to make a difference to your wealth. And if you do want to own Google, one of the most phenomenal growth stocks of our time, do you really want to risk many thousands of dollars in order to make just a few thousand dollars because of the pitifully small amount of share you can buy with those dollars. (I am perfectly happy if you want to imagine risking hundreds of dol-lars instead of thousands to buy Google, since I am indifferent about the relative amounts. I just want you to buy what you can afford to buy.)

As I write, Google is at $400. So let's walk through some simple arithmetic in order to explain the problem of owning common stocks before we get to the options solution. Let's say you bought one share of Google for $400 and it went up 50 points, a huge amount. What would you have to show for it if you took profits? Fifty bucks. Just fifty bucks! How much did you risk to win that $50? Four hundred hard-earned dollars. What is the rate of return on that $50? Let's see, you made $50 on $400, which is 12.5 percent. Okay, now let's say you have more to invest; maybe you have $4,000? You buy 10 shares. Google advances 50 points. You make $500. Not chump change, but you risked $4,000 to make it. Google's a volatile stock. What would have happened if the market repeated its awful action of 2007 and Google dropped to $300, a total possibility, right? You would have then risked $4,000 on just ten shares of Google just to lose $1,000. You would have lost a quarter of your investment.

Now, let's think really big. You want 100 shares of Google so each point can really make you some money. You have to put up $40,000 to get your 100 shares, a truly gigantic sum of money for almost everyone reading this book, not to mention almost everyone in the entire country, particularly just for one stock! Now, say Google goes up 50 points. Congratulations, you've made $5,000. That's terrific, but at the same time you have to ask yourself, how much of your total capital did you put at risk, and how much can you really afford to lose in order to make that $5,000? Did you risk almost all of your money to make that return? Ask yourself if you can afford to lose, say, $10,000 on your investment to make that $5,000, as that could certainly happen. After all, Google is prone to swoons and surges. Don't forget that in March 2009, Google fell from $378 to $290, so a 100-point drop from $400 is certainly in the realm of possibility. And it would smart like all get-out if it happened to you, believe me. That is in a nutshell the problem with buying common stock; the same holds true for stocks with much lower share prices than Google. Often, your money just doesn't go far enough, so when you win, the upside leaves much to be desired, as you probably couldn't buy nearly as many shares as you wanted. Even worse, in order to get that upside, you have to commit huge amounts of capital and take on tremendous amounts of risk. The Google example says it all: it takes $40,000 of your money to give you a $5,000 win, and you could risk losing $10,000 in the attempt.

Now, how about if I knew a way to wager just $5,000 to get that $5,000 win? How about if I had a way to let you profit from Google with a much smaller amount of money, which, at the same time, allowed you to invest the rest in a safer set of stocks or bonds? That's what options allow you to do. They allow you to get that $5,000 win at a fraction of the risk by giving you control over the 100 shares in the example for much less than you would have paid with common stock.

Again, here's the dilemma articulated in plain English, not Wall Street gibberish. When it comes to stock investing you want to "control" as much stock as you can, while putting up the least amount of money, to get the best risk reward. You want to find some way to have the upside of, using the same example, Google's run from $400 to $450, or 50 points, without the downside of 100 points, or even more. I bet the vast majority of you would say, "Can't do it, there's no way it can happen. There's no way to cut off that downside without ruining your upside." Well, you'd be wrong. There's a way to control all of that upside and contain that downside. Moreover, there's a way to profit from the upside and, if you want to learn some of the most advanced strategies I have to offer, you can also profit from the downside, too.

Miracle? Alchemy? No, just call options—call options used wisely and effectively to choke off risk while increasing the reward.

What we need to do is essentially "create" Google's stock in a different form, which takes into account all that you are willing to lose and yet still can generate a better percentage gain than the common stock can. You can create your own personal vehicle to run with the Google common stock express on the way up, but not on the way down. We want this creation to track as much upside and as little downside as we can.

I have not yet introduced any option terms, but I hope I have piqued your interest because now we are going to have to get our hands a little dirty. We can't create this personal options vehicle without going over some terms that allow us to run the thing smoothly on the Google expressway.

We need to talk the mechanics of call options and why you should learn them. I first started trading calls in my dorm room at Harvard Law School because when I had a great idea, I wanted to capitalize on it and I had only about $2,500 to my name. Initially, because I had so little capital, I bought a lot of down-and-out $1 and $2 and $3 stocks to try to get the most bang for my buck. But you know what? Stocks don't get to those prices because a company wants them to be down there. They go to those levels because the fundamentals are deteriorating or because the company's stock may be worthless or certainly working its way there. I used to buy many of the low-dollar stocks that I saw recommended in *Forbes* or *BusinessWeek* or in newsletters I would get and I quickly realized that you get what you pay for. I rarely made money and I rapidly lost money. Fortunately, I was writing briefs for Professor Alan Dershowitz—the Von Bulow case (if you have ever seen the movie *Reversal of Fortune*, I am in it as a composite character)—so I was able to replenish the money at about the same speed I was losing it in the market.

In the meantime I saw many companies with fundamentals that I really liked that traded at $60, $70, $80, and $90 or higher. But when I would buy ten shares of one of those, I didn't have room for much else in my portfolio. If I bought twenty-five shares, I was pretty much done; I had used all of my capital. And if I wanted to buy something like Google, at $400, I ran out of money at six shares, and I had risked a gigantic amount of my money on one stock! Totally unacceptable situation.

That left me in an awkward position. The best stocks I knew about and had studied could go up, ten, twenty, thirty dollars and I simply didn't make a lot of money on those stocks if I bought ten shares, yet I felt like I was taking a huge amount of risk. If I were going to take on that kind of risk I wanted a bigger reward. Plus, the more I analyzed the business of picking stocks, the more I thought that I really wanted to capture only the price appreciation of a stock, not its dividend, because at the time I needed to make money rapidly. That's because the initial capital I was using was my student loan money meant for law school tuition. I was simply trying to augment it, trying to make a little extra dough between payments, knowing that it wasn't totally reckless because I had the money coming in from my work on Dershowitz's cases.

Don't get me wrong: I am all for dividends, as I mentioned in earlier chapters, but I needed a way to make some profits that weren't just on a quarterly basis and that were much bigger than any dividend could pay. I had to forgo a key part of the long-term capital appreciation stream if I wanted to make some bigger money in a quick period. So I looked into options, which give you the ability to profit from a stock's rise without getting any dividends. I knew very little about these mysterious instruments when I started out. But I knew they tracked the stock and gave you a lot more bang for the buck than if you bought the common stock itself. Here is what I stumbled on. Let's say I wanted to buy Exxon, which is a $70 stock as I write. While Exxon has a reasonable dividend of 42 cents a quarter per share, frankly that's not what I was looking for because while it makes a ton of sense to hold Exxon for years, take in that dividend, and let it compound, I didn't have that luxury. I needed to make money at a faster pace.

At the time I was looking for rapid advances that I could capture. If I didn't think Exxon would advance rather quickly I would find another stock that would. Maybe I think Exxon at $70 is 20 points undervalued and I think that oil is about to take off and Exxon is the way I want to play crude's appreciation.

So let's go through the arithmetic of buying a common stock. If I bought 30 shares of Exxon at $70, for $2,100, well within my $2,500 budget, and it goes up the 20 points I am looking for, I make $600—$20 times 30 shares—for about a 28 percent return on my $2,100 investment. But what happens if it goes down $20? Then, of course, I am out $600. I always regarded these risk/reward situations as asymmetrical, meaning that it hurt far more to lose $600 than I could take, even as making $600 should have been a decent offset to that pain. The $600 was just too much for me to lose, especially when you consider the arithmetic. The loss may have been 28 percent but after that loss you need a 40 percent gain just to get back to even. (After the big loss I would have 30 shares of a $50 stock, or $1,500, down from $2,100 and to get back to even would require a $600 return on $1,500, something that's pretty darned daunting.)

That arithmetic and risk profile were unsatisfying to me, and the worries that I had about the losses drove me to explore options as a way to make bigger gains and take fewer losses. I had always heard that options by their nature could limit your downside and still let you capture the upside for a smaller amount of money. So I decided to teach myself how to use call options as a way to limit my risk and maximize my reward. All I knew about them, though, was that you could choose among many different levels of the stock, including levels above the stock, to start investing in the call. That meant that you had to know not just the price of the common stock to buy a call, but also something called "the strike price," the starting level of your investment. Beyond that I really didn't know anything much at all. What intrigued me though, was that, say in the case of Exxon trading at $70, there was a strike at $70 that I figured would allow me to get the upside from $70 but not lose anything more than my investment in the option if Exxon went below $70. It seemed like a good deal to someone who views risk asymetrically as I do, wanting the gain but not being able to handle the loss. I had a lot to learn.

The problem with teaching yourself anything about investing is that you tend to have to lose money first before you figure it all out. That's what happened to me at first in options because I didn't know how to use them. I didn't know how quickly you could lose money in them and how dangerous they can be if you don't know how to use them right. My experience cost me almost all I had and I want you to learn from it without repeating my mistakes. So let me show you how I originally got my head handed to me in calls so you won't do the same thing if you are tempted to use these instruments as a way to get back to even.

I certainly had the right premise for using calls. I would choose stocks that I thought would move quickly and I would establish a target price. Let's say it was June 1 and I thought Exxon, which was at $70, could go to $90 in a couple of months. I wanted to capture that gain one-for-one, without risking much to the downside. Given that when you buy a call all you can lose is the money you invest in the call, I would choose how much money I was willing to risk to catch that big move. I then wanted to figure out which call would give me the most upside, and it would track the gains in that stock as closely as possible. Remember, I knew that each call had what was known as a "strike price," the price where you would be starting your investment in Exxon. Back then you could find out the cost of each call only by calling a broker. These days you can get that information on any website that has options pricing, including Yahoo Finance. It is much easier now than when I was trading from my dorm room in the early 1980s, so I think that the method I am about to reveal is even more worth taking advantage of than when I used it to help pay for law school.

So, without the advantage of the Web I had to call my broker and ask for a menu with the prices of all sorts of call options struck at different levels that would allow me to cash in on the run I thought Exxon was about to have. I will re-create that menu here. Since it was the first day of June and Exxon was at $70, it seemed obvious that I should buy a June 70 call. What does that do? It allows me to profit with Exxon as it goes above $70, by the third Friday of the month when the call expires, without losing more than my investment if it goes down or does nothing. Seems reasonable. I could also buy the options struck at 75, known as the June 75 calls, which gave me the right to the appreciation above 75 by the third Friday in June. Then there were many strikes higher up, at five-point intervals all the way to $90. There were also strikes below the price of the stock, including the June 65s and the June 60s.

I was very cocky when I first started. If I liked a stock and I thought it would go up a lot, I figured it would start that move the moment I bought it. Options trade in monthly cycles, expiring, as I mentioned above, on the third Friday of each month. Given that it was June 1 and I thought Exxon would power higher immediately, I asked the broker to give me the prices for both the June 70 and 75 calls. He said that I could buy the June 70 calls for $1.30 and the June 75 calls for 25 cents. I didn't understand those prices at all. A dollar thirty? Twenty-five cents? Or $1.30 for one share? What the heck costs only 25 cents? I was totally mystified. I wanted to know what I got for $1.30. He said "nothing, because with a call option you are getting the right to the appreciation not of one share but of 100 shares, so you have to multiply the 100 shares by the $1.30 number." That meant if I wanted to buy one call, giving me the right to the appreciation of 100 shares starting at the strike price of $70, I had to pay $130. If I'd created the system, I would have just said "the price is $130." Calls are quoted in dollars and cents that must *always* be multiplied by 100 if you want to figure out how much you have to pay to buy the call.

However, when you consider how much less that call, which gives you control of 100 shares over $70, costs versus buying 100 shares outright at $70, you can see that it seems to be a real bargain: $130 versus $7,000. Now this was the bang for the buck I was looking for! If I was really sure of myself, if I really wanted to make a bet that this stock would rocket without putting down a lot of money, I could buy one call for $25 that kicked in and gave me the power of 100 shares when the stock went above $75. But, remember the date: June 1. My broker told me, wisely, that unless I thought the stock was just going to tear higher instantly I would probably lose all my money. That's because if the stock didn't move or it went down by the third Friday of June, I would lose all $130 on the June 70 calls. He suggested I go out another month, as there are always calls available not just in the current month (the one you are in)—June, in this case—but also the "near months," like the next month, July. He said, why not go out until the next month to give the idea more time to percolate. Instead of the call expiring on the third Friday of June, this call would expire on the third Friday of July, a much better deal because I didn't want to put a gun to my head. This seemed like a more reasonable amount of time for Exxon to work its magic.

Of course, I would have to pay more for the July call than for the June call. That's because options are contracts, like real estate contracts. I was buying a contract to have all of Exxon's appreciation above $70 by the third Friday in July, instead of the third Friday in June. If I wanted an option to buy real estate for eight weeks instead of three weeks I would expect to have to pay more to get it, too. Time is money.

I asked for the price of the July 70 call and was told it was $2.30, almost twice as much as the June call because I had more time to let Exxon run. Again, if you were going to buy that call, to figure out how much money you would be spending, you had to multiply $2.30 times 100. (Always think "multiply by 100," as soon as you hear the price, and it will get less alien, I promise.)

To me that was even more of a bargain than the June call because instead of spending $7,000 to buy 100 shares of Exxon I was spending $230 to get just the appreciation of Exxon for about eight weeks, and I didn't have any downside below $70 per share! What a great deal: there was risk to the common stock all the way to zero, but using calls my risk was only $230 if the stock went below $70.

Then I asked for the Exxon July 75 calls and the broker told me those cost 80 cents. Wow, now that seemed like a real gimme! The stock goes up big, and I get all the appreciation on 100 shares above 75 for just $80!

Fortunately I knew enough to go out one month as my broker suggested, something that I unlearned way too often in those early days, since I often felt my hunches were going to pan out faster. I can tell you that in almost every single case when I did that current month strike, I lost money. Almost every single time, whether it be in what I thought were gimmes, like the Exxon trade, or in situations like an earnings upside surprise that I might expect in a matter of weeks or even days.

Therefore, I would pull the trigger on one of the July 70 calls, again because I figured that the cost of riding up one call equal to the upside of 100 shares was only a fraction of owning the common stock, just $230 versus $7,000. So I told my broker to buy me a call on Exxon at $70. I passed on the July 75s since I was worried that they would "go out worthless" if the stock didn't appreciate fast enough to get above $75 by the third week in July.

Because options are tricky and my broker knew I was new at it, he taught me how to put the order in correctly. He said the right way to do it is to say: "I would like to buy one Exxon July 70 call for $2.30." (I never used "market" prices, as everyone who has ever read any of my books knows, because markets move fast and you can get picked off and pay far more than you ever intended if the stock bolts. Pick your price and stick with it. If you miss it, wait for another turn.)

And then he taught me some more terms. He said there were three kinds of calls: an "in-the-money" call, an "at-the-money" call, and an "out-of-the-money" call. I asked him what the heck that gobbledygook was. He said when you buy a call with a strike that is at the current price of the common stock, in this case a $70 call when the common trades at $70, that's considered "at the money" and you will be participating in the appreciation of the common stock immediately. That's what I was buying. When you buy a call struck at $75, that's called an "out of the money" because you are nowhere near being at the money. You don't begin to get appreciation until the stock goes up five points. After much trial and error I learned that these strikes should have been called out-of-moneys, not out-of-*the*-moneys, because of the money you lose speculating on a strike high above the current price of almost any stock. Finally there is an in-the-money call, with a strike that is below the price of the common, in this case, say the July 65 strike, which, he said, "is just like owning common stock." At the time I figured, who would ever need an in-the-money call? That's exactly what I was trying to get away from, something just like common stock, with more risk and less reward!

Ultimately, I couldn't have been more wrong about the value of the in-the-money calls because I failed to take into account the cost of the at-the-money $70 call in my calculations, a huge mistake that I should never have made. I was so enamored of the downside protection—loss cut off at $70—that I didn't fathom how difficult it would be to make money from where I started. If the July call costs $2.30 per call, you are not really getting the common stock at 70. You have to add the $2.30 you paid to the $70 strike. That means you don't start to make money until the stock exceeds $72.30. The best way to look at this pricing is to ask yourself, "Where am I creating my Exxon, my personal vehicle to take advantage of the appreciation of the stock?" What looks like a small amount of money is actually, if the stock doesn't appreciate quickly, a huge hurdle and one that most people don't grasp in time before they pull the trigger. I didn't.

Think of that real estate example again. No broker's going to sell you the right to the potential appreciation of property for that long a time for free. Same with common stocks; you can't control the 100 shares for eight weeks without paying something for that right to the upside, and in most cases it presents way too high a wall to mount before the gains can begin, even when you might ultimately be right.

You can perform the same function for the July 75 calls for 80 cents: we are creating the stock at $75.80 and we are spending $80 to do so (100 times .80).

So can you guess what happens? As is almost always the case when I executed this at-the-money kind of trade—and I did dozens of them before I figured out the problem—the stock did nothing. A week goes by, two weeks go by, three weeks, and there's no movement. The June calls, the current month, would almost always go out worthless in that short of a time period, so at least I didn't throw away the money on the June calls. Don't fall for those near-term calls; they're truly a sucker's bet.

But eight weeks isn't a long time, either. Next thing I knew it's the third Friday of July and I lost all of my $230, because oil stayed flat and Exxon either went down or did nothing. Quite a difference from what would have happened if I owned the common. Then I would still be playing, still be in, and I wouldn't have dropped a nickel. I had made a bad bet. The common stock would have been better, if I was willing to risk my money to buy it. I threw away $230.

The good news is that I bought only one call. Can you imagine if I had bought ten call option contracts, something that would have given me control over 1,000 shares? I could have afforded it because 10 calls, the right to control 1,000 shares, would have cost me $2,300, within my $2,500 budget. But if the stock had done nothing or gone down I would have been out almost everything that I had on my hunch that Exxon was going to take off. That's a horrible, hideous loss, one I couldn't afford, especially considering that if I had just bought 30 shares of Exxon I wouldn't have lost a thing. Sure, it's terrific to think that with the same amount of money that it takes to buy 30 shares I could buy the appreciation for 1,000 shares but that potential loss is unfathomable when you consider how often a stock just does nothing.

Now, of course, the stock could have gone up to $75, and I would have had more than a double on my at-the-money call, as I would have invested $2.30 per call and that call would have been worth $5. Five dollars minus my $2.30 cost equals $2.70, or $270 on a $230 investment, a great rate of return. And occasionally, I discovered, I could be that right. Yes, sometimes it actually did happen. But far more often, nothing happened and I paid a whole lot for nothing. That happened to me again and again when I started. I would buy an at-the-money call or an out-of-the-money call and the stock would do nothing or go down and wipe me out. One hundred percent loss. The one or two times it did work out kept me in the game for at-the-moneys, just like a lottery ticket buyer who occasionally wins a small amount of money and feels hooked on buying more and more tickets.

There was also a second scenario that happened quite often that was incredibly futile and equally galling: Exxon would go up $2 or $3 by the third week of July, and I would make nothing or next to nothing anyway, because my call cost me as much as that upside. So if Exxon went to $71 I would have lost $130. If it had gone to $72 I would have lost $30. Not a lot, but it adds up over time. That's all because I had created Exxon at $72.30 instead of leaving well enough alone and getting all the appreciation the common stock would have given me. It bothered me to no end that I could be right on the direction—the stock would go up a couple of bucks—and the common stock holder would make that money but I would see none of it. *None of it!* If your call option that you bought at the money finished in the money, as the July 70 call would be if the stock were at $72, you had the right, if you wanted to, to take delivery of all of that common stock. The contract says you control 100 shares for that period of time, and just as with real estate, if you want to, you can take delivery of the property. Here, of course, though, I would have to take delivery of 100 shares of Exxon and with the stock at $72 I would have to pay $7,200 for the common stock. I didn't have that kind of money, so I would simply sell the call at expiration and get some of my money back but nothing more. I had too little money to do anything else, and I wanted the quick return.

I tried to figure out how to avoid the situation where the stock started rallying right after the July expiration, a situation where I would be right on the direction but wrong on the time. This miss of a big move by a month or two would happen incredibly often. As an antidote to that happening I looked out in time to the next set of options available, and in this case there was nothing until October. Some stocks have new sets of options sooner than that but many do not have more than a current term option—the month you are in, in this case June—the next month, July, and then usually two months are skipped and you get calls in October.

I figured, why put a July gun to my head? There was only one problem, though: the longer you go out in time, the more a call costs, just as if you want to have an option on land: if you wanted the option for only a month, you wouldn't have to pay much because you were not tying up the potential seller long. But, as in the case of options again, if you wanted to control Exxon for five months—from June until the third Friday of October—it would cost a lot more. In this case the call struck at $70 for October cost $4.40. Can you imagine starting that far behind? I would have to make 4.40 points above $70 *just to break even*! No thanks. I would be paying $440 for the right to collect the appreciation above $74.40, which, again, would be fine if the stock galloped higher. But if it did nothing I would lose it all, and if it took its time getting to my target, advancing $5 by October expiration, I would make next to nothing. That's way too big a price to make the October at-the-money call worthwhile.

In all of these cases, over hundreds of trades later—hundreds of trades you don't have to make—I came to realize that the lower dollar price of the calls, whether they be at-the-moneys or out-of-the-moneys, was pure seduction with little to no payoff. The smaller dollar costs led me to believe I was putting little at risk but what I really was doing was making the odds against me too great because of the cost of the call added to the strike. Not only could I not afford the stock to go down, wiping out my at-the-money by turning it into an out-of-the-money, I also needed the stock to go up past $72.30 to start making money with the calls that expired in the third week of July. I needed all of these good things to happen in a period of time that was way too compressed. When I cataloged each trade, as I did like a maniac after each month, I found that eight times out of ten I was booting out near-worthless calls, or calls worth less than I paid for them, or doing nothing at all because the common stock went down, leaving me high and dry.

My trading diary—something I highly suggest that you keep if you are going to learn from your mistakes—showed that lengthening the buy until October gave me more time but made the hurdle too great because it cost so much more to control the stock over that period of time. The "time premium," as they say in the trade, was just too expensive. And in every case, no matter what the month, the out-of-the-moneys were a nightmare, as few stocks can power that high that fast except in exceptional circumstances. The low-priced call "bargain" was illusory and I simply was losing gobs of money by the month on rank speculation. The risk was less than owning the common stock because you could lose only a small amount of dollars, but they add up over time—and the reward was nil. These are important lessons, and I want you to learn from the thousands of dollars I threw away buying at-the-money and out-of-the-money calls.

However, I didn't want to give up with options because I had so little money and so often my ideas were right if they only had more time to germinate. After multiple losing trades it dawned on me that something I simply had dismissed out of hand might be a better buy, might make a lot more sense: purchasing deep-in-the-money calls instead of at-the-moneys or out-of-the-moneys. In almost every example of the bad option trades I looked at from my diaries, the in-the-moneys would have prevented the loss if the stock had stayed static or would have made me good money with the stock appreciating just two or three dollars.

That's right, I realized that perhaps a better bet was not to buy the at-the-money, struck at $70 on a $70 stock, and most certainly not to buy the almost always worthless out-of-the-money $75 call on a $70 stock, but to buy a lower strike, to create the stock I wanted to control. To avoid paying the excessive premiums, the in-the-moneys were the cheapest way to do so, even if they required more capital than the at-the-moneys. In the case of Exxon, the in-the-money July 65 calls, the first ones down from where the stock was trading at the time, cost me only $5.25. I was creating the stock at $70.25 ($65 plus $5.25) instead of $72.30 with the at-the-money July 70 calls. Now, there are a ton of in-the-money calls on every stock's menu, and you can buy them in five-dollar increments—or *often* even smaller increments for some popular stocks—all the way down, just as you could all the way up. In the case of Exxon you can buy the $65 call, the $60 call, the $55 call, and so on. However, I only needed 25 cents more than the $70 stock price to get the one-for-one appreciation I was trying to get from the July 70s but that the July 70s could never give me. (The June 65 calls had only 10 cents premium, creating the stock at $70.10 but again, that wasn't a long enough time for the appreciation to occur.) Obviously, to buy July 65 call selling at $5.25 requires you to pay more than twice the dollar amount you would spend if you purchased the July 70 calls trading at $2.30. The quick arithmetic goes like this: the July in-the-money 65 call, with Exxon trading at $70, costs $525 (100 × $5.25) versus the July 70 at-the-money call costing $230 (100 × $2.30). Both allow you to control the stock above $70, but I was getting a better deal now because unlike the at-the-money call, which didn't start making me money until the stock exceeded the cost of the call plus the strike—meaning that Exxon would have to go above $72.30 to start winning—with in-the-money calls I started winning almost immediately on every point above the strike, that is, as soon as Exxon traded above $70.25.

We like to say the in-the-money call trades almost exactly flat with the common stock even if you go out in time. So if Exxon went to $71, my call that I paid $5.25 for would be at $6.00 and I would be up 75 cents or $75 (again, remember always to multiply by 100 because one call equals the right to control 100 shares). If Exxon went to $75, I would get almost a double for my money, roughly the same *percentage* gain that the July 70s would have given me. Yes, I could lose the whole $525 if Exxon went to $65, but the alternatives, the stock doing nothing or the stock going up, made the risk acceptable. And if the stock went below $65? Well, I would lose all $525, but at least I would be stopped out at $65, unlike the common stock, which could keep falling below that level and keep costing me. Yes, it would cost double what the 70 call would cost if I lost everything, but that's a pretty big decline in the stock over a short time period and I was willing to risk it. So, I concluded, the in-the-money call, while certainly costing more and exposing me to more downside, gave me the best way to gain from any appreciation that I was expecting with less money lost if the stock did nothing. (I would lose only $25 if the stocks stayed at $70, but I would lose $230 on the at-the-money $70 call if the stock did nothing).

And, if I really wanted to have more time, I could always go out several months and buy the October 65 call, the next month available. However, once again you have to pay for the luxury of time. The call isn't nearly as "flat" with the common as the July 65 call: it costs $7 not $5.25. While that's still cheaper than where you can create Exxon with the July 70 call, I still think—thousands of trades later—that the July in-the-money call represents the best bet, and here's why: as you get closer to the July expiration you can do something called "rolling over" your contract to the next month. That's simply instructing your broker to swap your July in-the-money call for a later month as you get close to July expiration. If you are going to a near month, there will be, just as in the case of the original call, very little premium over the common stock. So if your stock hasn't moved yet and you still think it will, you can just keep risking the same amount of money. There's a price to pay. You've got a small commission attached to the rollover trade, much lower today, by the way, than what I paid at the time. And there's also a small spread between the sale of a call and the buy of a new one in a different month, but that spread is typically minimal and barely factors in the overall scheme of things. All in all, we are talking no more than pennies to roll over one deep-in-the-money call to another in a later month, preserving the trade at very little cost.

Now, you are probably wondering, why is this deep-in-the-money strategy so compelling if you're trying to get back to even? Because if you believe, as I do, that the market will fight its way higher, the best way for you to participate and get the best risk/reward is with these deep-in-the-money options. As in the Exxon example, you are able to control much more stock than you could if you owned common stock, with little premium to the common stock, and you can use the rest of your capital for other purposes or keep it in cash for when stocks take another swoon.

Again, think of it like this: for $525 you can own all of the upside to 100 shares of Exxon versus $7,000 for the right to the same appreciation as the common stock holder who buys the stock at $70, *but you are in a much less risky situation* than the common stock holder because in his risk profile the stock can go to zero, but using my method you are stopped out at $65. That's why this strategy, called "stock replacement," is so ideal for you. You can lose only what you put up, you don't need to put up much, and your remaining cash can be put to work in bonds or higher-yielding common stocks to make money back over time. That's why this strategy is so conservative, even if it seems riskier.

You can use this stock replacement strategy for just about every stock out there, including the one I told you about at the beginning of this chapter, Google, which requires you to put up more money per common stock share than any other stock save Berkshire Hathaway. I didn't want to reveal how to create your own personal Google stock replacement until you could see all the mechanics come together. That's because designing a call strategy for the wild-trading Google is a big leap from developing one for the staid Exxon. With Google it is much harder to find the right entry point, the right strike, because the options are "pumped," meaning they all have a huge amount of premium over the common stock, even if you go very deep in the money. That's because Google has immense volatility, Wall Street code for Google's gyrating up-and-down daily action. But this stock replacement method really shines with an equity as exciting at Google, as its $400 price tag is way too expensive for most people to buy and the potential losses from a high-dollar-priced common stock could be disastrous for you. Replacing Google stock with Google call options limits your downside and allows you to participate in almost all of the upside of this great company. In Google's case you have to go pretty far down the strike list until you find an in-the-money call option that trades roughly "flat" with the common, like the Exxon July 65 call traded with Exxon at $70. That's because people pay up for a call on a volatile stock like Google because they want the protection against the extreme downside and they can't afford to buy the common stock in a size that matters. Stock replacement strategy is a safer and smarter way to profit from Google than the common stock itself.

With Google, again, you have to check the menu of strikes before you leap into the call fray. And you have to add the cost of the call to the common stock, just as you do with Exxon, to see what price you are creating Google at. For instance, on the first of June with the stock at $400 you could buy one July 350 for about $55, which creates Google at $405. I know, that's a lot of premium, meaning that the cost of the call on top of the strike price, $55, is $5 more than you would expect considering the cheaper Exxon example, as $400 minus $350 is equal to $50. Again, because Google is more volatile and can have more vicious swings, making the possibility of short-term profits or losses more likely, people will pay more for the upside and the protection. Why not buy another call that is higher and closer to being at the money? Because the cost of that premium ruins the trade. It's even worse than if you buy an at-the-money for Exxon. Sometimes it is so bad that with Google at $400 you might have to pay $15 for a $400 call that might be on the verge of expiring, as speculators bid up the at-the-money call price to ridiculous levels. You must never pay up like that if you expect to make any money.

Why buy the $350s instead of the $360s or $370s? That's a bit arbitrary, I admit, but I have always liked to limit myself to the strike that has a maximum of only $5 premium and no more. That's about the biggest hurdle rate I can tolerate. My trading diaries reflect the fact that any time I paid more than $5 premium for any call on any stock, I failed to recoup that premium. I know that deep strike price might preclude those with a small budget from buying Google calls. This one call, which would have cost $5,500 to purchase, was out of reach for my $2,500 budget ($55 price times 100 shares). But still, for that $5,500 I could own almost the exact same appreciation in 100 shares of Google that would cost someone buying the common stock $40,000. You can control the same number of shares for one-seventh the price! That's a true bargain. It is a terrific and conservative way to invest in Google because if you bought $5,500 of Google you would have almost no Google—about 13 shares at $400 each. So if the price went up big you would have little to show for it. Google could go up 20 points and you would make $260 with the common stock. But you would make about $1,500 with the option because you would control many more shares.

Why wouldn't you make more? Why wouldn't you make 20 times 100 instead of 15 times 100? Because you must always remember the cost of the premium you had to pay to control that stock, which, in this case, was $5 (a twenty-point increase to 420 minus the $405 creation price). You have to deduct that toll from your winnings. But, even with the $5 premium, the reward with the call on a big Google surge of $20 is much more bountiful than the profit you would make with the common stock.

Now, how about the risk, though? This risk factor is where replacing Google common stock with a Google call option really proves its mettle. The common stock shareholders are responsible for every penny below the $350 strike. So you can lose, say, 100 points in Google, just a fraction of what it lost from its peak, and never be stopped out. But the call holder is stopped out of his loss at the $350 strike price. The owner of 100 shares of common stock loses $5,000 down from $400 to $350. The owner of the call loses $5,500 from $400 to $350—that $500, again, is the toll or cost of admission to the call world. But below $350 the common stock holder has huge risk. The call holder? Nothing. In fact, with Google at $350, there can be an actual value to the call owner. Here's how: if there were any time left at all before expiration—where the call would, of course, go out worthless unless the stock was above $350—the option would probably retain some value. For example, if Google were to suffer a quick plunge from, say, $400 to $350, someone might want to pay for your

$350 call because, alas, it is now at the money, and, as I have said many times now, irresponsible gamblers are always willing to over-pay for an at-the-money call. If there's more than a week's time before expiration, I bet that $350 call could fetch as much as $10. Even if Google plummets, say, to $340, with at least a week to go before expi-ration, the stock is so volatile that someone might pay up to $5 for the out-of-the-money just to bet on a quick bounce back of this volatile stock. In that way the Google in-the-money call holder actually re-coups the cost of admission. It's still one more reason to go deep, as it is called, because the holder of a call that is struck far higher would certainly be out the whole premium cost if the stock fell that far. Again, remember my $5 rule, because that is the contract that is deep enough so you don't pay a big toll but you are still stopped out after what I regard as an acceptable amount of downside, something I am judging from my two decades of trading options.

So, to review again—because you have to know this cold—the call holder doesn't lose anything below $350 and can possibly get the cost of his ticket back on a quick fall below the strike, while the common stock holder always faces huge downside. That's a conservative strat-egy if there ever was one. If you want to stay in control of Google and the move you are expecting hasn't happened yet, you can always roll your call over to the next month's contract. There's a little higher cost to roll over a Google call than there is on call options on most other stocks, because there's a bigger spread between where you can buy and sell an option on a more volatile stock like this one. However, it's not too high a price to pay for staying in the Google game.

Now you know why I think the best way to get back to even is with deep-in-the-money calls that "replace" common stock by en-abling you to "create" an instrument that gives you the right to con-trol far, far more shares and therefore far, far more upside than you would with a dollar-equivalent amount of common stock, with a stop-out at a price that leaves you far less vulnerable to a catastrophe in-volving the common stock, the company, or the market. Don't ever again let anyone tell you that stock options are inherently risky. When used correctly, options are conservative, and the common stock is much more risky. In an environment as choppy as the one we're in, with the possibility of a comeback once the economy returns to normalcy, I can't think of a better way to make your money back with less risk than this strategy.

8

TAKING OPTIONS TO THE NEXT LEVEL
Advanced Strategies

This chapter is really compelling but also a lot more challenging than what I normally put in my investing books. Why am I doing it? I think this chapter will show you how a pro operates. When I say it is challenging, this time I mean you've got real heavy lifting ahead of you. I am going to present the most advanced strategies I have ever offered. For anyone who isn't in the mood to work that hard right now, feel free to skip this chapter. Don't feel bad if you take a pass on it. The book should work just as well without it. But the strategy I am about to explain made me too much money in my career not to share it with you, and given the urgency to get back to even, it isn't fair to leave it out.

I know how difficult the strategy I just described to you might be to grasp. I hesitate to layer on another level. But in a stock market that got more than cut in half, in a market where many people believe there is more risk than ever, it might pay to have some insurance to the downside, something that will allow you to profit using the stock replacement strategy with *no additional cost*. I know, it sounds too good to be true, but what I am about to reveal is a quirk in the way options work, a quirk that no broker will explain to you—99 percent of them probably don't even understand it or know about it—and yet I think it is too great to be ignored.

You might be asking yourself, if I want to profit from a quick market reversal or the severe decline in an individual stock, don't I have to short the stock, which means borrowing someone else's stock first, then selling it and then buying it back to capture the gain? Isn't the risk too great? In most cases you are right, the risk *is* too great. That's why I am loath to recommend that short-selling strategy, because you could be shorting a tiger and because I believe in a recovery over the longer term. You might bet against a stock, borrowing it first, because, remember, you can't sell something you don't have, selling it short, and then have it go up big-time right in your face. Then you will have to put up money as it goes up against you and ultimately have to buy it back at a price that could wipe you out. Think of it like this: stocks stop at zero on the downside, but they can go up to infinity. I will never, ever, recommend a strategy that could produce unlimited, horrific losses. As a hedge fund manager, a seasoned professional, I rarely shorted stocks outright. There was just too much risk and not enough reward.

If I wanted to make a bet against a particular security, I always preferred put options. You can certainly do the same thing and while I expect the overall market to go higher in the next few years, many stocks just won't get there, and it never hurts to bet against a stock you know is going down. That's why I put a stock in the "sell block" every Thursday night on *Mad Money*. Puts work just like calls, but they capture the downside instead of the upside. You can buy a deep-in-the-money put option and benefit one for one with the downside, just as in the call examples I gave you earlier. Again, it is safer and better than shorting a stock because you get stopped out when the common stock goes *above* your strike price. Buying puts, unlike shorting stocks, can't wipe you out; you can lose only the money you wagered. Stocks you short can go to infinity. Also, a deep-in-the-money put in later months doesn't cost much more than a deep-in-the-money call does in terms of premium, so be sure to go out further if you want to make a bet that way. Remember, buying a deep-in-the-money put is a mirror image of a call, so just follow the rules I laid out above about the responsible way to use call options. It is a very efficient way to profit from the downside. Just as with calls, I caution you not to use at-the-money or out-of-the-money puts. My trading records are filled with blown put bets using the "ats" and "outs." Don't repeat my mistakes; go deep or don't go at all.

Some people use puts to insure common stock positions they own. That's a huge mistake. If you are worried about a common stock, sell it. If you don't like it, sell it. Do not insure it. It is not like a house; you don't live in the stock. The insurance is too expensive. Just sell it and buy it back when it is lower if you think it's likely to go down. Again, almost every single time I bought a put to insure a stock position I didn't like, I lost both on the put and the common stock. In many cases, the insurance was too costly and the stock had usually declined about as much as it was going to go down. It just wasn't worth it to do so. If you think a company's stock is so dangerous that it needs insurance, then you shouldn't want to own a share of it.

When you own a put and are making a bet against a stock that you do not own, you can ring the register the same way as you would in a call, taking profits by selling the put after the decline. I am all for that kind of strategy. But the premium on a put—the toll, the cost of admission—can still get in the way of your profit when you contrast it with the very advanced method I am about to show you.

Let me give you the better way to buy stock insurance, a cost-free way. I have figured out how to make even more money with the stock replacement strategy for in-the-money calls than I have explained already.

This method is hard to grasp—I never like to tell you that there are three steps to easy wealth, or tell you about a simple strategy to make you rich overnight. Those are lies, out-and-out lies. If you want to make your money work for you, you have to work for it yourself; you have to take control of it and do the things that I describe here, no matter how difficult it might be, initially, for you to understand.

This advanced method gives you another, hidden way to profit from stock replacement with call options. Let's go back to the Exxon example that I used earlier, the one where, at the first of June, with Exxon at $70, we bought the July 65 call for $5.25. As the stock appreciated, we could sell the call to lock in a gain. If the stock went up three points we could sell the call for $8 and subtract our cost. We could make about $300 on that call when we sold it. The trade would be over. Well done.

Now I want to show you another way to end that trade, one that I think is far more lucrative, but people don't do because they don't understand it. Consider selling common stock against the call and ultimately exercising the call turning it into common stock, not just selling it outright. I have to tell you up front: I have explained this strategy to countless people, but only a handful get it, so I am going to give it to you several times in several examples and also use the analogy to real estate, to buying a house, because I will stop at nothing to get you to comprehend this method. It can help you get back to even quickly, if the market has big advances followed by big declines, two post-crash possibilities for sure.

Remember, options are simply derivatives of common stock. You may treat them as separate instruments and never get your hands dirty with the common stock. You can say using common stocks is one strategy and using call options is another and never the twain shall meet. That was certainly the way it was when I traded out of my dorm room. I never exercised a call in my life. If the call was worth something at expiration, I sold it. If it went out worthless, there was nothing I could do. I never "took delivery," the technical term meaning exercising the call and exchanging it for common stock, because I never had the money to buy all 100 shares that I was controlling through options. It's amazing, isn't it, all of the technical terms, like *exercising*, that make this stuff so difficult? It's as though there is a vast conspiracy to keep you from profiting from calls, a vast conspiracy that's constantly scaring you away from a truly low-risk way to make money. What a disservice this does to such a conservative strategy that gives you so many ways to get back to even.

When I became more sophisticated, when I started to figure out the wonders of options, I stumbled onto something that made so much sense that I have been a proselytizer of this strategy to anyone who would listen although I have never revealed it in any book and never talk about it on any show because it requires a level of sophistication that few have. But given what you have learned already about my stock replacement philosophy, I bet you will pick it up fairly easily.

Let's go back to the Exxon call example. What would happen if I told you that instead of selling the call to ring the register, you mixed the call with common stock? What if I told you that instead of selling the call, you chose to sell the same amount of stock that you control with the call in a separate account—one call equaling 100 shares? What if I told you that you can literally have one account that is for calls and another account that you set up just to sell the same equivalent of common stock that you control? That's what I am suggesting you do with your winning call options. Don't sell them outright. Keep them in one account and sell common stock against them in another account. Technically you are shorting common stock against the calls, as you don't actually own the common stock until you exercise those calls. I told you I never want you to sell stocks short because of the huge risks inherent in shorting. But using my method, you are protected from the short since you have an offsetting right to the same shares you are betting against, so you are not taking on any short-selling risk at all. You are basically long in one account and short in another and you net out flat without any exposure to a skyrocketing short. Let me illustrate with an example.

Using the case of Exxon, let's visit the second choice that ends the trade in a more advantageous way than selling the calls outright. Instead of closing out the trade when the stock goes to, say $73, and you have that small win, let's sell 100 shares of common stock at $73. Of course we don't own the 100 shares to sell. So, technically, we would be short the 100 shares in our second account. But we do own the right to 100 shares in the first account. Why is that important? Because if Exxon climbs to $75 or $77 or $80, we would be losing money in our second account, which has sold the 100 shares. However, we would be making an equivalent amount of money with our one call option in our first account, so it nets out perfectly—that's the riskless short I was referring to above. At any given time if we want to formally book the profit, we simply call our broker and "exercise" the calls, which lets us take delivery of the 100 shares of common in our first account, matching the 100 shares that we have sold in our second account. We are flat, the gain taken, the same gain we would have had if we had just sold the call outright. No additional money is needed. You don't have to pay for the Exxon common stock because you have offset it with a common stock short one-for-one.

But what happens if we keep the one call in our first account and we sell the 100 shares in the second account and leave it there until expiration, not closing it out earlier? You see you are allowed to own a call and be short common stock of an equivalent amount simultaneously. You can't lose money doing this. If the stock goes higher, nothing happens, because we own a call option that appreciates one-for-one. After we have made money in the call, we are simply locking in that gain by selling the common stock "against" it at the price we chose to end the upside. It's the same as if we had sold the call. If we sell the common stock in the second account when the stock is at $73, we will have made almost $3 in the call option and we have capped our gain, since every time the stock goes up a dollar we make another dollar in the call but we lose a dollar shorting the common stock in the second account. In other words, selling 100 shares of common stock at $73 gives us the same amount of profit as selling the call option at $8. They are a mirror image. We are simply choosing to keep the trade "open" until expiration forces it to be closed out at no additional cost.

Now what happens if, suddenly, oil plummets, dropping, say $100 a barrel quickly, in a matter of weeks, as it did in late 2008? Or what happens if Exxon reports a huge shortfall and gets hit dramatically? There are dozens of reasons why a stock, even a stock as steady as Exxon, could get hammered. It is entirely possible that Exxon might fall as much as 12 or 15 points or more, even if we get the recovery I expect.

Remember, in our example you own the Exxon July 65 call in the first account, and you have sold the common stock in the second account at $73 with a few weeks to go before expiration. You know you are already going to make about $3 on that July 65 call when the position nets out at expiration. You have locked in the gain by selling the common stock. You can't lose money now. But then, kaboom, the bad news hits in the oil patch, and Exxon drops 12 straight points. That takes Exxon, which you sold at $73, ostensibly to flatten out the trade, down to $61—$73 minus $12. Your July 65 call gets killed, probably dropping all the way to about a dollar or lower. (It most likely retains some value as long as the sell-off doesn't happen toward the last days of expiration. If it is near expiration time, the call would most likely be worth next to nothing and would not be worth bothering with. Remember, if you sell it, the commission will eat up whatever is left of it, so just let it go out worthless.) Your dollar cost on that $5.25 call was $525, so you are out almost all of that money as the new, crushed $61 price of Exxon is too far from your now "out-of-the-money" July 65 call. (Yes, an in-the-money call can become out of the money in a severe decline of the underlying common stock.)

But what happened in your second account, the one where you sold 100 shares of Exxon at 73? Exxon's plummeted to $61. You are now up 12 points on that second account, because the price you sold it, $73, minus $61, the new price of Exxon after the fall, produces a decline of $12, all of which you are entitled to, because you sold the stock short at $73.

You can then buy the 100 shares back at $61 and make $12, or $1,200. You are wiped out on your call, because, remember, you didn't sell the call and finish the trade, but instead sold 100 shares against it and kept it open. So you lost the $525 on the call. (Again unless it is close to $65 and the call is therefore at the money and retains some worth.) But you just made $1,200 on your common stock! When you subtract the $525 you spent on the call from $1,200, you have a gain of $675.

Think of that! If you had sold the July 65 call outright when the stock was at $73, you would have made about $275 ($8 sale price minus $5.25 invested equals $2.75 times 100, as always). That's a terrific win. But by simply selling 100 shares in the second account against the call and holding the call, instead of selling the call outright, you gave yourself a chance to profit from a market collapse or an Exxon disaster for no extra cost! You literally found an additional $400 for doing nothing but keeping the trade open rather than flattening it out by exercising the call against the common stock you had sold or having just sold the call outright.

Consider this strategy an insurance policy against the downside below $65 where your call is struck. But unlike insurance, it costs you *nothing*.

Here's another hidden gem with this strategy: there could be a few more dollars on the line in your new second account. When you sell the 100 shares of Exxon in the second account, it actually does bring money into that account, even though you technically don't own the shares you sold. You get $7,300 in cash (100 times the $73 price) in what is known as "phantom income." If you ask—and only if you ask, because remember, it's another issue your broker won't bring up—his firm should pay you interest on that $7,300 in what is known as a "short interest rebate." You should get that interest—just as you would if you placed $7,300 into your account—between the time you sold the common stock and when expiration flattens out the trade between the call and the common stock. I have found that brokers like to pay that interest only selectively to heavy traders; they choose whom they want to pay it for. I became a huge client so I got that short interest rebate routinely, and it amounted to a substantial sum when the current rates the firm paid on your cash deposits were high. Don't forget the short-term rates, the rate you get on overnight money, have been low for a long time, but they can go up when the Federal Reserve raises rates. If you go for the free insurance, it is worth requesting the short interest rebate to earn the money on the deposit the sale of Exxon brings into your account, but they do reserve the right not to give it to you.

Do you need the insurance? Is it worth the hassle?

You might say, "Jim, what is the likelihood, really, of Exxon going down 12 points in a straight line. It might not be worth the effort to do the option account/common stock account thing." Aside from the fact that it costs you nothing more than a small exercise fee when you net out the trade versus a commission when you sell the call outright, I can't think of any reasons not to do it other than laziness and a bizarre desire not to make as much money as you can. You might not think the market or Exxon can collapse like that, but why not take the free insurance? If you still doubt me, let me give you a few more examples that make the case for the free insurance more compelling.

This time, I am going to use the high-dollar-price stock of Google to show you the benefits of this ultraconservative strategy of buying a call instead of common stock and then opening up a second account to sell 100 shares of common stock short against that call. Even if you are a doubter, I want you to be a believer that this is a much more conservative strategy than owning common stock, that it has a great deal more upside and profit potential.

We know Google is a wild stock that can swing in big increments, one that could vacillate much more easily and have a much bigger loss than Exxon. A 50-point swoon with Google is pretty much a monthly occurrence! So let's see how you could profit from the downside of Google as well as the upside, which my stock replacement method allows you do to.

Let's presume that Google is at $400. We scroll down the menu looking for a strike that pretty much approximates the common stock without too much premium. In this case, as I look on June 1 through the menu of July calls, I spot that same July 350 call for $55 with a maximum $5 toll—or premium—over the common stock. I will be putting up $5,500 to control 100 shares of Google. Remember, if I wanted to buy 100 shares of Google it would cost me $40,000. If I wanted to spend $5,500 in Google I would buy about 13 shares. That July 350 call is about the best I could do to control as much stock with as little money as possible. Any strike closer to $400, if you approximate the July prices from the beginning of June, will cost me an absurd amount of premium, with the $390s costing me $21—eleven points of premium, almost impossible to make back—the $380s costing me $29, all the way down to where I finally get the premium to around $5. I can go lower than the July 350 strike, but then I have to spend more money to get control of 100 shares than I want to spend and I still will have a decent amount of premium to contend with.

Now, let's say the stock suddenly leaps to $425, on a better-than-expected quarter or on a huge tech rally that includes GOOG. What is your call worth? The premium over the common stock of a deep-in-the-money call shrinks as the common stock goes higher, in part because fewer undercapitalized speculators can bid it up and in part because you have to put up more money and therefore more capital is at risk, something call buyers are loath to do. It's just too much like common stock—too much of a cash outlay—to attract buyers. After a $25 point leap in the common stock, the call you bought for $55 will now probably be worth about $77, as again, the premium goes down the deeper the call becomes, but it is never entirely erased. So, you have now made 22 points, 22 multiplied by 100, so your gain is $2,200 on a $5,500 investment. Not too shabby, especially when you consider that a 25-point gain on 13 shares is $325 with unlimited downside, instead of your downside that stops at $350 where the call is struck.

You are free to sell the call and lock in that $2,200 gain. You are always free to make that choice and move on.

But I think that would be foolish. You should, instead, open that second account, where you sell 100 shares of Google common stock short against the call and do not exercise your call. Keep it open until expiration automatically flattens the trade out for you and the gain on the call is taken.

Of course, you can exercise the call anytime you want, and that will put 100 shares of Google into your first account—remember that's how much you control—and you will already have sold the 100 shares short from earlier in the second account. That "nets" it out, as you match the short common stock to the 100 shares that you got when you exercised the call. You are flat with the trade done and the gain made whenever you chose to close out the trade regardless of how high Google goes. The risk is over, but the reward? It's still open using my method because you are now carrying insurance if the stock plummets. That's right, you are going to be able to cash in on a Google crash!

Here's how: You sold 100 shares of Google at $425. You own the Google $350 call. Suddenly, in the time frame of the next eight weeks, Google just gets clobbered and goes down to, say, $325. A 100-point decline in this stock can not only not be ruled out, it might even be a given these days.

What do you have? You sold Google stock at $425, and it is now at $325, so in that second account you buy back Google and capture 100 points, profiting from the huge decline. You have made a $10,000 profit in the second account on those 100 shares you sold short! Sure, it is possible that you would have lost a huge amount on the call that you own in the first account, but this example should show you the real beauty of this stock replacement method and the concomitant decision not to close out the trade but to sell common stock in your second account to offset the call. You have $10,000 in profit in account two already and there is a likelihood that your July 350 isn't worthless. In fact, this once-deep-in-the-money call is now an out-of-the-money call that someone will certainly pay up for. So there's more money to be made with that left-over call.

Traders know that Google is a coiled spring. So with the stock at $325, where you bought back the common, they might pay a lot for your July 350 call, especially if there are a few weeks or a month before expiration, as Google could snap right back on an upgrade or on positive news about the Web. Depending upon how much time is left before the July expiration, the call could be worth a great deal. I think traders would be willing, if it were even at the beginning of July—remember, calls don't expire until the third Friday of the month—to pay as much as $10 for that call or even more! Of course, I would never buy a now-out-of-the-money call like that because of that hefty premium associated with all out-of-the-moneys, particularly on wild traders like Google. But some sucker will definitely want that out-of-the-money, betting on a quick Google snapback, and you can count on a sucker being born in the options market every second! So, if someone were willing to pay that much for the newfound out-of-the-money July 350 call that gives me a couple of choices. I can immediately sell the call for $10 and take a loss of $45—remember, you bought the July $350 call for $55. But I would have a gain of $10,000 on the common stock I sold and bought back in the second account. That nets out to $5,500. If you recall, if I had simply ended the trade and sold the call when the stock was at $425, I would have made just $2,200 ($77, minus $55 for the call). In this method I make *more than twice as much* with *no* extra risk.

Even if this Google crash occurs the day before expiration of my call, I would still make the $10,000, but I would lose all the worth of the call, so I would "only" make $4,500 (the $10,000 gain in the second account from the common stock minus the $5,500 cost of the call). That is still more than twice the simple strategy of ringing the register by selling the call and making $2200.

I stumbled on a pile of Intel gold once just like this. More than fifteen years ago I had bought 1,000 Intel June 100 calls with the stock at $95 for about $7 and two months to go before expiration, an investment of $700,000—hey, I managed $500 million; that's about the right amount to spend if you are going to move the needle. I was banking on a great quarter and, sure enough, I got a preannounce-ment to the upside as Intel told the world its earnings would far ex-ceed Wall Street estimates. The stock ran up 10 points quickly, where I could have sold the calls I bought and made $8. (Again the arithme-tic: the calls had created Intel at $102 and when it rallied to $110, I could have sold them for an $8 profit.) If I had sold the calls outright I would have made $800,000 on an investment of $700,000—not bad for a couple of weeks' worth of work.

Instead, though, I didn't sell the calls. I kept them in my first ac-count. I sold 100,000 shares of common stock against the calls in my second account and I kept the trade open, not exercising the calls. Remember, the brokers paid me a short interest rebate on all of the money I made when I sold 100,000 shares at $110, or $11 million. I was able to pick up a couple of percentage points of interest on the days I had that $11 million from the sale of Intel in my account. That's a small amount of interest, but every little bit helps. In fact that was an additional reason why I chose to have 100,000 shares sold in one ac-count against 1,000 calls owned in another; I certainly didn't foresee anything bad happening to Intel, after it had just reported great news.

Sure enough, out of nowhere, right after I sold the common stock against the calls, Intel lost a key legal case against rival chipmaker AMD. It was a total surprise. No one monitoring the case thought Intel would lose and no decision was due for some time. Immediately, Intel dropped to $65 a share! It lost 45 points from where I had just sold it, an unheard-of move for the giant chipmaker. I quickly bought back the 100,000 shares of common stock that I had sold at $110 and

I made that $45 on the 100,000 shares, or $4.5 million. I didn't want to let the stock roar back upward, which, by the way, it did when cooler heads examined the court's findings. I just wanted the gain. Of course, I got wiped out on the $7 I spent on the calls. Remember, I had spent $700,000 to buy them and that's a total loss in this case because the stock had fallen to well below the strike, so no one was going to pay me anything for them. But I made $4.5 million just on the common stock decline. All in all, netting things out, I made $3.8 million in profit on $700,000, pretty fabulous considering that I liked Intel! Again, I could have made the quick $8, but instead I went with this more abstruse insurance method and I made a real killing. The gain was so bountiful it was almost unfair, but that's the wonder of this free insurance that comes from stock replacement if you sell common stock in the second account against the calls held in the first account.

I know that for anyone who has never toiled with options, this payoff sounds too good to be true. It would be like buying an option to purchase a $3 million house. The option, the right to buy the house, say, over the next six months, costs $3,000. If the house appreciates $10,000 in that time, I should be able to sell that option for $7,000. But that's all I can make. In the option world, I can sell it for $7,000 or collect a fortune if the house burns down even when I don't own it. An option in real estate only entitles you to the upside. But an option in the common stock world allows you to profit from the downside, too, if you are smart about it and use my method.

Now there are all sorts of permutations I could throw at you using my stock replacement method. If you go back to the Google example, where, at the first of June, you buy the July $350 call at $55, creating Google at $405, and it shoots up 10 points immediately, you could sell a nearer month call, say the June 410 call, in your second account, and probably pick up about $8, since the call premium would "pump" from the big move as speculators got excited and paid too much for the call. You would then own the July 350 call in your first account against being "short" the June 410 call in your second. If the stock does nothing from there on in and it stalls out at $410, you pick up $8 when June expiration occurs because the contract you sold went out worthless. You win; the profligate, irresponsible buyer of the out-of-the-money call loses again. Then you can start doing the same thing with the July calls, selling a July 410 call against your call in the second account. Of course you can always instead sell your July $350 call to close out the trade or you can sell the common stock the way I described and bet against Google. If, however, you sell the June 410 and the stock keeps rallying past the strike and finishes above the strike at expiration time, you're in the analogous situation to having sold stock yourself, creating the short at $418 (you sold the June 410 call for $8 and you add that to $410 to figure out the price of the short in the second account). That's because if you sell a call that finishes in the money, that call becomes common stock that you have sold since it is automatically exercised. That's still a nice gain because you created Google originally at $405 and you can keep the long-call, short-common trade on for the insurance. There are dozens of strikes above your $350 call and months to do what I just described, known as "calendar" spreading. However, those methods require almost hourly monitoring to get the best prices and I am presuming you don't have that level of time or intensity.

You can also do a "partial," selling, say, 50 shares of common against your call, and let the rest run. I like the partial sale, which I call "trading around" a core position of Google, because it allows you to profit from the ebb and flow of a choppy market. Trading around a position requires total immersion in the market, and I don't want to sentence you to watching the price of Google every minute. That's the province of full-time professionals.

I share these difficult strategies with you because I used all of these methods to rack up giant gains at my hedge fund. They are hard, but I wanted you to see the "real deal" and get you thinking about new ways to make money that no one else talks about. All of them tied up small amounts of cash, allowing me to own T-bills with the rest of my money to make a good return away from this conservative strategy. These were my "secret sauce" strategies that enabled me to make fortunes every time the market swooned and it was the *key* to how I could have been up 36 percent in 2000 when almost every other fund lost gobs and gobs of money. To the pros, I always told people I was "long-call, short-common," with the first account owning the call and the second account selling the common "short" even as it had none of the risk of actually being short because I owned the call against it.

Should you try this strategy? At a minimum I want you to use stock replacement for some of your money to better your chances of getting back to even. If you can do so, don't close out the trade after a win, but sell a like amount of common stock against your calls in a second account. In other words, be long-call and short-common against it, to use the nomenclature. Try to get the broker to pay you a short interest rebate on your money in the second account, even if it is just a few dollars—at a minimum it can defer commission costs, especially if the cash rates set by the Federal Reserve move higher. Make sure the money that you would have otherwise invested in common stocks like Google goes into the dividend payers I discussed in a previous chapter so you have income coming in, or go into the even more conservative option, the bond market.

I promise you, this method is the fastest way to get back to even that I know. My options strategy has been tested through twenty-five years' experience from that graduate school dorm to the paper exercises I perform regularly in my blog on RealMoney.com, where I detail long-call–short-common strategies all the time. Sophisticated investors love them, and I want you to be sophisticated! Now you know how to play like a pro without the vicious and costly learning experience that I had to go through. Before you use real dollars, map out how you would go long a particular call at a particular price of a common stock that you think might appreciate rapidly. Pick your in-the-money strike, monitor the possible gain, and mythically sell the common stock against it in the second account to close out the trade. After you have practiced on paper, then you will be able to use real money and make a real profit.

Congratulations. You just learned how to use the best, most conservative strategy ever invented to profit from the stock market, all for the cost of this book. It was an expensive experience for me, but it cost next to nothing for you!

9

HOW YOUR GENERATION SHOULD RESPOND TO THE CRASH

You have the tools you need to protect your portfolio and at the same time make enough money by investing in stocks to rebuild the wealth you've lost and start working your way back to even. You have some fresh concepts that will help you navigate your way through this difficult and often misleading postcrash stock market landscape. I've even stuck my neck out and told you what I think will be the two most important and lucrative themes in the not-too-distant future, something only a madman or someone with a mad devotion to helping you make money would commit to print, because if I'm wrong, the record will be there for everyone to see. But I think not doing everything in my power to help you recover the money you may have lost in the market is a much bigger risk than potentially embarrassing myself. In short, I've now told you everything you need to know in order to get to work and start getting back to even. So it's time to address the elephant in the room, the one thing that must have some of you worried more than anything else, the question that could invalidate just about everything you've learned so far in this book: Do you have enough time?

My methods will allow you to get back to even, but that really doesn't matter if they don't get you back to even fast enough. If you're on the verge of retirement, or you've already retired, and you've got huge losses in your retirement portfolio, then timing is everything. In the horrific declines of the last year, as in any other large-scale pasting of stocks, you can pretty much assume that the older you are, the more it hurts because you have less time to make back your losses and much more to lose. You don't just need to get back to where you were before the crash, you need to do it quickly. The same goes for anyone who was hoping to pay for college for their children or buy a home. Ideally you want to be able to make enough money to cover those expenses before it's too late. And failing that, because some of you are going to be in situations where there simply isn't enough time to get back to even before you think you have to—at least, not without taking on totally unacceptable levels of risk—you have to know the best way to allocate the cash you have left, balancing what you need to cover your most important expenditures against what you need to save in order to have enough money to make investing in stocks worth your time.

Let's deal with the most urgent problem first. You could be the most assiduous saver, you could have done all the right, responsible things with your money so that you had enough to pay for a comfortable retirement. Then the market got chainsawed, and despite your best efforts, it now seems like you might have to postpone your retirement and work for years longer than you ever expected to. I'm sure that many of you who are in this position must feel like no matter how intelligently you invest, no matter what you do going forward, it just won't be enough to recover from your losses. Maybe you think that nothing short of a miracle will ever be enough. I'm not going to tell you that the prognosis is good if you're in your late fifties or sixties and the severe decline wiped out much of the money you had saved for retirement, because the truth is that you really got crushed by the timing of the market's collapse. Hopefully you had most of your money in bonds rather than stocks at this point and avoided the worst of the damage, but I know there are many people out there who saw their retirement savings get cut in half. There simply isn't a good way to recover from a 50 percent decline on an ultrafast timetable.

This is a case where simple arithmetic is totally stacked against you, since it takes a 100 percent gain, a double, to come back from a 50 percent loss. If you had $1 million saved for retirement, a 50 percent decline would leave you with just $500,000, and from there you would need a $500,000 gain—100 percent—to get back to even. It's a lot easier to lose money than it is to make it back, which is one of the main reasons why the conventional wisdom on retirement, and this is a sentiment I basically share, is that stocks should take up a smaller and smaller percentage of your portfolio as you approach retirement, with bonds, which are less risky than stocks but also have more limited upside potential, taking up a larger percentage. So if you've lost half of your retirement money and had planned on retiring in a year or two, you're either going to have to work longer or live on a smaller budget once you've retired, something that may not be possible.

But you know what? Except for the absolute worst cases, your situation is probably a whole lot less dire than it might seem. The most important thing is that you resist the urge to panic. Even with the stock market's incredible recovery in spring 2009, your losses if you held from the peak in October 2007 are still likely to be pretty devastating. In the past, after other horrible bear markets, there's been a tendency, especially among those who are close to retirement, to abandon stocks altogether because the experience of the decline makes people feel like they're way too risky to rely on. The same thing has happened this time around, and it's important for you to realize that this is precisely the wrong thing to be doing. After taking mammoth losses, you almost always want to say, "Okay, I learned my lesson, stocks just aren't a safe place to keep retirement money. I won't get fooled again," and then move all of your retirement savings into bonds or even cash in order to keep what's left of your money safe. If you do that, you're giving up on ever getting back to even. Stocks may be risky, but they're the one asset class that is both easy enough for non-professionals to understand and capable of delivering the kind of upside you need to rebuild your retirement fund. Far from giving up on equities and hiding out in a bond bunker, the best way to get back to where you were before the crash is to take a certain portion of your portfolio and invest it in the right stocks, ones that provide you with both safety and income, which means stocks with big dividends that companies can easily afford to pay. Earlier I told you that dividend-paying stocks aren't just for retirees; they can be nearly as exciting as the fastest-growing tech stocks. But that doesn't mean the conventional wisdom about them being correct for elder investors is wrong. High yielders are fine for anyone who is approaching retirement or already there.

I could spend ages pontificating about what you should have been doing before the crash, but while that might be helpful for younger investors who still have decades to save for retirement, it's not exactly useful if you hope to retire in just a handful of years, or if you're already retired. And I don't want to repeat what I've already told you at length in my previous books. So many of the books about money that have come out since the beginning of the financial crisis have seemed, at least to me, like opportunistic attempts to capitalize on the fear and panic by repackaging the same exact advice, the same bromides that the authors were dispensing before, in a new, more timely and opportunistic package. I'm trying to do just the opposite. The real estate collapse, the financial crisis, the crash, and the incredible rally off the bottom have changed the playing field. We're in a unique situation that comes with a unique set of problems, and those problems need to be addressed, not swept under the rug in some catch-all recapitulation of the usual tactics and strategies. For an in-depth discussion of everything you need to know about preparing for retirement, you should read the "Planning for Retirement" chapter of *Stay Mad for Life*. This book is about getting back to even, so here's what you need to know to recover from the worst selloff since the Great Depression and not be forced to toil for years longer than you had ever planned.

We'll need to go over some of the basics, but the first thing you must recognize is that however much it may feel like you're under the gun, or in some kind of financial ticking-time-bomb scenario where you have only a very limited period of time to make enough money to retire before your window of opportunity closes forever, it's simply not true. You don't have as much time as someone much younger, but that doesn't mean you're operating under a time limit. Sure, you lose your paycheck when you stop working, which is your principal way of adding more money to your retirement account, but that doesn't mean the game is over or that there's no longer anything you can do to rebuild your lost retirement savings. The whole point of investing is to have a source of income that's separate from your paycheck. Why is it so important not to feel like you're under the gun? Because trying to mend a broken retirement fund when you're so close to retiring is a very delicate balancing act. On the one hand, you have to protect the capital you have left by being very conservative with most of it. On the other hand, you will have to take some risks with a portion of your retirement money in order to generate the returns necessary to come back from your losses. If you feel like you need to have enough money set aside before the buzzer rings, then you're going to be tempted to take on too much risk so you can try to generate higher returns and get back to even sooner than you need to. There is no clock. The pressure is imaginary.

How on earth can I make a statement like that and expect to be taken seriously? Isn't it self-evident that the clock is ticking loudly, particularly if you're staring forced retirement at sixty-five right in the face and you don't have enough money saved to cover the costs of retirement because the market gave your portfolio a real beating in 2008? Absolutely not, and I'll tell you why. When you retire, and trust me, this is relevant, I advocate having about two-thirds of your retirement portfolio in bonds—the best way is through a bond fund that owns either U.S. Treasurys backed by the full faith and credit of the U.S. government or, if your income puts you in a high enough tax bracket, you want municipal bonds as they are tax-free. Put the remaining one-third in stocks. Although as long as you have between 60 to 70 percent bonds and 30 to 40 percent stocks, I think you're on the right track. This view is actually pretty heretical, as most people who dispense financial advice will either tell you to own no stocks when you're on the verge of retiring, or to make sure that stocks take up no more than 10 percent of your retirement portfolio. They think stocks are too risky for older investors, and all you need is the safety offered by bonds. This view has only gained more traction since the crash, which is too bad because, frankly, and you know me as a plain speaker, it's nuts. When you put your money into Treasurys, into the bond bunker, you're effectively taking it off the table as capital—you're saying, "This money? I'm not going to use it to generate more money. I just want to keep it safe and perhaps, I can get a return that outpaces inflation." As I write, the rates on ten- to thirty-year Treasurys are beating inflation ever so slightly and short-term Treasurys are giving you virtually no return at all. Neither is a bargain; the short-term approach is the lesser evil because you will have the flexibility to invest at higher rates when a stronger economy develops, and the Federal Reserve Bank begins to raise interest rates again.

For those of you who are especially concerned about inflation, the government also issues Treasury Inflation-Protected Securities, generally called TIPS, which give you some protection against inflation eating away at the purchasing power of your returns, what's known as "inflation risk." TIPS have considerably lower yields than regular Treasurys. That's the trade-off you make for the protection. With TIPS, the principal, what you'll ultimately receive when the bond matures, increases to keep pace with inflation. TIPS pay interest at a fixed rate, so when the principal rises, the dollar amount of interest you receive will also rise, and the yield always stays the same. How does this work? The principal is adjusted based on changes in the consumer price index, one of the most widely used measures of inflation, so an increase in the CPI will increase both what you're paid at maturity, and the interest you're paid every six months. A decrease in the CPI, on the other hand, which indicates deflation, causes both principal and interest to decline, so these bonds will lose value in a situation where the CPI declines. But when TIPS mature they never pay less than the amount of principal you originally invested even if there's been rampant deflation. I know that there's a lot of interest in TIPS, and if you're terrorized every night by dreams of hyperinflation reminiscent of Weimar Germany, then purely as a psychiatric, antianxiety measure, it might make sense for you to buy them, which you can do either through a bank or broker, or directly from the government electronically through the Treasury Direct website. I do not think that TIPS should be a factor in your game plan, though. I have tremendous faith in the ability of the Treasury Department and the Federal Reserve to rein in the stimulus to void all worries on inflation. But given how little return you get from TIPS, even if inflation goes awry we can find something better, which is why I prefer to stay short-term and redeploy when rates go higher. And if, as I expect, inflation turns out not to be a problem, then you will make a whole lot more money in higher-yielding stocks, especially because you pay lower taxes on dividends than on interest from bonds.

What else is on the fixed-income menu? Treasurys are giving you virtually no return at all. Neither is a bargain; the short-term approach is the lesser evil because you will have the flexibility to invest at higher rates when a stronger economy develops and the Federal Reserve Bank begins to raise interest rates again. You can own high-quality corporate bonds, issued by excellent companies, that have a better chance of providing a return that could exceed the inflationary rate. But right now we have to accept the conclusion that you are going to get skimpy income even from corporate bonds with little "credit" risk, meaning a chance of default. You could own bonds issued by corporations that are hurting and desperate for money—high-yielding bonds—but frankly those are simply too dangerous to be involved in with such a difficult economic landscape upon us. That's the bargain you have to accept if you don't want to risk losing your principal. Your safest and best hope for now for your cash is a short-term, two-year certificate of deposit kept at a bank that is insured by the Federal Deposit Insurance Corporation. The FDIC will insure your account for up to $250,000, so if you have more than that to invest it's a good idea to buy CDs in different banks for your own protection and peace of mind. By the time the CDs roll over there will be a better chance to get a higher rate on something safe than there will be for the time being.

The meager returns bonds give you is why I say that when you stop using your money to make more money by investing in stocks, you lose your most potent tool for rebuilding your lost wealth. Either you cling to safety and at some point in the course of your retirement you may run out of money, or you take some risk in stocks and go for the higher returns that will enable you to get back to even. Capital preservation, keeping your money safe, should never be a financial suicide pact. It's possible the all-bond approach made sense thirty or forty years ago, but with people living longer and longer and racking up huge medical bills in the process, it does not make sense today. If anything, not having a decent chunk of your money invested in stocks when you retire is the risky approach. Unless you've got enough money to support yourself for the rest of your life, in which case you can send it all into the bond bunker, you are going to need the higher returns from those stocks to pay your bills later in life. By not owning enough stocks you're essentially betting against your own longevity, and you'd have to be totally crazy to make that kind of "heads I lose, tails you win" wager.

So why does any of this mean you shouldn't feel as though you're operating under any kind of rigid time constraints if you're quickly approaching your retirement without enough money to support yourself all the way through? How does keeping a third of your portfolio in stocks make it so that you aren't under immense time pressure? Simple: The stock component of your retirement fund means that you don't have to get back to even before you retire to still be in good shape. If you continue to invest in stocks after you stop working, then that gives you a way to generate substantial upside, to make significant amounts of money. It means the game isn't over just because you're no longer getting a paycheck; instead you get to go into extra innings. You can keep making money in the stock market for decades after you've stopped making money from work, so there's no reason to take unnecessary risks with your capital in the years leading up to your retirement. You may not have as much time when things go awry to mend your portfolio as someone in their twenties or thirties, but you still have more time than you probably think, decades even. You should have enough time not only to recover from this financial debacle, but to bounce back from another one, too. How? You start out by drawing on the money you've kept in bonds to cover your cost of living, and only after that money is exhausted should you use the capital you've earmarked for stocks to support yourself.

Before I discuss the kinds of stocks and strategies that make sense at this point in your life, we should go over the retirement tools that do have a limited shelf life and what you need to do with them in order to get back to even while you still have the chance. I'm talking about your individual retirement account, or IRA, and your 401(k) plan if your employer offers one, or 403(b) plan if you work for a public school or some nonprofits, or a 457 plan for state or local government employees. Your 401(k) and IRA should be the foundations of your retirement portfolio because of their tax-advantaged, or as I like to say on *Mad Money,* tax-blessed status. The contributions you make to a 401(k) or IRA come from your pretax income, so you don't get taxed on the money that goes in. And, even better, while your money stays in, none of your gains are taxed—no capital gains tax, no dividend tax—and your money can compound for years, tax-free, in a 401(k) or IRA, giving you much larger returns over a long enough period of time. When you start withdrawing money from a 401(k) or IRA, which you can do without paying any kind of penalty once you turn fifty-nine and a half years old, it's treated as ordinary income for tax purposes, and thanks to this tax deferral you ultimately end up giving the feds far less money than you would have if these investments had been in an ordinary, non-tax-deferred account.

In addition to the tax benefits, your employer might also match your 401(k) contributions, at least up to a certain percentage, although more and more companies have cut back on this perquisite since the recession started. Please be careful to stay diversified in retirement accounts and not have too much stock in the company you work for. The era is littered with the stocks of companies that people banked on and that became worthless when those corporations went belly-up. Just ask the retirees from the Tribune Company who went "all-in" during the company's failed buyout, if you want to know how disastrous this strategy can be. Diversification is even more important for retirement money than for your *Mad Money* stock account.

You have to start making withdrawals from your IRA and 401(k) starting April 1 of the year you turn seventy and a half or the IRS will hit you with a fat penalty. The penalty varies depending on how much money you have in your account. But once you retire, you can't keep contributing money, as 401(k) plans are offered by employers as replacements for tradition pension plans, and while you can start up an IRA with pretty much any bank or brokerage, you're allowed to contribute only up to 100 percent of your earned income annually, and once you retire, you have no earned income.

Once you stop working, you stop being able to take advantage of these great tax-blessed vehicles, so it's imperative that you take full advantage of them while you still can, especially after losing large sums of money in either account. Luckily, there are provisions that allow workers over the age of fifty to make larger than normal catch-up contributions, something you need to take advantage of if your retirement fund was hit hard by the crash. For 2009, if you're fifty or older you can contribute $6,000 to your IRA, $1,000 more than the $5,000 ceiling for everyone else, and with your 401(k) plan you can contribute $22,000, which is $5,500 more than the $16,500 limit for everyone else. Make the larger contributions so that more of your investments can benefit from their tax-deferred status.

Should you invest in your 401(k) plan or your IRA first? If your employer is matching your 401(k) contributions, then start there until you've exhausted the match. After that, you shouldn't plan on putting any more money in your 401(k) until you've maxed out your IRA contributions. Why? Because 401(k) plans have some serious downsides, especially compared to a traditional IRA. You'll hear people cite high management fees and administrative costs as a problem, and these definitely eat away at your retirement funds, no question, but the worst thing about most 401(k) plans is that they typically offer you poor choices and not enough control over your investments. Ideally you want to own a diversified portfolio of five to ten individual stocks, but most 401(k) plans don't give you that option. Instead you usually must choose between no more than a couple of dozen different funds, some for stocks, some for bonds, and even though you can lobby your company's human resources department to add better offerings, most of what you have to choose from isn't all that grand. An IRA, on the other hand, doesn't have the high management fees of a 401(k), and it lets you invest the way you want to, making it superior to a 401(k) in every way except for the free matching money or stock you might get from your employer with a 401(k) plan and the larger amount of money you're allowed to contribute to it every year. Only after you've contributed the maximum $6,000 to your IRA should you then increase the amount of money you contribute to your 401(k).

Within your 401(k), usually the best option you have for investing in equities will be a low-cost index fund that mirrors a broad index like the Standard & Poor's 500. Since there's hardly any chance that you'll be allowed to pick your own stocks, you should try to get your bond exposure from your 401(k), but only if it contains a decent bond fund. Your IRA is a different story entirely. Here you can pick stocks that will help you get back to even, and your best bet, both from the perspective of safety as well as generating income, is to buy some high-yielding stocks, including some that I have mentioned earlier.

Three groups of stocks that I would specifically single out for your IRA are the master limited partnerships, or MLPs, in the energy business (also known as energy trusts), oil tanker stocks, and real estate investment trusts, or REITs. The trusts are structured so as to avoid paying any corporate taxes, which they can do by distributing the vast majority of their profits back to shareholders in the form of massive dividends. I already highlighted Kinder Morgan Energy Partners (KMP) in this group, because it's a pipeline operator, not a producer of oil or natural gas, which means it has far less exposure to the vicissitudes of the economy or even oil and gas prices. It's basically a toll-road operator, like a utility, which allows it to pay a very consistent, very high dividend—as I write it yields 8 percent. I also like Enterprise Products Partners (EPD), which is in the same business with the same conservative model and yields about 8.3 percent. These are pretty interchangeable companies, similar in just about every way, so if you check and find that one yields more than the other, go with the higher-yielding stock.

For potentially even more bountiful yields and more direct plays on the prices of oil and natural gas, I like the energy trusts that are producers of those commodities. They pump oil and natural gas out of the ground and give their profits back to investors in the form of mighty big distributions. However, because those distributions depend on the prices of oil and natural gas, they tend to vary a lot more than what you would get from the more consistent, utility-like Kinder Morgan Energy Partners or Enterprise Product Partners. All these names are money machines, though, and at their best, the production MLPs yield a lot more than the pipeline operators, albeit with a lot more risk to potential dividend cuts. My favorite is LINN Energy (LINE), which yields more than ten percent as I write. That level should remain consistent unless there is substantial stock price appreciation, because LINN is fully hedged out three years, meaning it has already sold all of its natural gas forward in the futures markets for dramatically higher prices than it would get now.

I also prefer Permian Basin Royalty Trust (PBT) and BP Prudhoe Bay Royalty Trust (BPT), each of which is more directly levered to the current price of crude, which I think is going to stay high for years because we can't find enough to sate the Chinese buyers. I can tell you that these two trusts usually have yields in the double digits when oil is going higher and they have long-lived production, meaning you won't have to worry about them running out of reserves for at least the next five years as they have enough energy in the ground to continue to give you outsized returns. Do not worry that they change their payouts regularly to reflect the current price of oil or natural gas, because if you believe, as I do, that prices will stay permanently higher than the days before China became a great power and excessive energy user, you can rest at ease that you will get a better consistent return with them than in just about every other investment on the horizon. Don't forget it's not as though we are finding new, cheap oil around the globe anymore. Those U.S. trusts are low-cost producers of oil and gas that give you handsome returns when energy costs rise.

Using the rule of 72, which we discussed before, the dividends alone from KMP and EPD will allow you to double your money in less than nine years, while LINN Energy, if it can maintain that distribution, would double your money in an even shorter period, and that's assuming that the stocks stand still and there are no dividend increases—unlikely given the dividend-raising track record of these companies. Those gains would all come from their gargantuan yields, but for MLPs, the payouts or distributions aren't taxed as dividends. When it comes to royalty trusts, you should talk to a tax professional because paying the taxes on these distributions can get very complicated. Some percentage won't be taxed because of depreciation, some could be tax-deferred because the distribution is treated as return on investment, but the part that you have to pay taxes on will be taxed as ordinary income, not at the low dividend tax rate of 15 percent. So unless you're in the 15 percent or below tax bracket, you benefit from putting these royalty trusts in a tax-deferred account like an IRA. Every year you'll take in those big payouts, and then you can reinvest them in the stocks, allowing them to compound, tax-free for ages. Now, that's a great way to get back to even. Plus, the very presence of the dividend creates yield support, where the yield increases as the share price falls, eventually leading buyers to come in and prop up the stock for the dividend alone, which makes these high yielders less risky than other, non-high-yielding stocks. Think of the big yields as trampolines that spring your stocks back to higher prices if they get hammered.

How about the tanker stocks for retirement accounts? These companies are legendary for their huge dividends, as their managements love to aggressively return value to shareholders. My favorite stock in the group by far is Nordic American Tanker (NAT), which yields 11.5 percent as I write, and has paid out an average yield of 15.1 percent a year for the last eleven years, by far the highest return of any tanker company. Nordic American is in the best financial shape of any of the tanker corporations, since most of them have taken on way too much debt to recommend here. People misunderstand this business constantly; it's all about the supply and demand for ships, not the price of oil. We just came through an oil tanker pricing trough where there were too many ships hitting the market at once, which caused some tanker companies to go belly-up. Nordic, run by the brilliant Herbjorn Hansson, a frequent guest on *Mad Money*, took advantage of the temporary ship glut to pick up some tankers for far less than they cost just a few years ago and much less than they would cost to build now. I believe these new tankers will generate outsized returns for years to come with Nordic American the biggest mover of Middle Eastern oil to China. Occasionally Nordic American will do an equity offering to pay for new ships, banging down the stock price and upsetting current shareholders, which, I will tell you, is almost always a great time to buy if you don't own any. Every time the company has done one of these deals, it has been a windfall for shareholders because the new ships have allowed Nordic American to increase its dividend by more than enough to offset the dilution caused by the new shares. For older investors looking for income from a company that is very conservative about it deploying its resources, Nordic American Tanker may have exactly what you want. While other tanker stocks periodically give you a higher yield, I trust only Hansson, because he has never overextended the company and has *always* delivered for his shareholders.

Real estate investment trusts, the other group of stocks that make sense for your IRA, especially when you're trying to get your retirement portfolio back to even, pay out large dividends that are taxed as ordinary income. So, again, unless you're in the 15 percent tax bracket or lower, you get a special advantage from putting these in an IRA. Just make sure you also like the fundamentals of the REIT, not merely the fact that it has a juicy dividend and you can defer paying any taxes on it within an IRA. Don't fall into the trap of thinking these are just real estate stocks. You've got medical REITs—stocks that own the land under hospitals or research facilities, which I would not own under the Obama administration, given the president's commitment to health-care reform and containing costs, neither of which is good for profits. You've got timber REITS, which own timberlands, too risky in this weak home building environment, where lumber and demand is low, and then you have REITs that own residential real estate, or commercial office buildings, including shopping malls. Many mall, apartment, and residential real estate developers got too bullish at the top of the market, loading up their REITs with way too much bank debt. But not all real estate investment trusts overstepped their bounds or borrowed too much money and some are in fantastic shape to take advantage of the losses of others. Perhaps the hardest-hit group of real estate investment trusts, the one that has seen the biggest bankruptcy, General Growth Properties, is the shopping mall sector. I predict there will be a terrific opportunity for solvent, well-managed shopping mall REITs to feast among the General Growth malls, and the malls of others I expect to fail, and the one that will be in the best shape to pick will be Federal Realty. This real estate investment trust, with a 5 percent yield that is perhaps the safest of all REIT dividends, is run by Donald Wood, a conservative manager who passed up on expanding or building in the last few years because he thought prices had gotten out of control. With no one tenant representing more than 2.6 percent of mall square footage, FRT understands the need to diversify and not bank on what could be some indebted and troubled retailers. While other real estate investment trusts have been cutting their dividends furiously, FRT has increased its dividend for forty-one consecutive years, the longest record in the real estate investment trust industry.

If you're looking for stocks to help get your retirement portfolio back to even, remember that you can own them for years and years after you've retired, which makes those equities with high yields even more attractive for investors who are approaching retirement or have already retired. You can reinvest the dividends back into those stocks and allow them to compound for years. That gives you the kind of upside you need to support yourself in retirement, especially if your retirement portfolio has taken a lot of damage, but even if it hasn't.

One more point about how you should try to get back to even if you've already retired. Believe it or not, your best bet for safely making enough money to get your portfolio back where you need it to be is with the very same strategy that I employed at my hedge fund: using deep-in-the-money call options as safer replacements for stocks. I've explained this in depth already, so you understand how, even though most people think options are just for those who are willing to take huge risks, this strategy is actually deeply conservative, requiring little money down. That allows you to keep the rest of your non-stock money in cash or bonds and gives you a limited, well-defined downside, as well as a bigger percentage return than if you owned the common stock. Remember, the strategy allows you to allocate much less in equities and more in fixed income because options require much less capital than common stock for the same amount of punch. You might think that this strategy is best suited for young people who are full of adrenaline, but the most important thing you need in order to get it right is time. When you're retired, time is something you have in spades. So if you're retired and need to get back to even, you are in a better position than almost anyone else to take advantage of the best strategy I know, as you can sit in front of your computer all day checking the quotes, or of course, monitor them through the ticker at the bottom of the screen on CNBC! I talk about all of these MLPs, REITs, and tanker companies constantly on *Mad Money* because I worry about your retirement, so that's the best place to keep up with their prospects if you don't have the time or inclination to do the homework yourself.

For the Young, the Young at Heart, and the Extremely Lucky

For anyone who's in their twenties or early thirties, the crash and its aftermath have created a situation that's just about the polar opposite of the jam that older investors nearing retirement have found themselves in. The monstrous decline was catastrophic for everyone who had a lot of money invested in the stock market and needed that money to support him or herself in the not-too-distant future. These days you won't catch anyone over the age of forty talking about the brutalized stock market as anything other than an absolutely terrible and terrifying destroyer of wealth, a tarnished asset class that will never regain its presubmersion luster. But if you're much younger, if you don't have a lot of money invested anywhere, if you expect to work and support yourself for decades to come, then you should be thanking your lucky stars for virtually every single bad thing that's happened to the stock market and every other asset class save gold and U.S. Treasurys.

I believe that we had a once-in-a-generation buying opportunity in early March 2009, when the Dow Jones Industrial Average was trading at 6,500, a period that lasted for a little less than two weeks. That's in the past, and I don't think we'll be revisiting those levels anytime soon, but for everyone who was either on the sidelines or who could afford to take huge losses because they have decades to make that money back, the bottom was a truly great moment to pour money into stocks. It will be again, if we happen to return to those levels. For older investors without much capital on the sidelines, that horrifying early March 2009 was a heart-attack-inducing experience, and even as stocks moved higher, the losses from the top were still enormous. If you're in your twenties, however, and didn't have much capital committed to the stock market, then your greatest advantage is that you have no need to get back to even because you're not down. And while the generational buying opportunity moment may have passed, the averages are still way off their highs and have given up most of their gains for the last decade. The only obstacle standing in your way is that you might not have that much money to put aside to capitalize on some bargain-basement prices—or at least first-floor prices—given the move off the lows, and still be able to feed, clothe, and shelter yourself.

The same goes for anyone who's older and managed to sidestep the decline, either because you saw it coming and adjusted your invest-ments, or because you just weren't keeping your money in stocks. Maybe you missed the crash because you were at one time considered to be irresponsible or a bad financial planner and are now just consid-ered real lucky. Doesn't matter. However you got here, you've arrived at a fabulous buying moment, at least as far as the stock market is concerned. Opportunity isn't just knocking, it called in the SWAT team and has one of those police battering rams ready to smash in your door. Look, I know that it can be difficult to force yourself to save money and then turn around and invest it in stocks when it seems like the benefits to you are so far off. I'm sure you want your youth to be enjoyable, and the idea of spending an hour a week per stock doing homework on top of your day job, or if you're still in school, between classes, may not sound like your idea of fun. But you know what? I can pretty much guarantee that if you don't take ad-vantage of this truly incredible moment to start investing, you will be cursing yourself ten years from now. At any other time, I'd be willing to entertain the argument that there's no rush. I'd like to be able to tell you to avoid the financial cyber-pages, and go have a good time to insure that your youth isn't wasted. Then, when you've got the reckless enthusiasm hammered out of you, there will be plenty of time to start investing. Unfortunately, I just can't do that now. I believe that's a bad argument even in normal times because you're passing up extra years of compounding—the sooner you start saving and investing, the longer your money has to grow and the more money you'll have down the road. But these are not normal times. Many stocks are still priced for an endless recession or a decades-long slowdown, and they can be purchased for much less than they will be worth in the not-too-distant future. I can't let you pass on that chance to get very rich on some fantastic stocks that I am about to mention, especially because I don't expect these marked-down prices to be around very long. Don't pass up this moment, not with stocks this low.

I have said it to thousands of students at colleges where I have taken *Mad Money* on the road, and I will write it here: every young person who doesn't squeeze every last penny out of his or her paycheck and use it to invest in stocks at what are still historically inexpensive prices for as long as these values last, is robbing him- or herself in the most foolish possible way. The downside after such a hideous decline is much less than usual, and the upside far greater. This gives you a tremendous chance to make a lot of money in the market in a very short period of time. You got lucky because the worst stock market crash since the Great Depression happened in 2008 and not in 2018 or 2028. It happened when it couldn't do you much financial harm, and you could benefit enormously from the low prices the downturn has created. I would have killed—or at least maimed—for an opportunity like this when I was in my twenties, so please, don't cheat yourself. From my experiences with students and people just out of college or graduate school, I know that younger folks understand they should be saving money, but they often moan that they just can't afford to do so. With stocks at these prices I am telling you that you can't afford *not* to do so. The arguments are simply much more compelling with the Dow Jones averages down huge from their highs and many stocks well below where they would be if there weren't such distrust and revulsion about the overall market.

And it gets even better than the simple fact that stocks are trading at 1998 or 1999 levels. This is not just about valuation, although the prices of many stocks are so compelling that valuation ought to be enough on its own. It also just so happens that this market is almost perfectly tailored to the young and the young at heart. What do I mean by that? In general, younger investors—like older risk-tolerant investors—can afford to take risks that, say, a retiree just can't. You know that I believe dividend-paying stocks are fantastic, especially the accidentally high yielders, which can also deliver tremendous up-side, and there should be some high yielders in everyone's portfolio, no matter what their age. But I also know that growth stocks that don't pay any dividends right now offer some truly incredible upside potential, perhaps the best in decades. These stocks are a lot more risky than something with a dividend, not just because they lack yield support, but because when a growth stock that has been power-ing higher on lots of momentum misses a step—if, for example, it reports a quarter that's only so-so, that doesn't beat the Street's ex-pectations or shows signs that its growth might be on the decline—then the very same money managers who furiously bought the stock on the way up will sell it just as furiously, and even short it, on the way down.

When stocks fall from dizzying momentum-driving buying, you can really get hurt. Some of that decline comes from a recognition that the earnings growth won't be as terrific as buyers thought, but a larger, more insidious portion comes from something called multiple contraction, where investors stop being willing to pay a premium multiple—a much higher price than for most stocks—for the prospec-tive earnings stream because they think the increases in earnings are slowing or perhaps even vanishing over time. Multiple compression can take years to play itself out as momentum-seeking investors pay less and less for progressively slower earnings growth, until they've all been shaken out and the valuations have sunk to levels where in-vestors who care more about the value of the enterprise—what an-other company might pay for it in a takeover, for example—finally

decide that these now-broken stocks are cheap enough to start buying. That's the growth-to-value risk, and it's a brutal one.

The reward for finding and sticking with high-earnings growth
equities right now, though, is tremendous, because there are lots of
excellent companies with sanguine growth prospects that have weathered the economic tsunami well, yet are valued as if they have lost
their way or their growth is about to end any minute. Which companies am I talking about? What's really worth buying out of this growth
cohort?

Younger investors aren't just going to benefit from the lower valuations of many of the major industrial and financial companies I have
described here. They also have a once-in-a-lifetime opportunity to
invest in something that I think is so big that it makes me envy the
investing moment for all of those who are in their twenties and early
thirties. This is true, genuine financial jealousy not only because
youthful investors will be able to get the full gains that I am about to
describe, but also because they can afford to make some riskier bets,
knowing they have plenty of time to recover from any losses they
may incur early from a rocky stock market. Moreover, as you'll see in
a moment, unlike so many bad technology bets that befuddled investors have made over the years, younger stock buyers have the added
advantage of actually using and understanding the technologies and
the applications of the huge investing trend I am about to describe.
That's a welcome change from speculating in abstruse products for
wide-area networks or gate arrays or high-speed switching and rout-
ing that have burned uninformed investors time and time again.

But before I tell you what it is, let me just say straight out I have
not been a fan of technology stocks since the great dot-com flameout
in 2000–2001. There have been moments when they were investible
but tech companies have pretty much given you the worst performance for a prolonged period of time because they have little to dif-
ferentiate themselves, have overpaid managements who often lavish
themselves with options, and have little to no dividends. Those three

negatives have been the hallmark of almost all technology companies worldwide. Plus, with the exception of Apple and Google, most tech companies don't have any real growth, or their best years of growth have seemed to be behind them. I cut my teeth trading IBM, which had explosive growth in the early 1980s, and I then segued over in the late 1980s and early 1990s to the great personal computer investments with Intel, Dell, Hewlett-Packard, and Microsoft, and then to the networking and storage companies like Cisco and EMC. All of these businesses were constantly reinventing themselves, Microsoft with Windows and Vista, Intel with 486 and Pentium, and Hewlett-Packard with big servers and high-speed printers. But, without exception, these product cycles have run their course and given us companies that tend not to grow earnings any faster than regular industrial companies. In the parlance of Wall Street they have become "cyclical growth stories," not "secular growth stories," meaning that they need strong economies worldwide to show real earnings power. At times they are terrific, and I think the stock market's malaise has made both Cisco and Hewlett-Packard just too cheap to ignore as both have strong 2010 growth prospects. They will get expensive, though, when the next big economic expansion eventually ends. The others? Frankly, I would rather own an industrial with a good dividend and management that's paid commensurately with how it performs for shareholders.

Right now, though, for the first time in a decade we are seeing the beginning of a brand-new product cycle, one that is truly gigantic and represents the first true secular growth trend in a decade, that the market will ultimately fall in love with, the kind of trend that can cause enormous, multiyear runs in the stocks that are plugged into this product cycle. What's the trend? The product? It's something that young people, really anyone from the age of twenty to as old as thirty-five—you can see how I'm showing my age here—are uniquely able to understand and perhaps not able to live without. It's something that should be accessible to you in an intuitive way, even as it's very difficult for older money managers and analysts to grasp because they didn't grow up with personal computers, the Internet, and cell phones. I'm talking about the mobile Internet, an idea that encompasses many different devices, but is exemplified by the smartest of the smartphones—the iPhone from Apple (AAPL), the Palm (PALM) Pre, and the whole line of BlackBerries from Research In Motion (RIMM).

What do I mean when I say these smartphones embody a new product cycle—the biggest product cycle that we've seen from tech since the initial rise of the Internet and maybe even bigger? I mean that devices like the iPhone, which contain a multitude of different applications and allow you to be constantly hooked up to the Internet and to navigate it just as you would on a computer, are fundamentally changing the way we use technology. Owning a smartphone is not a luxury or a fashion statement, which is how Wall Street understands this move; it's in fact a necessity. The premise here is that some ideas are so powerful that they can dramatically change the technology in a given industry, or allow us to do something that was previously impossible, or make something that had been incredibly difficult and expensive into a process that's easy and cheap.

In his book *Only the Paranoid Survive,* Andy Grove, the brilliant former CEO of Intel, called moments where these ideas took hold 10X changes or 10X tsunamis, because they allow us to do things ten times better.

Mobile Internet is one of these 10X tsunamis—it's not just about the iPhone or the Pre or the BlackBerry. Mobile devices that allow you to access the Web have so proliferated that the way we interact with the Internet and with information has fundamentally changed. It's not that all of a sudden we have cool new products like the iPhone; it's how these devices are becoming a huge and indispensable part of our daily lives. As more and more people feel the need for these products, that demand will drive sales at Apple, Palm, and Research In Motion, as well as their suppliers, the parts makers, the software writers, even the retailers and vendors of the products, much higher than anyone would ever have imagined. Younger people can understand this concept—this theme makes sense as part of your everyday lives. The idea that the mobile Internet could be every bit as revolutionary as the switch from snail mail to email, and just as important and game-changing as the move from the typewriter to the personal computer, or from print to the Web, makes intuitive sense to you. But few older people, especially on Wall Street, can see this groundbreaking new technology for what it is, something ten times bigger than any trend out there, something worth potentially hundreds of billions of dollars in revenues and ultimately in stock market wealth creation. That gives you a huge edge on the investing competition.

It doesn't hurt that these are the companies you're intimately familiar with: Apple, Palm, Research In Motion. You like their products, you buy their products, you understand their appeal. That alone is never a good reason to own a stock, because what we care about more than anything is the fundamentals, how a company is performing, whether it is actually making any money. But it is helpful if you already believe the fundamentals are strong and getting stronger. These smartphones are becoming every bit as necessary as, say, our ability to read newspapers on the Internet, as surely as we text instead of call and take pictures with phones and not cameras, and just as surely as we now watch TV on our computers, even our handheld ones. Devices like the Pre, the iPhone, the BlackBerry are the little gadgets that do everything, especially now that so many applications have been released on the iPhone, turning it into the Swiss army knife of smartphones. These revolutionary products essentially make just about every other gadget out there irrelevant: camera, check; music player, check; email, check; phone, check; Web browser, check; and countless other less important things. They represent exactly the kind of technological leap that takes everyone by surprise—everyone except for younger investors, who get it.

Yes, I am transparently trying to entice you into the stock market by using hot, interesting stocks that you know and like, but they also constitute one of the strongest product cycles I have seen in ages. Nobody on the Street is expecting that everyone will need something like an iPhone in the same way that it's now expected that virtually everyone has access to a personal computer, but that's exactly the way things are going.

Which is the best to own? Palm is the most volatile and perhaps the most risky. It has the shortest track record of the three—from the time the Pre launched, it's been a darling but the company's long-term record doesn't give you much comfort. Still, this is the company that is most likely to be acquired for its technology by an outfit like Nokia or Ericsson or Samsung because it is so revolutionary. Apple is simply the best-run company in America, with or without Steve Jobs, and in many ways it is the complete package since the iPhone just complements Mac computers and the iPod/iTunes business. I would own it in a heartbeat if I were younger and wanted to bet that the company will maintain its market leadership and expand it beyond individuals to corporations, something it has been unable to do until now. Research In Motion is more problematic. It's losing share to Apple and I fear a new Nokia "BlackBerry killer" could be on the horizon. But the company's always reinventing its devices, and I think it will keep pace for years to come.

When you get a product cycle that is strong and multiyear, it spreads and lifts all kinds of ancillary plays—everything that goes into one of these phones or supports the networks they rely on can go higher. As I say on *Mad Money* when I go to my soundboard and press the sound of a bowler nailing a strike, there is tremendous "pin action" off each of these devices. So, if you think that Apple, Palm, and RIMM are too overexposed or expensive, I can give you a menu of the stocks of other companies that go into their devices, that are also part of the mobile Internet product cycle, and you can do an hour of homework to determine whether you think any one of them is worth owning. What's being carried along by this huge mobile Internet wave? Starent Networks (STAR), the enabling structure to allow phone companies to deliver multimedia services on the phones; Analog Devices (ADI), RF Micro Devices (RFMD), Skyworks Solutions (SWKS), Texas Instruments (TXN), and TriQuint Semiconductor (TQNT), the builders of smart chips that allow the devices to maintain and transmit so much data; Broadcom (BRCM) and Marvell Technology Group (MRVL), which make technologies that integrate broadband into the devices; and SanDisk (SNDK), which allows them to store information and retrieve it with lightning speed. Perhaps the best way to invest in this new product cycle is with Qualcomm (QCOM), which is the largest position in my charitable trust, which you can follow along at ActionAlertsPlus.com. Qualcomm is the company that created the technology that makes so much of smartphone intelligence possible—it's the reason you can get such terrific Internet access on your phone. It's the brains of not just one but of all the wireless outfits. Wireless infrastructure is being built around the globe to support Qualcomm's brand-new chips, so the company's role in this tech tsunami is just getting started. It's got the best of what is known as 4G (fourth generation) semiconductor patents so it could have great long-term prospects.

Why am I confident that we have so many years ahead of us for this smartphone product cycle? First, only about one in one hundred cell phone users has a smartphone that can surf the Internet and handle most of the more intensive and addictive applications. Second, most developing countries are skipping landlines entirely and putting in infrastructure that enables these phones to work everywhere, including a $40 billion program just kicked off by the Chinese government. Finally you have the backing of our own huge telco carriers—Sprint in support of the Pre, AT&T in support of the iPhone, and Verizon Wireless in support of the BlackBerry, although Verizon Wireless covets an iPhone deal, another reason why I like Apple more than RIMM. Plus Apple is just scratching the Chinese surface, with China Unicom as its backer, another gigantic carrier. Without these new phones these telco companies can't expand or perhaps even survive. Therefore, they can be counted on to subsidize the purchase of mobile Internet devices for years to come.

If you're young, or young at heart, I seriously recommend checking out and investing in one of these stocks. You can't build a portfolio just out of the mobile Internet trend, since it would be all tech and totally undiversified, but you can afford to take a big swing at one or two of them because you have your whole investing life ahead of you. That's right, think of it: you have not one but two incredible opportunities as a young investor, the chance to buy stocks that have been knocked down to insanely low levels, and an intuitive understanding of what could turn out to be one of the biggest moves of a lifetime, a huge new product cycle in tech based around smartphones and all their accoutrements. If you can't decide which ones, I would go with Apple for the iPhone and Qualcomm, the intellectual brains and property behind the outfit. If this mobile Internet theme is anything like the previous product cycles in tech, and it seems akin to if not bigger and better than the largest ones, it will take years to play out and will make fortunes for those daredevils who plunge in now.

Still, don't lose discipline. Don't be greedy when these stocks are up. Younger investors can afford to let their gains run longer and not be as sensitive to taking profits in their winners, especially in a scenario where I expect multiyear profits. Nevertheless, even if you're young, you should still gradually sell off parts of your position in any of these stocks as it goes higher. Scale out slowly over time. Don't sell all at once, but incrementally with big percentage distances between sale prices as much as 25 percent higher each sale so that eventually you're playing with the house's money, meaning whatever money you have left in the stock comes not from your original investment but purely from the profits you've already made. Then don't touch what's left; you're playing for free! Younger investors can afford to wait longer before you start taking stock off the table, but anyone who's older and reading this must adhere to my method of scaling out, because unlike someone in their twenties, you simply cannot risk turning big investment gains into losses. If you want to, you can use call options as stock replacement to limit your downside, but that requires more time and effort. Anyone can profit from the tech tsunami, but for those of you who are still in your twenties or early thirties, I can't make it any more simple than this: there has never been a better time for you to start being an investor than right now. Promise me you will take advantage of it.

10

TWENTY-FIVE NEW RULES FOR POST-APOCALYPTIC INVESTING

I will not rest until I have done everything in my power to equip you with the knowledge you need in order to get back to even, the same knowledge and strategies that will give you a good shot at using the market to make yourself rich after you've undone the financial damage that's practically become the hallmark of this era. I've explained how you can stop the bleeding if you're still losing money and what we've learned from the horrible, but also transformative experience of the crash. I've gone over the basics about building a portfolio and understanding the nature of stocks and the proper way to invest in them, so that you won't be blown out the first time you experience a setback. Most important, you now have the tools you need to start putting together your back-to-even portfolio, including everything you could possibly learn from dividends, which have become our new yardstick for assessing stocks, not just the ones that deliver the most income to older investors; and how to use dividends to locate stocks with tremendous amounts of upside waiting like a coiled spring.

You know the two most important, and, if history is any guide, most profitable themes that will dominate the markets in the near future: the global economic recovery and the rise of smaller regional banks across the United States as they take advantage of the financial crisis to gobble up their weaker competitors, with the stocks I think are best positioned to play each theme. And, for those of you who are willing to spend more time than just one hour per week per stock, using your capital to rebuild lost savings and create new fortunes, you now know what I have never before revealed in any other venue: the very strategy of using call options as stock replacement that I used successfully at my hedge fund. If you can make the time, and you should, using my deep-in-the-money call as stock replacement strategy can deliver greater-percentage returns than investing in common stock, while your downside is limited, and all for less money, so you can keep what's left over in cash and bonds if you want to feel safe. So, you have the tools you need to get back to even, but I'm still concerned.

Why? When the Securities and Exchange Commission adopted Regulation FD, or Fair Disclosure, which went into effect back in October 2000, I felt that it was safe for regular people to invest in the stock market and basically be on an even footing with the professionals. Regulation FD really leveled the playing field by making it illegal for companies to reveal any information to the pros that they don't also reveal to you. Unfortunately, two things make me think that it's gotten harder for regular people to invest and that the deck is once again stacked, not in your favor. The crash was frightening, but even more terrifying was watching the destruction caused by short-sellers, newly liberated by an SEC that repealed one of the oldest safeguards we have against bear raids, the uptick rule, the best protection ever devised to stop the shorts from sowing fear. When stocks were in free fall, it wasn't just the declines that worried me, it was the velocity of those declines and the strong sense that the short-sellers were in complete control of the market.

The second thing that troubles me has been the reaction of the media, not to the crisis, but to the incredible, once-in-a-generation rally that we experienced after the bottom in March 2009. There is so much misinformation, disinformation, and misinformed speculation by the financial press that is compounded tenfold by the dishonesty of many of the expert money managers who are brought on to talk about the market every day. So I have developed twenty-five new rules to help you deal with hedge fund hegemony, to keep you grounded in a world where the press never stops throwing misdirection plays at you and no one ever admits when they've gotten something wrong, and to follow in the tradition of my rules in *Real Money*, *Mad Money*, and *Stay Mad For Life* to teach you what's changed from the incredible events of the last two years. These are the most important lessons that I have learned from both the crash and the rally off the bottom. These rules will help you understand what's happening in the market and allow you to make money from it even though you are being bombarded with exaggerations and outright falsehoods.

1. **Be careful of upside surprises.** Whenever a company reports its quarterly results, and its earnings per share are higher than what the analysts on Wall Street who research the company for a living had, on average, expected, then all the headlines about the quarter will describe it as an upside surprise. Stocks are supposed to go up when the underlying companies they're attached to deliver higher-than-expected earnings, but what the headlines call an upside surprise and what truly impresses the professionals in a quarter are two different things. This distinction can get confusing for people because sometimes when a company reports an upside surprise for the wrong reasons its stock will actually go down. For a regular investor looking at the coverage of a quarter, the market probably seems totally arbitrary and capricious. If an upside surprise can't reliably send a stock higher, then what the heck can? And I'm not talking about situations where management also lowers its guidance, what it expects to earn in the future, at the same time as it delivers higher-than-expected earnings. Then its stock will go down, and that's not really baffling—when we buy shares in a company, we care about what it will earn in the future, not what it has already earned in the past.

No, I'm talking about the confusion that results from the headline writers not drawing a serious distinction between a high-quality upside surprise and a low-quality, illusory, almost sleight-of-hand upside surprise. We like companies that can deliver the first kind, but the second kind doesn't attract much interest. How do you tell the difference? Simple: one's organic, and the other is manufactured. A high-quality upside surprise, a real better-than-expected quarter, is generated by higher-than-expected sales, which then leads to better-than-expected earnings per share. Stronger sales could mean a few different things, but they're all good: they could signal that the industry is improving and more people overall are buying a company's product, or it could mean that the company is taking market share from its competitors, or that it has growth coming from an entirely new business. So a real upside surprise tells you either that the environment has improved or the company has improved, both of which indicate that it should be able to grow its sales and its earnings at a faster clip in the future, and that's a reason to buy, since the big boys on Wall Street ultimately still value stocks based on growth. It's very rare for a stock to go down off of this kind of high-quality, sales-driven upside surprise. Even in the depths of our recent garden-variety depression, these revenue upside surprise stories advanced, as you can see by looking back at Apple's phenomenal run, which has produced upside after upside almost entirely on much-better-than-expected sales of the iPhone and the iPod.

What about the low-quality, sleight-of-hand kind of upside surprise? It's easy to tell it apart from the first kind, even if the press doesn't bother to draw any real distinction. A low-quality bettering of research analysts' earnings estimates is based purely on a better bottom line, the earnings per share, than the top line, the sales number. Here the upside surprise is generated not by improved business, but because management cut costs, manipulated the tax rate through aggressive but legal accounting treatment, or bought back stock. The bought-back-stock earnings surprise is now regarded as almost totally illusory by market professionals, as the increased earnings per share only indicates a smaller share count and not profits that were genuinely better than what anyone was looking for. Many of the food and drug companies like to generate sleight-of-hand upside surprises when they can't manage the real thing. And this is the dirty little secret, the reason the big boys don't care about those so-called upside surprises, even if journalists think they matter: any large enough company with halfway competent management that's in a predictable line of business, like the food and drug companies, can almost always ensure that its earnings per share "beats" the street's expectations, as long as the quarter isn't totally abysmal. The food and drug companies often tend to fire a lot of people or use buybacks to generate their earnings-per-share-based upside surprises or repatriate as much profit as necessary from their foreign markets—the amount is entirely at their discretion—to beat the estimates. It doesn't take anything special, it doesn't indicate that things are in any way better, it just tells you that management is shrewd enough to make sure its earnings number doesn't disappoint anyone. If creating the "upside" is that routine, then it's hard to consider it much of a surprise. Now you can tell what the big boys at the Wall Street fashion show want to see in a quarter, and you won't make the confused assumption, as the press does, that the headline earnings-per-share number is all that matters. A company's ability to deliver better-than-expected sales counts for a whole lot more.

2. **The indicators that matter can change in a heartbeat. Never stop trying to find out which ones matter most.** I've always believed that before you can start picking stocks, you need to piece together an economic worldview, a sense of where things are and where they're headed using all the available facts at your disposal at any given moment, something that's much more an art

than a science. The reason is that the indicators you're using, the various pieces of information that have some kind of predictive value, never quite tell you the same thing twice, and sometimes they stop telling you anything useful altogether. Imagine the contrast with someone piloting a plane. When you're a pilot, you look at your instrument panel, which shows you all the necessary indicators for flying a plane, and even though it might be displaying thirty different things, you know that the significance of each one is always the same on every flight. Now suppose on your next flight, each separate reading on the instrument panel, meaning each particular indicator, measures something slightly different or even totally different from before, and on top of that some of the indicators have become more important and some have become less important, while others have stopped working.

And that's not even the hardest part, because the real issue is that even though what you're getting from each indicator is different from before, the instrument panel looks the same as it always did. There aren't any new labels telling you what's changed; you have to figure that out on your own. Now, luckily you're not under the same kind of pressure as an airplane pilot and you don't have to process nearly as much information all at once, which is why it's actually much easier to formulate an opinion about where the economy is headed than it is to learn how to fly, except in the narrow sense where your instruments are unreliable. However, despite the desire by some analysts and portfolio managers, and especially those technicians who analyze charts, we can never be on autopilot. Your portfolio might crash if you just let the plane use the data it thinks it needs and you sit back and relax.

So how do you make sure that the indicators you're using are still doing what you think they do? First, we only use something as an indicator if we think there is a decent correlation between the indicator and something we think is worth measuring. For example, gold prices have historically been a good indicator of how frightened investors are of economic instability or inflation. When we're scared we buy gold because it represents safety, especially since gold prices tend to increase when financial assets go down, as gold keeps its value in inflationary times, and paper assets lose value. When I was back at my old hedge fund, gold prices were a fantastic indicator of the level of fear in the market. But over the last nine years since I retired, gold gradually stopped being a good stand-in for terror and eventually reached a point where a move higher hardly told you anything at all. What changed? Many things: more demand from newly developed nations—you start making money, you start buying gold jewelry; more investors buy gold to hedge the once almighty dollar; more commodity hedge funds try to invest in gold as an asset class all by itself, like real estate or bonds; and even ETFs that buy up the bullion directly. A move in gold might be caused by any one of those things, and that means gold no longer matters as an indicator—not of fear, not of stress on other asset classes, not of a darned thing.

If you're trying to determine which direction the stock market is heading, then gold is far more likely to confuse you than it is to impart anything close to useful information. Investors who watched gold's run-up in 2009 and made the mistake of thinking it was an important sign would have been selling stocks precisely when they should have been buying them. They would have missed a huge move in stocks because they used the old rules and followed gold to an illogical conclusion. That's not so different from a pilot flying through heavy fog who relies on the instruments to maneuver, only to discover that someone replaced the altimeter with a random number generator, and so he almost crashes into the ground. However, investors who took the wrong cue from gold have no excuse for relying on an indicator that hasn't worked in years.

How about identifying newly important indicators? Okay, when China became a global economic superpower, you had to start paying more attention to the Baltic Dry Freight Index, which tracks shipping rates around the world and is a terrific reflector of Chinese demand for just about anything that can be carried in a dry bulk ship, for example, iron ore or coal or grain. In March 2009 we saw the first bottom ever called by the Baltic Dry Freight Index. It turned and rallied well ahead of the bottom in our stock market, and if you knew to look for something that would measure Chinese trade with the rest of the world, this index gave you a great edge, even better than simply tracking the Chinese market. You probably had never heard of the Baltic Dry Freight Index before a year ago, or even before you picked up this book, but I guarantee you, we'll all be paying very close attention to this index for years to come, as it's the best way to track imports to China. Even if you didn't pick up on its importance yourself, you had to be flexible enough to realize that just because something was unfamiliar didn't mean it wouldn't become significant. I now regard the Baltic Dry Freight Index as more important than almost all U.S. data save the monthly unemployment numbers. That's saying something.

Myriad other indices flit in and out of contention for importance and attention. The VIX, an index that measures volatility, can come into play when the system is stressed, with a high reading telling you to be careful. On the other hand, if the system isn't stressed, people don't even bother with the VIX and it comes off the instrument panel. And above all the others, I still favor any index that measures the number of stocks that have gone up versus the number that have gone down, such as the Advance/Decline Index, which shows the total difference between the number of stocks that are advancing and the number that are declining every day, but, unlike the Baltic Dry Freight Index, which can predict a return to world trade, an advance/decline test simply confirms what you may already know about a market's widening or narrowing breadth.

The moral of this story isn't that you need to follow the Baltic

Dry Freight Index religiously from now on; it's that the indicator you might be following, the tell you think is letting you discern the next big move, may not be anywhere near as helpful as you think, and it could even do you harm by sidetracking you from the next big move entirely. The best way to protect yourself is by knowing precisely what the indicator you're following measures and then drawing the connection between what it literally tells you and what that might mean for the market.

3. **Know your fellow shareholders.** One of the most important takeaways from the crash is that knowing about the company whose stock you own can be less important than knowing who else owns it, who is buying or dumping it. It's imperative that you keep track of your fellow shareholders because they have more power to destroy a stock than anybody else, including management and Uncle Sam, at least in the short run. You already know that at times there's only a gossamer-thin thread connecting a company's short-term earnings prospects and assets with its stock. If your fellow shareholders turn on you by liquidating large positions, selling their shares at fire-sale prices, then even that link will be severed and the stock, now totally untethered from anything except the relentless selling pressure, will sink like a stone. Remember that not everyone sells because they want to; sometimes people sell because they have no other choice. That makes them dangerous, as forced selling can wreck the stocks of even the best companies in spite of strong fundamentals and great prospects.

So how can you distinguish a bad fellow shareholder, someone you definitely do not want as your neighbor in any stock, from a good one? What should make you suspicious? Stocks that are owned by a lot of hedge funds can be very dangerous in a down market. After a big sell-off you can bet that a lot of hedge funds will have lost serious money, and when that happens those funds will often get hit with a great deal of what are called redemptions.

That's confusing hedge fund speak for when your clients tell you to give them their money back. A hedge fund that's been forced to liquidate can weigh on a stock for months, as it can take that long for it to unwind its position. One of the reasons the declines in September and October 2008 were so severe is that numerous hedge funds got hit with massive redemptions, forcing them to sell, or even liquidate all their assets, in order to pay their clients back. All of that forced selling created a whirlpool underneath the market, sucking stocks lower at the worst possible time.

At my hedge fund I had a lockup period to prevent this kind of thing from happening—my clients could ask for their money back only at certain times. But these days many hedge funds not only don't have lockup periods, they take money from fund-of-funds managers, a type of financial intermediary that I consider a totally unnecessary tax on the system and causes more than its fair share of forced selling. What the heck is a fund of funds? It's basically a fund that takes money from rich people, collects a little cut, and then invests that money across multiple hedge funds. If you're a hedge fund manager who needs money, taking money from fund-of-funds managers can seem attractive. But fund-of-funds money is the slickest, least sticky kind of money around, so if your hedge fund starts to underperform, the fund-of-funds guys will demand their cash back faster than anybody else—after all, they have to justify their cut to their clients, causing yet more forced selling at the hedge fund. That's why I shunned fund-of-funds money at my hedge fund, but lately these fund-of-funds guys have proliferated like mad, which made the forced selling during the crash so much worse.

Now, while the forced selling from one big hedge fund that's been forced to liquidate can do a lot of damage, what you should really worry about are the situations where you have lots of hedge funds concentrated in the same stock or group of stocks. Money managers tend to think alike and make similar bets, so once the losses in a group get rolling, they snowball until the forced selling is finally over. Just look at the commodity collapse that started in July 2008 and accelerated in September and October. The prices of everything from oil and natural gas to wheat, fertilizer, and copper got crushed. But the stocks of the commodity producers fell even harder. Why? Because the hedge funds had all made big bets on energy, on agriculture, on minerals and mining; they were all concentrated in these groups, which were reaching the end of historic multiyear runs. So when the stocks started going down and the losses mounted, many hedge funds were forced to sell these names to pay back frightened clients.

One of the most daunting prospects that you can face as a shareholder is when you know a stock is great but these forced sellers keep pounding it. That's how the natural gas stocks got overly trashed as well as the copper, fertilizer, and steel stocks, including some of the best ones, at the end of 2008. It is hard to find out who your fellow shareholders are and how weak their hands are. Most Wall Street firms don't write about weak or strong shareholders. But Goldman Sachs put out a piece of research in the summer of 2008 warning about the high concentrations of hedge funds in several stocks, including some I liked a great deal, such as National Oilwell Varco (NOV), the drilling platform manufacturer, and Freeport McMoRan (FCX), the copper company that I recommended in *Stay Mad For Life*. Both stocks went on to lose about three-quarters of their value or more because of forced selling. Of course, the sales produced great opportunities to buy, but you didn't know that until the hedge funds were finished selling, and they finished only when the year was over and they had to return money to their now beleaguered investors. Another way to find information about who owns which stocks is to go to www.stockpickr.com, a site we set up at TheStreet.com to show you who is doing what and whom to worry about or emulate. We cross-check holdings with hedge-fund filings and help you determine whether your stock might be in bad hands. Also www.topguntrader.com, a great newsletter by renowned technician Rick Bensignor, specializes in identifying which stocks are held by shaky shareholders. Both Stockpickr and Top Gun Trader alert you to who is buying and selling and how quickly and desperately they want to get out. I use Top Gun Trader on *Mad Money* to flag these worrisome holders and get ahead of the damage.

When the market is improving, you can worry less about who else owns the stocks you buy. But you should always remain vigilant. Don't forget the damage that hedge funds can do when they collectively abandon a group of stocks in which they're heavily invested. They rolled back tremendous multiyear gains in the commodity stocks in a matter of months. When you crowd lots of hedge funds together into a single stock or a sector, you have a disaster waiting to happen, and the worse the market's doing, the more dangerous your hedge fund fellow shareholders become. At the same time, you should also remember the other side of this story: if you have conviction about a company, and you know that there is forced selling and not some kind of problem with the fundamentals that's ailing its stock, you will get some great opportunities to buy high-quality merchandise at low prices. I don't want to hype my television show or tell you that you must watch *Mad Money*, but my series on "hedge funds gone wild," which I ran at the end of 2008, highlighted some of these needlessly trashed stocks and was the single best place to get this kind of information. I will reprise the work if it happens again.

4. **It pays to follow the *dumb* money.** People are constantly trying to figure out what the so-called smart money is doing so they can mimic the investing habits of well-informed, professional money managers who ostensibly know what they're doing. I have a much easier and far more reliable way of capturing quick gains. All you have to do is figure out what the least-informed and most amateur-

ish investors are doing. Find out where the dumb money is headed and you've got a chance to rack up the kind of easy wins that you should be looking for, especially if you need to get back to even quickly, either because you're about to retire and your retirement fund has been shredded, or you have other large, unavoidable expenses, such as paying for college tuition or a new home. How come this works? Because when you get right down to it, the amount of dumb money in the market is just staggering, and the investors whom I'm insensitively, if not unfairly, lumping under the rubric of dumb money are very predictable.

How predictable is the dumb money? Let me put it this way: when the market's in bull mode, individual investors love to pour their money into mutual funds, and those funds turn around and put most of that cash to work on Mondays. Back at my old hedge fund we used to call it Mutual Fund Monday because, thanks to the influx of dumb money, the market seemed to levitate, week after week, going up often for what appeared to be no apparent reason if you didn't know what was happening behind the scenes. It doesn't get much more predictable than that.

So how exactly do we profit from following the dumb money? The kind of investors I'm talking about endlessly seek the most sizzling mutual funds to put their assets in. Whenever one diversified mutual fund that invests in stocks is beating the stuffing out of all the others over a fairly short period of time—think over the last quarter, or even the last month—then the person running that fund will get gobs of money, much of it of the dim-witted variety, coming from people who are trying to chase the hottest mutual fund. You can find that information all over the Web. Now, if that mutual fund is large enough, you just got yourself a shopping list. How large? It has to be managing at least upwards of $50 billion, because with that much money, there's no way a mutual fund can buy a meaningful amount of stock without giving it a nice boost higher.

Look up the fund's largest holdings, especially the stocks that it has bought more of recently, information that's also easy to find on the Web. If you see any names where you also like the fundamentals, those are the stocks to buy. How do I know this? In their own way, mutual fund managers are just as predictable as the dumb investors who chase them, and maybe even more predictable. Whenever a fund manager gets a huge influx of cash, most of the time he'll use that money to buy more of stocks he already likes—he'll take his biggest positions and make them even bigger, usually in a style so aggressive that the stocks leap up big on his own buying. That's your chance to ride his coattails to profits. These guys tend not to buy different stocks with new money, they just buy more of the same, staying true to their investing style and beliefs, which makes it easy for you to spot the stocks that they'll likely move with their buying. I know that this sounds like circular reasoning: you should like the stock because it's going up because the mutual funds that own it are taking in money and putting it to work in these stocks. But sometimes you don't want to overthink it; this one has been battle-tested time after time and it always comes up aces. One caveat: be sure to monitor these trends quarter to quarter. The moment one of these funds has a bad three months the money will come pouring out of those stocks and so will your trade's profits!

Following the smart money? Those guys are wrong half the time anyway. The dumb money, on the other hand, can be a source of quick and easy tag along gains, over and over again, as long as you know where it's going.

5. A "bear market" rally is still a rally. After the stock market bottomed on March 6, 2009, and as it began its light-speed snapback, a rally in which the S&P 500 and the Dow Jones Industrial Average each gained more than 36 percent three months after the March 6 intraday low, the business media created a new uncertainty: was this a "real" rally or just a rally in a bear market? Even

several months later someone or other with access to the public stage continued this so-called debate. I can't even begin to express how damaging the premise of this argument is, because it encourages people to stay on the sidelines *in spite of* the fact that they think stocks are heading higher. Think about it like this: what are you supposed to do differently depending on which kind of rally it is? If the rally is genuine, I assume that means you should go out and aggressively buy shares in the stocks that have led the market higher. And how about if it's actually "just" a rally in a bear market, how does that change your game plan?

All the talking heads and business writers who make hay about the differences between "real" rallies and "bear market" rallies are pretty clear on the idea that you should steer clear of rallies in a bear market. It's self-evident, isn't it? A bear market rally isn't real, it won't last, it doesn't mean the market or the economy is on the mend; it's just a way to trick gullible investors into buying stocks at the wrong time, as if they're out of season or something. I find that those who say "it isn't going to last" typically missed it; those who say "wait for a pullback" are usually on the sidelines desperately hoping for lower prices so they can get in on the action; and finally, those who dismiss it entirely with the "bear market" label, have, by and large, been stampeded by the bull, and their last chance of staying in business is to hope the market comes back down so their underperformance isn't so glaring. Do not listen to the painfully self-interested and wrong!

As an investor your goal is to make money, so why the heck should you care about any of these things that make a "bear market" rally worse than a "real" rally? Won't last? Hey, you have to sell in order to book your profits anyway, and besides, you could say the same thing about every broad-based market-wide rally that took place over the last decade, because we've given up all those gains. Also, a rally in a bear market doesn't mean that either the economy or the underlying companies are truly improving. Again, how does that relate, in any way, to whether you should try to take advantage of the fact that lots of stocks are going higher? What are we left with? I guarantee you that your bank will happily take money made during a bear market, even during a bear market rally; the teller doesn't know the difference, believe me. If you're struggling to get back to even, you can't afford to spurn a rally just because "we're in a bear market." But that's exactly what the people who try to minimize a rally's importance by throwing "bear market" in front of it are pushing you to do. It's just like people who think money made by trading stocks over a short time horizon is inferior to money made (if there is any) from long-term investing, or the people who would rather make no money than make money speculating. Those who spurned the rally in 2009 missed a 36 percent rally in three months and protested until the end that all those points of upside weren't worth harvesting, to which I would ask, "Then which ones are?"

The other glaring problem with the sadly widespread idea that it's perfectly okay, even a good thing, to miss out on rallies during a bear market is that the whole bull/bear thing is a metaphor. Yes, some markets are harder and some easier to make money in, but you can't just use animal symbols to guide your investing decisions. If for some reason you think it's critical to have set definitions of bull and bear markets, then at a certain point a large enough rally will turn a bear into a bull. Is there a special line where a "bear market" rally that supposedly isn't worth your time turns into a "real" rally that is, a sort of Pinocchio moment?

If a rally happens during a bear market, do stocks still go up? From reading some of the stuff written by people who believe a rally during a bear market somehow isn't real, you'd think the answer was somewhere between "no" and "who knows." I don't care when it happens, you don't want to opt out of a big rally, or even a small one. And that's not the same as betting against a rally and being wrong. It's totally legitimate to be wrong, but to believe stocks are going higher and also think that it's not worth doing anything about that fact—that's nuts. You'll never get back to even if you're knowingly, willfully blinding yourself to opportunities.

6. **Don't assume that commentators who dislike the market are any more honest or any less self-interested than those who talk up the market or individual stocks.** Whenever we hear someone touting a stock on television, we instantly accept the idea that they own it and treat everything they say with a healthy dose of suspicion. At least, after this vicious bear market, we have learned that much. But we hardly ever reserve that level skepticism for people who badmouth the market. More often than not, investors will assume that people who criticize the market either don't have an agenda or must not be pushing one. Why, they must be pure! To most people, expressing a negative view of the market is a way of automatically bolstering their credibility. To me, as someone who brought in about half the profits at my old hedge fund by shorting stocks, this attitude is totally surreal.

People who criticize the market on television or in print are not necessarily trying to help you. When someone says they like a stock they're immediately branded a tout, but when someone says they hate the entire market, how often do you think, "Wait a second, this person might be shorting the market or underinvested in it and hoping to knock stocks down in order to buy them at a lower price"? It's easy to recognize that many investors need stocks to go higher, but perhaps because the idea of shorting stocks is less familiar to most people, it's much less common to make the connection that some people need markets down at times, too. They're no more on your side than the longs who recommend stocks. In fact, their ability to instill fear without ever admitting that they themselves are afraid of the market going higher, not lower, gives them less legitimacy in my eyes. Money managers who attack the market on television should disclose their level of investment, their performance, and especially whether their dislike of the market has caused them to underperform the competition and put them under tremendous pressure to deliver results by any means necessary. But they would rather die than answer those questions.

In my professional opinion, there's probably more chicanery and dishonesty coming from the shorts in their interactions with the media than the longs. You have to remember that there are people out there who want to push prices down every bit as much as the touts want to drive them up and perhaps even more so. You do not want to fall into the trap of assuming that the people who knock the stock market have your best interests at heart, or that they're more altruistic than those who sing the market's praises. Believe me, they aren't worried about you. If you bought a stock based on the rosy picture of its future that some portfolio manager who happened to be in front of a camera kindly painted for you while he was long, and then the same guy promptly turned around and sold the stock into strength, you would probably feel as though you'd been taken advantage of, and you'd be right. How is that any different than if someone went on the air and convinced you to sell everything with some scathing critique of the market only to then turn around and buy stock aggressively after they've been knocked down or use the weakness to cover a short position? Don't let yourself be duped. The other issue is that, while the money managers who come on television have to disclose their positions in any stocks they talk about, they never have to tell you, "I'm underinvested so I'm lagging the benchmarks and getting left in the dust by my competitors, so it's vital that I try to knock the market down in order to give myself a decent entry point." If they don't own anything and aren't short anything, there's nothing to disclose, but they still might very well have an interest in knocking stocks lower. You're just never going to hear about it.

At any given time there are plenty of people in the industry who would benefit from a broad stock market decline and be more than happy to go on television and make the case that the decline is going to happen and encourage you to get out while you still can. As stocks become stronger and a bull market really gets going, all of the hedge funds who were either net short, meaning that on the whole they were betting on stocks to go down with more short positions than long ones, or simply underinvested and are now underperforming become more and more desperate. Money managers who've been left behind by the market and their competitors start to feel like cornered rats getting ready to be slaughtered by a feral feline. Many hedge funds can't afford even one year of underperformance. It takes a lot of built-up goodwill with your clients, meaning you'd have to have a pretty darned good record, if you want to explain to them how you barely made any money at a time when stocks everywhere were soaring, and still have a business by the time you're through. You have to be careful because when stocks are at their strongest, many of these hedge fund managers, the ones with the fewest scruples, will happily plant negative stories in the press and try to take advantage of the media to spread as much negativity as possible to get stocks down so they can buy. They also sometimes pressure analysts to come on television and badmouth stocks, in part because heavy commissions might depend on it, not that any analyst who bowed to that kind of pressure could ever admit why in public. Many brokerage houses cater to the big traders, the hedge funds, which want to make money on both the long and short side. These hedge funds pay hefty commissions to brokers and push the firms they do business with to go negative on the stocks they are shorting. Research analysts who want to get business from the hedge funds go on television and badmouth stocks they know the hedge funds are betting against. This negative cycle happened relentlessly with the bank stocks all the way down. Of course, no analyst would ever admit to doing this as it's illegal. Their opinions are not supposed to be influenced by the brokerage side of the business. Everyone involved will deny it, and I'll probably be disinvited from all the good parties and attacked mercilessly for having written this, but as long as the brokers need to attract hedge funds to make money, you can bet they'll do whatever it takes.

I wish this weren't the case; it would be wonderful if we lived in a world where everyone was honest and no one ever tried to manipulate the market. But since that's not the world we live in, the best way I know how to protect you from this kind of chicanery is by shining a light on it and making sure you know what to watch out for. So be on your guard. The people badmouthing the market aren't any more altruistic or honest than the people who tout specific stocks.

7. **Don't just look at the averages; breadth is just as important.** People usually look at where the Dow Jones Industrial Average and the Standard and Poor's 500 close every day to get a feel for the health of the market, but the truth is, as much as we like to cling to these totems, they don't necessarily capture the real state of the market. To truly get a feel for how we're doing, you always want to take breadth into account. What's breadth? Simply put, it's a measure of the number of stocks that are going up versus the number that are going down. Good breadth means there are many stocks in many different sectors moving higher, and bad breadth is when we have more stocks going down than are going up. The averages can go higher even on narrow breadth, and when that happens you want to be careful. Similarly, they can go down or do nothing when the market's breadth is good because of a larger percentage decline in one or two areas, even if those areas aren't particularly important.

How important is breadth? It can be a kind of polygraph, letting you know whether a rally is telling the truth. And given how far the Dow Jones Average lagged behind changes in the U.S. economy and seemed unable to catch up—remember, when we headed into the garden-variety depression in September 2008, AIG (AIG), Alcoa (AA), Citigroup (C), and General Motors (GM) were still leading components of the Dow—you need a polygraph more than ever. Only Alcoa really came through that period more or less alive, but a pathetic, indebted aluminum company doesn't tell us much of anything. Meanwhile, the other three emerged as wards of the state. Think about that: if the averages are powering higher only because of strength in a handful of groups, and some of those groups could be as bogus as the AIG, GM, and Citigroup welfare line, then you need to be cautious. Every market has leaders, such as the sectors that have been the strongest, but if those leaders don't gather any followers, if the strength doesn't create strong breadth, then your rally might be on thin ice.

You need to look at breadth to know whether a bull market is truly robust. The lack of breadth in the great rally of 2007 that took us to new highs was a harbinger of the problems to come, since the market's leaders at the time were fertilizer, natural gas, and mineral stocks, all of which were collapsing as their stocks went higher. This was a narrow and ultimately unsustainable bull market.

New bull markets, however, do usually start out on thin breadth, which is why the market bottom in March 2009 managed to slip past so many prognosticators. But that rally turned out to be genuine as more and more sectors joined the original survivors of what could be one of the most important "lows" of the ages. When a bull market is genuine, as the March 2009 one was, then you will see more and more sectors join in and the breadth will improve. And that's not always detectable in the averages. We started to recover from the crash as stocks rallied off the bottom in March 2009 with narrow strength in just three groups: tech, the banks, and the oils. In fact, it was even narrower than that: a couple of semiconductor stocks, a bank—Wells Fargo (WFC)—and some oil service stocks, notably Schlumberger (SLB) and Transocean (RIG), an offshore driller, were the first to pop their heads out of the deep, dark trenches. Then, starting in the second half of that April, even though the averages stopped powering higher at quite the same pace, the market's breadth improved, with strength coming from more than just the three leadership groups. That marked a very important point, and it was something you had to look at breadth to notice.

At first, much of the move higher was caused by hedge funds covering or buying in long-established short positions, in this case bets against the banks based on the belief that they would be nationalized. As soon as it became clear that the Obama administration would not let another important bank fail after witnessing the fallout from the Lehman Brothers disaster, the hedge funds went at the business of short-covering with a level of fury never before seen in the stock market. Then the mutual funds decided to abandon defensive stocks: the foods, such as General Mills (GIS); the drugs, such as Johnson & Johnson (JNJ); and the consumer products names, along the lines of Pepsi and Procter & Gamble (PG), which had hung in there during the huge downturn. Instead they started pouring their money into more economically sensitive stocks, especially the three leadership groups. That produced a big move in the averages, because these stocks, especially the banks, had been beaten down and were ripe for large-percentage moves skyward, whereas the stocks that were being sold down declined far less in percentage terms. When the rally developed more breadth, expanding into many more sectors, that signaled that there was increased interest in buying stocks across the board, with significant amounts of money flowing in from the sidelines as smaller investors didn't want to miss the first legitimate rally in years and the hedge funds, many of which had made bearish bets all the way down, started to declare victory after the worst bear market since the 1930s had carved a 53 percent chunk off the top from two years before. What breadth ultimately tells you is whether a move is truly bringing most sectors higher, or when the breadth is thin, if it's a zero-sum activity, with money rotating from one group of sectors to another. Never again, I believe, will people so blindly trust the high-profile averages as a way to gauge a market's health or determine its direction, and for good reason. If you have to follow an average, at least take your cue from the Russell 2000, which encompasses far more stocks and is more representative of the American economy than either the Dow Jones Industrial Average or the Standard & Poor's 500.

8. **Don't trust buybacks.** I used to think that large buybacks, where companies repurchase their own shares on the open market in order to take them out of the equation, reducing the number of shares outstanding and boosting their earnings per share, were worthwhile, and that bad buybacks were the exception, not the rule. Buybacks became increasingly popular in recent years: from the fourth quarter of 2004 through 2008, the companies in the S&P 500 spent a total of $1.73 trillion on stock buybacks, almost twice the $907 billion they spent on dividends. However, it's clear that buybacks simply haven't given us the value we thought they would. Traditionally buybacks are cited as a way of returning value to shareholders, but from their recent track record you would think that the point of buying back stock is to destroy value by wasting hard-earned cash. There's a much better way to return value to shareholders, and that's by increasing the size of your dividend. A large company with a dinky dividend and a big buyback should ring some alarm bells.

In the wake of the crash, it's easy to find companies that bought back lots of stock at higher prices only to have their share prices continue to tumble, leaving shareholders with next to nothing to show for the billions spent buying back stock. Some have been far worse than others. For example, the HMOs, companies like Aetna (AET), WellPoint (WPT), and UnitedHealth Group (UNH), stand out as some of the worst buyback offenders. These are the kind of large, mature businesses that you would expect to pay mammoth dividends. Instead they kept their dividends puny in order to finance buybacks on a massive scale in 2006, 2007, and 2008, even as, in some cases, insiders were selling their stock at the same time as the company was buying it back. It would be one thing if the HMOs were all paying out big dividends, but as I write Aetna pays out a puny 4-cent annual dividend, UNH has a 3-cent dividend, and WellPoint pays you nothing. That's not because they've had to cut their dividends; they never had substantial ones in the first place. However, all three companies could have paid out dividends that would have given them yields in excess of 4 percent using the money they had spent repurchasing stock. So why do executives seem to like buybacks so much? There are a couple of reasons.

The HMOs were among the worst cases of companies buying back shares in order to generate cheap earnings-per-share growth. Since a company's earnings per share is just its net income divided by the total number of shares, a buyback can be a great way to create the perception of growth. I also wouldn't be surprised if it turns out some of the HMO companies used buybacks to keep their stocks higher in the short term so that their executives could sell stock at inflated prices. Whatever the reason, the buyback craze helped wreck their status as once-safe entities and distinguished them as enemies of long-term shareholders, the same people that at one time flocked to this sector for safety.

What about the perception that a buyback can help cushion a stock's fall by ensuring that there's always a buyer ready to step in and purchase stock? The evidence says otherwise. Short-sellers, or just ordinary sellers in a panic, can almost always overpower a company trying to prop up its own stock, especially as there are restrictions on how much companies can buy on a given day. Again, a dividend does a much better job of limiting a stock's fall by creating yield support. No group was more aggressive when it came to buybacks than the banks, but the buybacks didn't do an ounce of good at holding the stocks up when they faced off against the rapid-fire onslaught of short-selling that hammered down every bank in sight. As soon as the shorts were armed with a new-found power to bang stocks down over and over again, the buyback game was over. That power, by the way, was granted to them by the Securities and Exchange Commission when it repealed an old, Depression-era regulation called the uptick rule that had previously forced short-sellers to wait for above-market prices before they could sell stock, a repeal that let the shorts hammer down every bank stock in sight to merciless and often unjust levels.

You'll also see executives try to call a bottom in their own stocks by announcing major buybacks. This attempt at a Babe Ruth–style called shot almost always fails and turns out to be a waste of shareholders' money. The executives trying to call the bottom often understand the stock market, and their own companies, much less than you would have expected. The New York Times Company (NYT) spent hundreds of millions of dollars on useless buybacks, depleting its much-needed reserves of cash, as its executives tried and failed to use this expensive method as a signal that their stock was done going down. They didn't realize that their business was in long-term secular decline and that the company would have been much better off husbanding its cash.

Dividends have another advantage over buybacks. They can always be cut if the company needs to save cash. Dividends can slowly and steadily deplete a company's capital, but they can be held back easily. The New York Times Company could have sliced its dividend much higher than it did—it waited until the mid-single digits, but it was the endless buyback that did the serious damage to its balance sheet as the Times ultimately borrowed money to keep the buyback going. You never want to own the stock of a company that's borrowing money, or using cash it might need later to survive, just to prop the darned thing up. That's the height of arrogance and stupidity. And you shouldn't rely on even the largest buyback to help steady a stock if the situation becomes too dire. They are a false sign of health, and a waste of shareholders' money. In the end the companies with the biggest buybacks had the least amount of rainy-day money to weather the economic hurricane, and many of them will never come back.

9. **Technicals matter.** I'm the first person to tell you not to pick stocks solely based on what you can learn from their charts, or what's known as technical analysis. You can't use the charts as a way to bypass doing your homework and researching a company's fundamentals. Charts are not a crutch. But technical analysis can still be a very useful tool, and you shouldn't spurn it just because divining a stock's future moves from its past action can seem like voodoo or astrology, or mumbo jumbo chicken gumbo, as I call it on *Mad Money,* just to remind people that it's not the way we make decisions, that it's only one piece of the puzzle, not the be-all and end-all of investing as it is for so many people who cling to the charts. Technical analysis done by an expert can be every bit as rigorous as fundamental analysis. You just have to understand what that analysis is telling you. We know that at certain times, far more important than the fundamentals is what the big-money guys are doing with their shares.

Unfortunately, because of the secrecy of Wall Street, you can't just call up your broker and ask whether Fidelity or State Street or T. Rowe Price or Alliance or Janus are buying or selling today. That's confidential information and your broker would get fired for revealing it to you. The technicals are your substitute for direct knowledge of what the big money is thinking and doing. Given that the big mutual funds control so much of a stock's trading, it is foolish not to know what they are up to if you can possibly find out. The chartists give you the necessary clues to detect their actions. Plus, the institutional investors rely on the charts when they make decisions, so knowledge of the charts, as divined by the most consistently correct chartists, can give you a virtuous circle of performance; they like the chart, so they buy, you like the chart because it shows that they're buying, so you buy, too. You are essentially piggybacking off their own work. Think of technical analysis as your window into the Wall Street fashion show, helping you figure out what's in and out of style, not by asking the big boys but by analyzing their footprints. A good technician helps you by using the charts to find sophisticated patterns that mimic the actual minds of the major institutional shareholders without ever asking them what they're doing. Think of the technicals as *CSI* for investors, and a good technician as a kind of stock-picking Sherlock Holmes. That's why I now devote a segment of *Mad Money* called "Off the Charts" to understanding the work of various different technicians and comparing it with my opinion of a stock's fundamentals every week.

What does this mean precisely? Good technicians, people like Dan Fitzpatrick, my colleague at TheStreet.com's paid sister site, RealMoney.com (I blog side by side with him), and Rick Bensignor, another colleague who writes the subscription-only Top Gun Trader newsletter, and whose work I regularly discuss on my show, can tell you when a stock's big institutional buyers have become exhausted, meaning they're sick of paying for stocks or they're running out of money to buy with or tell you when the big boys are finished selling, all by looking at information that's hidden in plain sight in a stock's action through a process of ratiocination similar to what Edgar Allan Poe described in "The Purloined Letter." Not only does this stock chart analysis allow them to predict when big moves will stop and start, it can even predict good or bad news coming before the rest of us have the slightest notion what that news might be. For example, Fitzpatrick predicted an upside surprise followed by a major rally in Big Lots (BIG), the nation's largest closeout retailer, just the day before the company reported, based purely on the technicals. Bensignor nailed the bottom in Bank of America (BAC) for nearly a triple in less than three months, because his work enabled him to see that at $3 the Bank of America sellers were just plain spent, exhausted, and finished dumping their shares. These are just some of the winning technical analysis based calls we've featured on our Tuesday "Off the Charts" segment of *Mad Money*, by far our most-watched segment each week. (Remember that Top Gun Trader newsletter is the best way to spot hedge-fund forced-selling liquidation, one of Bensignor's specialties.)

One big caveat: You should never buy a stock based solely on the technicals because if it fails to go up you have absolutely no reason to own it. In fact, if its price fails to hold at its support lines, the technicians say you have to sell the stock, even if it is a company that's actually doing well and deserves to be bought, something that happened with an important technical failure of the stock of Goldman Sachs right before an almost immediate double. The stock took off like a rocket just when it was supposed to crash and burn! When you buy a stock because you like the fundamentals, you have a good justification for buying more as it goes down and so you have a much stronger sense of security than a chart can ever give you. But you should certainly listen to experienced technicians to develop an understanding of what the big institutional investors are doing so you have a better idea of when and where to buy or sell the stocks you like.

10. **Don't dig in your heels when you're wrong.** In the immortal words of the late, great economist and equally accomplished investor John Maynard Keynes, "when the facts change, I change my mind. What do you do, sir?" One of the easiest mistakes to make, and I know this because I've done it often myself, is to refuse to change your stripes after the facts are in and you've been proven wrong. It's natural to dig in your heels and refuse to concede when you think you're right but the market's gone against you. It's also a quick and easy way to lose money. I recently made this mistake myself when I was negative about the bank stocks for too long. But when Wells Fargo and JP Morgan said at the bottom in March 2009 that they were going to make money, you couldn't ignore this new information no matter how much you hated the financials. On

the other hand, I stayed too long in natural gas stocks because I wanted to believe in clean energy. Even as natural gas prices were collapsing in 2008, I hung on when I should have sold.

I have been blasted into reality over and over again whenever I dug in my heels on either side. You are always angry when you get run over and you are always willing to take it out on the people who are on the other side, the ones who got it right. For example, I got an incredibly heavy volume of hate mail after the market bottomed in March 2009 and then rallied much higher. When the Dow Jones Industrial Average was down to 6,500, close to the bottom, I came out and said that the downside was minimal and you had to start buying. Some of my belief that the big selloff had ended stemmed from a bold call made by a noted bear, Doug Kass, on RealMoney.com, saying that he, at last, was going bullish. When the biggest bear on Wall Street goes bullish and says we could be at "generational lows," as Kass did, you have to pay attention. But I also knew there just couldn't be much downside and we were bottoming because I had put together a doomsday scenario, basically a model of where I thought the market would go in case the worst really was at hand. I tallied all the members of the Dow Jones averages, and presumed that every single financial in the averages went to zero, including Bank of America (BAC), General Electric (GE)—yup, people consider this one a financial because of its big GE Capital division—Citigroup (C), and JP Morgan, and on top of that, I also took into account the total elimination of dividends at Caterpillar (CAT) as well as 3M (MMM), then I added in the potential bankruptcy of Alcoa (AA) for good measure, all pretty dire assumptions to say the least. And you know what? Even under those ghastly conditions, I still couldn't see a low that took us down significantly from where prices already were. From the moment I made that call there were people telling me that I was crazy and that I had no idea what I was talking about. But a month later, with the Dow 1,500 points higher, those people were still there, sending me emails that were even more impassioned and claiming that it was still too soon to tell. If you find yourself making that kind of argument, you're probably digging in your heels when you should be changing your mind. This is something that's hard for the most emotional investors and traders out there to come to terms with, but it's also crucial if you want to get back to even.

People do this all the time with stocks, but we would never allow ourselves to make the same argument about, for instance, sports. Would you claim that your favorite basketball team still had a chance of coming back from behind to win an hour after the game ended? What about a week? A month? Of course not. If anyone did that you would think they were insane. I'm just urging you to apply the same level of rigor to stocks that you would to sports. The facts are always changing in this business, and at some point you need to be willing to acknowledge that the game is over and you were wrong. I'm not trying to be glib about this; it's part of the emotional side of investing that, while difficult to measure, is just as important as the intellectual side, even if very few people in the financial media will talk about it. Swallowing your pride is never easy, but the more time you spend digging in your heels, the less you have to take advantage of the new situation and profit from it. How can you know for sure that it's time to say, "game over"? If you find yourself feeling the need to come up with more and more excuses and reasons why things will go your way, then it's probably a good time for you to instead start pondering why they haven't.

11. **Don't take your cue from the alibis of an inferior company.** There are strong and weak players in every sector, and the weak players will almost always seek to pin the blame for their failings on the entire industry. Believe them at your peril. When Dell (DELL) says things are bad and Motorola (MOT) says things are bad, you shouldn't sell your computer hardware or cell phone

stocks based on that. You shouldn't sell Apple (AAPL) or Qual-comm (QCOM), which have little to do with Dell and Motorola, other than the fact that they are all considered "tech." This is typical worst-of-breed behavior and you can't generalize from it. You will never hear a company say, "We're doing poorly because our competitors have better execution, they're grabbing our market share, and generally eating our lunch." No CEO in his right mind is going to come out on the quarterly conference call with a Shakespearean "the fault, dear shareholders, is not in our stars but in ourselves" revelation.

You need to be able to recognize an excuse when you see it. When a Motorola or a Dell, or any company that's gotten into the habit of serial underperformance, tells you that their shoddy results were caused by a shoddy environment, the odds are good that you won't hear the same story from their stronger competitors. Bad news for Motorola may be bad news only for Motorola. If they tell you it's raining, the odds are pretty good that when you hear from Apple or QCOM, they'll likely tell you that it must be raining only on Motorola's side of the street, because business is just fine where they're standing. You can't just assume that all companies in the same industry are equivalent. Sometimes there just isn't any pin action, meaning you can't extrapolate from one company's results to the rest of the industry, and that's most frequently the case when that company is one of the losers. This happens in every industry; it's not just tech stocks that hide behind others in a sector when they drop the ball. We saw it with General Mills (GIS), the cereal company, when it had just gotten beat by Kellogg (K), despite its claims that things were just a tad slow. We also saw it with Procter & Gamble (PG), which claimed that the world was rebelling from high-price products while in fact Colgate (CL) was running circles around it in almost every market where the two companies competed with each other. We even saw this phenomenon play out in fast food, where Burger King (BKC) lamented that the consumer couldn't afford a hamburger today, but it could tomorrow, the day when McDonald's told us it was selling them by the billions. Same in the supermarkets, too, where Safeway kept complaining that the consumer was moribund, but Whole Foods was kicking butt and taking names, while Wal-Mart stole food shoppers away from traditional supermarkets.

12. **Inventory matters, especially when credit is tight.** This rule is something that my father taught me when I was much younger, but I didn't realize just how far-reaching the implications were until the credit crisis set in and it was harder for companies to borrow money than at any point I can remember in my thirty years as an investor. It starts with an anecdote. When I was a little boy, my dad used to take me to what we called "the place," his warehouse where, to this day, he still sells wrapping paper, boxes, bags, five-inch by nine-inch jewelry boxes, and two-inch by twelve-inch shirt boxes. He would always work impossibly hard right through Christmas season and sometimes we would go to the place the day after Christmas, the day after he had spent seven straight weeks driving his station wagon to retailers to meet their holiday paper demand, and we would look upon the enemy, the nemesis of all business: excess inventory. We would see reams and reams of Christmas paper that hadn't been sold. I would say, "Dad, so what? You can sell it next year." And my father would sit there and patiently explain to me what he described as the most important thing I will ever need to know about business: that inventory has to be financed, that you have to pay banks, you have to have credit to keep inventory, that no business has enough cash on hand to pay for excess inventory, and now he would have to sell this Christmas paper for much less than he bought it for simply because he couldn't afford to finance it. Until he did, he couldn't bring in any Valentine's Day paper, wedding paper, or Easter or Mother's Day paper.

If you want to know when an industry is going to recover, if you're looking for a bottom, then you need to look for companies that are working off the equivalent of my dad's gift wrap dilemma. Business can't improve until companies eliminate their excess inventory, until they get rid of "the enemy," by cutting prices furiously because they can't afford the finance charges. They need to put their version of the great Christmas paper inventory glut behind them. Not just retail, but housing, technology, commodities, automobiles—if it has inventory, if it's not a pure service provider, then this rule applies. Normally these industries will bottom when they've finally gotten rid of the excess inventory and can start ordering again.

This inventory cycle bottom is what caused people to realize that the semiconductors, literally after years of being overinventoried, hit a bottom in January 2009 and started going up that March. In fact, the first company that saw a bottom was the lowest-level one, Taiwan Semiconductor, which makes simple chips for TVs and cameras. They were just out of chips, having dumped them below cost. When customers finally cleared their own inventory, Taiwan Semi, a stock I recommended on *Mad Money* when I saw the restocking begin, was finally able to charge full price for its newest semis. There weren't enough old ones left to discount. All of its "Christmas paper" had been sold; so had everyone else's. When Best Buy (BBY) says that its inventories are low enough for it to begin restocking its shelves, that helps everyone on down the tech food chain as the companies that sell to Best Buy place more orders with their component suppliers, and so on. You hit a bottom in everything from Corning, which makes the glass for computer monitors, to Apple and Texas Instruments, the guts of most modern electronics. For a time during the credit crisis, when banks were desperately struggling to raise capital and the economic outlook seemed so bleak that it didn't make sense for them to lend to most companies that needed it anyway, there was a wrench in the gears. It's not just enough that you work off your old inventory; the banks also have to be able to lend so that you finance the new stuff. Once the banks were on surer footing, when we started hearing that bankers were again making money simply by coming in every morning and turning the lights on every day, then a massive new cycle could begin anew that exceeded anything just produced by a semiconductor bottom. Once banks could issue letters of credit you could even see the group most levered to world trade, the shippers, put in a bottom and jump back from the near dead to the winner's circle. Inventory matters; sell stocks with too much of it and buy stocks that are running out. The former, whether it is a tech company or a retailer, will be cutting prices and hurting earnings. The latter will be raising prices and boosting earnings.

13. **Beware of stocks that shouldn't be stocks, even if they're household names.** Don't assume a stock is viable just because it's listed on an exchange. In this country we allow stocks to keep trading that, in any other nation with a developed stock exchange, would have been suspended in a heartbeat. These zombie stocks, which belong to companies that are almost certainly or in some cases just plain certainly headed for bankruptcy, are the worst kind of pretend pieces of paper. They probably aren't even worth using as wallpaper, but we allow them to trade anyway because they generate enormous volume and that means more profits for the exchanges where they're listed and more commissions for the brokers. So far the worst examples have been General Motors (GM), AIG (AIG), Fannie Mae (FNM), and Freddie Mac (FRE). Nobody had the guts to cancel these stocks, even when it was apparent that they would become next to worthless, because they routinely traded tens of millions of shares a day. The common stocks of these companies are the living dead, but still no one stopped them from trading.

Let me explain just how irresponsible it is for the regulators or the exchanges to allow these zombies to keep trading. The common stock of General Motors, for example, was allowed to continue trading even after the public learned the details of who the company's new owners would be after it entered an inevitable pre-packaged bankruptcy. You could keep buying the old GM shares even though everyone from the executives and the unions to the government itself knew that the common stock that was trading would be canceled, worthless, and that a new common stock would be issued in its stead to the new owners, with the government taking 70 percent and labor and the bondholders splitting the rest. Once we knew who was about to own the company, it became absolutely cynical and outrageous that GM's old common stock was still out there, hurting innocent if ignorant investors who thought they had a play on some kind of turnaround.

The old common stock that kept trading really didn't represent anything like a true ownership stake in the company. It was the height of irresponsibility not to suspend or cancel the common stock when it looked like even GM's bondholders were going to get a raw deal, and remember, in bankruptcy the bond bullies get paid before the shareholders—they're ahead of you in line, they're the ones who usually get whatever spoils are left of the darned company. Fannie and Freddie were allowed to keep trading despite the fact that buying either of them was more like investing in the FHA or the Federal Home Loan Bank Board, that is, outfits that are more public trusts—or mistrusts—than companies that should have stocks. And AIG? The idea that somehow the owners of the common stock would get the upside after it works through the $200 billion in bailout funds keeping that rogue outfit afloat has always been absurd. Yet, in a truly cynical ploy, as the stock neared $1, management orchestrated a twenty-for-one reverse split, enticing even more suckers to this most likely worthless equity.

The regulators have proven that they don't care if you get taken advantage of in cases like these. So in the future, don't be one of the dupes who buys anything in a similar position to the common stocks of these companies. Owning these kinds of securities is no different from betting on the loser in a fixed horse race, and sadly, Wall Street is far less lightly regulated than any type of gambling.

The Nevada Gaming Commission would never allow this kind of travesty of a mockery of a sham to happen, but the Securities and Exchange Commission probably doesn't even realize there's anything wrong with it. It's too bad. In no other developed country are these kinds of shenanigans permitted. The government steps in and halts the securities pending news. Our government doesn't do that, perhaps because there's too much money to be made by letting these pseudostocks keep trading, money for everyone but you. Until this country puts a stake in the heart of the zombies, do not be fooled by stocks that obviously aren't stocks, as anyone reading the financials or the front pages of *The New York Times,* where the big-business obituaries get reported, would know. We should take our cue from the British authorities, who routinely "suspend indefinitely" the trading of these kinds of stocks so the unsuspecting don't get hurt. We should demand that kind of protection here.

14. **Bull markets are all about leadership.** Every bull market, every market that's ultimately headed higher, has leaders, a group of sectors and within them groups of stocks that give it definition, and more important, that control or at least predict its behavior. If you know what the leaders are and understand how they behave, then you won't get blown out and you won't panic like so many others, at exactly the time you should be buying. There's a progression to the way the leaders move, a pattern that I have seen over and over again in my thirty years of trading, and your life as an investor will be a whole lot easier once you become familiar with it. You shouldn't have much trouble identifying the leaders. They're the first sectors that start to rally off the bottom and the ones with the strongest performance and the most upward momentum once the rally gets under way. Their charts move in a V form, their gains are visible intraday when all other stocks are down, and most important, they start roaring right from the opening bell even when the rest of the market is heading south. These

are Stonewall stocks, visible and standing tall like the Confederate general Stonewall Jackson in the heat of battle at the beginning of the Civil War, and other stocks rally around them, which is why I always identify them as generals on *Mad Money*. In the great bottom in 2009 we saw leaders assert themselves in tech, oil, and banking even as all other groups remained in chaos.

Why do leaders matter so much? Because others follow. Look at the bottom of 2009, when Google, Apple, and Research In Motion troughed one after another. The rally for each was the impetus for so many others to move higher as well. Google's recovery from the bottom caused people to start buying the other stocks in the cohort: eBay, Ciena, Broadcom, and Web speed promoter F-5, as well as networkers Cisco and Juniper, the backbone of the Web. Apple's rise from the bottom emboldened us to buy a whole host of companies, from desktop computers to Intel and AMD chips, to Hewlett-Packard and even Best Buy, where computers are sold. Research In Motion's strength caused a bottom in cell phone chipmakers Qualcomm, Skyworks Solutions, and ON Semiconductor, as well as in Motorola, Nokia, and Palm, all of which started to bounce back. The rally in oil leaders Schlumberger and Transocean caused everything else to rally including the natural gas stocks like Anadarko and Apache and oil giants like BP and Chevron, along with the other drilling-related plays, National Oilwell Varco and Halliburton. Once Wells Fargo, widely perceived to be the swing bank because of its heavy concentration of mortgages in the hardest-hit area, California, hit bottom, it gave us the impetus to buy Bank of America, JP Morgan Chase, USBancorp, and State Street, right down the food chain. Leadership is remarkable; the buyers come in bidding up the not-so-hot and emerging players right behind the generals. Now that's leadership!

And leaders can tell us a great deal about where the market is headed. Even in the best of times stocks never go up in a straight line, and every bull market I have ever seen has experienced shallow pullbacks that tend to follow very similar rules. These pullbacks cause a lot of people to panic or at least decide that the bull run must be over, but the leaders are usually just taking a breather before they head even higher. If you understand that they're part of a pattern and know how to follow it, then you'll be much less likely to jump to the wrong, bearish conclusion and scare yourself into missing positive moves that you really need to take advantage of if you want to get back to even. Let me tell you what a standard bull market selloff looks like. First, the hottest group tanks, and one after another the leaders roll over. With the leaders down, everything else then proceeds to get crushed. And as all of this happens, more and more people will come on television explaining how this is just the beginning of a big correction, a really monstrous move that will take us much lower. By the time all the leaders are down, you've got a wall of worry with a bunch of supposed experts telling you the time has come to abandon all hope and sell like crazy because the market is now bereft of leadership. That's an important market-bottom moment in itself.

You have to remember that in bull markets the leaders don't get taken out back and shot, they just briefly return to the ground in order to refuel. That's why, unless the fundamentals have changed dramatically, the leaders hardly ever pull back by more than 5 to 10 percent before they start climbing back up. And when I say "unless the fundamentals have changed," I don't mean, "if you think the fundamentals are bad at the moment." They may seem bad to you all the way up; the issue is whether anything has happened to make them worse, because if the stocks are going higher, obviously someone thinks they deserve to be bought. Even if you don't agree with the bullish thesis, if the stocks have been going higher in a sustained manner, you should try to figure out why and believe enough to play the pattern I'm describing. Usually the first group to fall will be the first to recover, although they may briefly flatline until we get a piece of data that can be seized on as a reason for buying them again. In each case, the techs, the banks, and the oils bottomed *before* the fundamentals turned, so don't lose faith before the darkest-before-dawn moment.

These pullbacks are your best opportunity to get into the strongest, hottest sectors out there as the market recovers, but this is the moment where you'll be most afraid that they're run out of steam. You know I like to buy in stages. When you see the leadership falter, start buying your first increment down 5 percent, leave room for it to decline to 10 percent before you buy any more, and then relax as it crawls, or as is more often the case, as it roars back to above the level where it started its fall. For those who need to see the examples in action, the best off the 2009 bottom were Apple and Google, which peaked, swooned, got written off at the bottom, and climbed right back again. I have seen this pattern work for three decades, and this last time was no different. I am so sure of this theory of leadership that if the stock you picked to play the rebound fails to bounce, you should assume that you have bet on a private or—worse—a soldier from the wrong army!

15. **We are no longer the center of the universe.** It's become increasingly apparent that China is far more important to the global economy, and therefore our economy *and* our stock market, than our own economy is. This is simply a fact of life, and we have to get used to it. If you try to invest with the mind-set that the United States is still the most important economic power in the world, then you will miss some of the biggest moves going forward, making it much more difficult for you to get back to even. Plus, unless you acknowledge the supremacy of China, nothing this market does will make a lick of sense to you. As the world's economies rebound, China is leading the way as the engine of the recovery. Hopefully the United States won't get stuck as the caboose, but we're certainly no longer in the driver's seat, particularly because we are the issuers of trillions of dollars in debt, and only the Chinese, with a national balance sheet brimming with capital,

have the capability to buy everything we issue. Their banks were never in trouble, even as ours teetered on the precipice or went under.

Chinese demand, particularly for natural resources, powered much of the bull market that peaked at the end of 2007 when our housing bust and incipient financial crisis started dragging down the market like a lead weight. But even as we careened toward banking Armageddon, the strength of China supported many of our industrial manufacturers and infrastructure companies. Everyone knows that the failure of Lehman Brothers on September 15, 2008, a date that will live in infamy, hit our economy and our stock market like a wrecking ball, but the falloff in Chinese demand for just about everything at roughly the same time helped push us into the brief garden-variety depression that lasted until the beginning of March 2009. And it was a Chinese recovery that helped pull us out of our deep morass. The Chinese stock market turned before ours did, rallying to double-digit advances while we were still hurtling to double-digit declines, and the indicator that best predicted our recovery was the obscure Baltic Dry Freight Index, which I've discussed and which turned into almost a direct measure of what the Chinese are buying.

China's $585 billion stimulus package has had far more impact on both the global economy and American companies like Caterpillar (CAT), Joy Global (JOYG), and Bucyrus International (BUCY), the big three of industrial earthmoving and mining equipment, among many others, including much of the coal and steel industries, than our own only slightly larger stimulus plan. Their demand for raw materials drove a host of our industries, including the grains, fertilizer companies like Mosaic (MOS) and Agrium (AGU), the coals like Peabody (BTU), the steels like U.S. Steel (X), and the rails like Union Pacific (UNP), CSX (CSX), Burlington Northern (BNI), and Norfolk Southern (NSC), which move the goods to the coast for shipment. Most important, its demand for oil stopped a headlong dive in crude prices that would have led to a collapse in all of the oil-producing countries, not to mention our own substantial worldwide drilling and oil industries. Its separate $40 billion wireless infrastructure package has been a huge boon for technology companies the world over, especially Qualcomm (QCOM), Broadcom (BRCM), Texas Instruments (TXN), Apple (AAPL), and Nokia (NOK).

The Chinese communist government knows that it's in trouble if it doesn't get its economy back on track so it's doing everything in its considerable power to ensure a swift recovery. A recession in our country might mean political leaders get voted out of office; a recession in China means political executions. No wonder they had a swifter recovery in China. It's time to face the facts: the People's Republic of China, the last bastion of communism, has become the most important capitalist country in the world.

16. **For the right price even inferior merchandise is worth buying, as long as it's not deteriorating.** In the crash, but also in its aftermath, some of the best opportunities came from holding your nose and buying the stocks of companies that you never imagined you wanted in the first place because they'd just become so darned cheap. I will never endorse a stock when I think the fundamentals of the underlying company are deteriorating, and I won't go near anything that could be headed toward bankruptcy, but there's a whole lot of space between a best-of-breed company and one that's uninvestable. In normal circumstances, though, the stocks of the lowliest companies that still pass the smell test sell for much more than I would ever be willing to pay for them, usually because there are too many hopeful investors speculating unwisely and buying barely adequate merchandise because it appears cheap when in fact it's just selling for the appropriate discount. However, if the price drops far enough, then it's perfectly okay to buy a stock if you merely have a low opinion of the underlying company. That's how much price matters. I get enormous volumes of hate mail on this subject, normally from people who are upset that I

recommended selling a company that I'd previously said I liked after a big increase in its share price. Just as even best-of-breed companies become too expensive at nosebleed heights, there are levels where worst-of-breed companies are cheap enough to be worth buying. Notice, worst of breed is different from just plain worst; a worst-of-breed business might not look like much compared to its best-of-breed competition, but it can at least get into the dog show.

How do you know when the price is right on something you wouldn't otherwise buy? Obviously there's a sliding scale here: the better the company, the more you should be willing to pay. If you're speculating, then it's worth looking for companies that have been left for dead, even though they still have a perfectly strong pulse on closer inspection. There's no price you should be willing to pay for a company that could potentially go under; there's no circumstance under which a stock that has even a 30 percent chance of going to zero is inexpensive. But if you're truly convinced that bankruptcy isn't on the table and the Street just has it all wrong, then buying an unattractive company at an attractive price could make a whole lot of sense. At the bottom of the barrel, Bank of America (BAC) and Sprint (S) were both knocked down to prices that were ludicrously cheap if you thought the government wasn't going to seize the first and that the second would be able to pay its bills. At less than $4 in early March 2009, even if you liked other banks a whole lot more than Bank of America, as long as you thought it would survive then it was priced too low to ignore. Sure enough, the stock more than tripled in the next two months. Your key to buying Bank of America was, of all things, an interview with Fed chief Ben Bernanke on the television show *60 Minutes* saying no major bank would be allowed to fail. What a great time to jump on a bank that everyone was betting would be seized by the government before the interview. The next day Bank of America's magnificent run took hold. As for Sprint, this one looked ·

touch-and-go at the beginning of 2009, with its stock starting the year under $2 a share, but even after it told us that it had enough cash to pay its debts when it reported a bad but better-than-expected quarter on February 19, you could still pick up the stock for $3.25. Even though Sprint was hemorrhaging subscribers, it was still solvent and looking more and more like a takeover candidate every day, making the price was just too good to ignore. If you were willing to hold your nose, it gave you a 69 percent gain in just three months. Sprint actually turned out to be the best performer in the S&P 500 for the first quarter of 2009.

When it comes to higher-quality stocks, it's harder to find situations where something that doesn't interest you suddenly becomes worth buying because the price is right. There aren't many times when a halfway decent stock will get hit that hard. But keep your eyes peeled for companies raising money through equity offerings; this won't take much effort since so many are trying to raise capital. You can often find great deals on stocks that you never would have looked at once, let alone twice. I'll go into much more detail later on about the right way to play a secondary offering, and what separates the good from the bad, but just in terms of price, on the same day, May 13, 2009, both Ford (F) and BB&T (BBT), a southern bank that's similar to the five regional banks I endorsed except that it has many more bad loans, sold stock at radically discounted prices. Ford's secondary offering priced at a 5 percent discount to the previous day's close, and a 24 percent discount to the previous week's, and BB&T's sold at a 10 percent discount to the previous day's close and a 27 percent discount to the close a week before. Before BB&T got the deal done, the underwriters—the issuers of the stock—had "softened" the market, knocking BB&T down so the price could spring back after the secondary. That, plus the fact that the company was worth a heck of a lot more after it raised the money than before because bankruptcy was no longer a risk, made the secondary offering a steal.

Both deals immediately made you money. Even if you'd had no prior interest in either Ford or BB&T and thought they were both mediocre at best, at discounts that steep both stocks were clearly great buys. Always keep your eye on the price, because even less-than-stellar companies can turn out to be big winners if you get a chance to buy them low enough.

The ultimate example of this worst-of-breed buying opportunity was AMD at its bottom at the end of 2008. Here's a company I have hated for more than twenty-two years. But when it hit $2 after agreeing to sell its problematic foundry division and after its graphic chip division began to take share from market leaders Intel (INTC) and NVIDIA (NVDA), the opportunity was too great. I called this a "hold-your-nose-and-buy" situation. You caught a double in a matter of months.

Price forces you to make new judgments about bad merchandise. Just as some fixer-uppers have a price that makes them worth buying, stocks can get so cheap that they become diamonds—rough diamonds, but diamonds just the same.

17. **Just because someone has a Ph.D. or even a Nobel Prize in economics doesn't mean he knows anything about investing.** Of all the armchair players who constantly opine on the stock market or the banks in the press, I think the professors are by far the most dangerous. They are very intelligent, very articulate, very well credentialed—in short they are capable of being very convincing—while at the same time they rarely have any skin in the game, which means they often know little to nothing of how the stock market works and not much more about the real-life operation of corporations or the nitty-gritty details of the economy. They have maximum influence but minimal understanding, which is why you have to be incredibly wary when you listen to anything they say. I don't mean to demean academia or the study of economics, but being a professional economist has little or no relation to being a professional investor. There's just not much cross-

over for the most part, although you'll almost never hear anyone admit that in public. If I started critiquing academic papers in peer-reviewed journals of economics, then most people would correctly write me off as someone without the necessary experience to be taken seriously, but for whatever reason, when economists talk about stocks, they're shown enormous deference.

I am sure that if the academics had to put their money where their mouths are, and didn't have the sanctity of tenure, they would have disappeared from the airwaves rather quickly when the market turned positive. Nevertheless, they are a factor, a confusing one, and they have added to our minefield of an investing landscape, so you have to rule them out before they do too much damage to your portfolio.

Ultimately, until they have some skin in the game, unless they invest in stocks themselves and have plenty of experience as investors and post their records, then you should take everything they say with a grain of salt, if not an entire box of Morton's, whether the person is a professor of economics or marine biology. Professors like Nouriel Roubini and Nobel winner Paul Krugman were some of the loudest proponents of nationalizing many of our largest banks based on the premise that they were insolvent. They ended up looking pretty silly when every major bank that needed money was able to raise private capital after the Treasury Department's stress tests, including banks, such as Fifth Third (FITB) and Key (KEY), that I wasn't sure would survive. Even if the facts hadn't made that entire line of argument irrelevant, I don't think the professors ever understood the far-reaching and calamitous effects of nationalizing the banks, because they never had any real skin in the game. Even if we make the absurd assumption that the government would do a totally bang-up job operating a bank behemoth of byzantine complexity like Citigroup (C) or Bank of America (BAC) through nationalization, we would have wiped out its preferred shareholders, and we probably would have crammed down its bonds, too. Since preferreds are one of the main ways banks go about financing themselves, and since other banks are the largest holders of preferred stock in American banks, followed by many pension funds, the collateral damage could have been as severe as half a dozen Lehmans going under. Wiping out all of their bonds would have destroyed trillions of dollars in savings globally. I'm not sure that the professors who demanded nationalization ever had any idea about this huge unintended consequence of doing so, and in a way, I think it's worse if they didn't know. People who don't have any money where their mouths are just care less than those who do. If you don't have any money on the line, then not only can you afford to be wrong—one of the reasons why so many professors were telling you to stay on the sidelines as stocks bounced back from their lows—but you can also promote disastrous public policy without having to worry about the consequences of your actions. So be careful not to give too much credence to those with impressive credentials but little actual experience. (I'm not allowed to own individual stocks, but through my charitable trust, which you can follow at ActionAlertsPlus.com, I have money on the line and know how it can focus the mind and make you a realist about pain and gain.)

18. **Keep your eye on the big picture. Don't let the press fool you into believing the fate of the market always hangs on whatever planned-for piece of data is coming out next.** As an investor you can't let your mind-set be defined by the stories the media decides to focus on. Too many stories are ginned up because journalists need something to say on a daily basis and want it to seem as important as possible. I can tell you why and how the news gets manufactured so you can keep everything in perspective because I've been a journalist for even longer than I've been an investor. When you're a reporter, every week you look at the calendar and you count out events that fall on different days in order to fill out all the pages. Back when I was a daily reporter we used to call this the daybook, and we would plan in advance what

the big stories were going to be, based on what the calendar gave us. Since you're desperate to produce exciting news that grabs eyeballs, you have to make whatever's coming up seem as dramatic, to say nothing of melodramatic, as possible.

Financial journalists play this game, too. Just look at that, the momentous Case-Shiller Home Price Index! Existing home sales? Huge, totally huge! And then the next day, *new* home sales—wow, that's some superduper data that trumps everything. Then forget about anything truly important that might have come before Thursday, just put it out of your mind, because the amazing, incredible, market-totally-hanging-on-every-decimal-space durable goods number awaits us! Retail sales? Stop trading because it's more relevant and cogent than any other report before it. Not all these reports are created equally, but the desire to have something important to say never changes, so everything gets hyped to ensure you have an earth-shattering story every day. Breaking news is really broken news; so don't fall for it. There are more important issues at stake.

Or to put it another way, there is no perspective in the press because there can be no perspective. In the business media we have to have something to talk about, and that something is the data that comes out each day, which tends to be much less important than it sounds. So it's absolutely vital for the commerce of journalism that we take every macroeconomic number and blow it totally out of proportion, even to the point of obscuring elements of the big picture that are far more important, because the goal is simply to make every second seem as consequential as possible.

The only time I wasn't a slave to the daybook was when I was a homicide reporter in Los Angeles, forced to cover unpredictable events out of everyone's control. But at every other time in my journalistic career I was told to make it clear to the readers or viewers that what I was talking about was of immense importance, even if I didn't think it was.

When I started TheStreet.com in 1996, I would become furious at editors and writers who tried to stress and highlight unimportant data. They would just come back at me and say that I ordered them to report the news and, by golly, they were going to do it. They didn't care that I didn't regard what they were reporting as news; it was just ingrained in them and might as well have been in their DNA for all they could control it. I couldn't do much about it even when I owned the darned thing, so believe me, there's not much hope that traditional financial journalism will change any time soon.

But you know what? As an investor, you don't have to be a slave to the daybook. Forewarned is forearmed. You now know what's driving the distortions and you don't have to trust the journalist's context, which happens to be deadly as far as your money is concerned. Always remember that you have to keep everything the press throws at you in perspective. Measure the bits of data that come out against the more holistic themes that are truly significant. No matter how much the press tries to hype each piece of news, it's rare that any one piece of macroeconomic data matters that much on its own. Think of these things as being like the skirmishes between the rebels and the Union in the unimportant days leading up to the battle of Gettysburg, or like potshots fired a week after the Battle of the Somme in World War I. If you don't, if you fall into the trap of believing that every new report is as momentous as it's made out to be, then you'll find yourself panicking and getting shaken out of the market just when it's heading higher because of some not-so-important data from the Commerce Department, or you'll end up riding your stocks all the way down into the teeth of the buzz saw when things get bad, because you won't have an ounce of perspective. It is undeniable that some pieces of information are more important than others, especially the unemployment report at the first of the month, because that can affect Federal Reserve policy. Too few jobs created, the less likely it is that the Fed starts hiking rates. But otherwise, just try to take all of the data in and remember that you may be hearing this or that piece of "breaking news" because there's nothing else to say to fill up the airwaves.

19. **Beware of hysterical historical analogies. We are not Japan, and we certainly aren't Weimar Germany.** These are the two nightmare-scenario historical analogies that the bears have invoked to try to frighten anyone who will listen. Every time you hear them articulated I am sure you want to sell everything and move to a shire in New Zealand. But there's no need to be afraid because neither comparison makes any sense. Ever since the crisis started, we've been dogged by arguments that the United States was repeating the Japanese "lost decade" experience in the 1990s, where for about ten years after their stock market crashed, Japan's economy experienced little to no growth. And there are some apparent similarities: thanks to a brutal downturn in real estate, the Japanese financial system collapsed and its banks hobbled along as government-supported zombies for a decade of almost no economic growth. The Japanese economy hadn't recovered for very long when the latest crisis hit and everything came tumbling down all over again. Japan's Nikkei 225, the main index that measures the performance of the Tokyo Stock Exchange, declined by 82 percent from its peak at 38,915 in December 1989 to its trough of 6,994 in October 2008. You can see why the "we are Japan" argument would be so frightening; it looks so much like where we were at the beginning of 2009.

But the fact is, the United States is very different from Japan—always has been, always will be. Our businesses made the hard call and quickly cut back on their inventories. Recessions don't end until we clear out excess inventory, which makes our experience different from Japan, which just prolonged the downturn by refusing to take the tough measures and the losses that were necessary to take. And on top of that, consumer spending in our country rebounded much more quickly than in Japan. They never started spending over there, but it looks like we never stop here, and that's great for our economy. The fear and the hoarding the downturn produced in Japan, along with the insistence on propping up all the banks, including the ridiculously insolvent ones, is the toxic brew that we know now isn't being sipped at the U.S. bar. All of our large banks that needed to have been able to raise private capital, unlike Japan's, where they stumbled along like the living dead for a decade, unable or unwilling to provide the credit needed to turn the country around. Japan's banks refused to recognize huge losses for years, while we're making the worst of our banks eat their losses, as painful as that has been for the shareholders of these institutions.

Beyond our initial response to the crisis and the apparent health of our financial system relative to Japan's, the huge structural differences are just too great to ignore, so huge that the "we are Japan" argument was always completely bogus and unbelievable. The main difference is demography. Japan's economy could sit in neutral for years because Japan's population is stagnant. From 1980 to 2008 the population of Japan grew by just 9 percent and it's projected to start decreasing in the not-too-distant future. In the same period the U.S. population grew by 34 percent. The very fact that we have more and more people gives us more resources and puts enormous pressure on our economy to grow—Japan did not and does not have that. Some of the reason is their lower birth rate, but most of it has to do with differences on immigration policy. Ours is generous—net migration in the United States is 4.31 new immigrants for every 1,000 members of the population. In Japan that number is near zero because their immigration policy is so restrictive.

And it's not just the number of people, it's also how old they are. In America the average age is 36.7 years, while in Japan it's 44.2 years. Japan is a country with far more senior citizens. That means lots and lots of retirees, people who aren't producing anything for the economy and are afraid to spend. America is a much younger country. Our economy is not that dependent on exports while Japan's is almost totally export oriented. Vastly different situations. Saying that we're going to have a lost decade because it happened in Japan is nothing more than an argument by analogy, totally without rigor, that the bears have used to try to club the stock market lower. Don't let it panic you as it's panicked thousands of investors who look at the chart of the Japanese stock indices and just want to jump out of our market, if not the window. The two countries truly have little in common with one another.

The Weimar Germany comparison: the idea that the United States is about to experience a level of hyperinflation that will destroy the real value of equities and wreck our purchasing power because our government has been borrowing and printing so much money is another canard. You don't go from increased commodity prices, which are largely a product of phony demand from hedge funds speculating on the prices of raw materials and not real demand, and a slight increase in Treasury yields that's barely noticeable on a ten-year chart, to hyperinflation, even when this is the worry du jour. And frankly, the idea of worrying about inflation before the economy has even recovered seems completely backward to me. You can't go from severe deflation such as we experienced straight to hyperinflation without some growth happening in between. As I'm writing we don't have that growth yet. But since the hysterics want to up the emotional ante and create drama and sow panic, perhaps because they need stocks lower to beat the market, they're sticking with Weimar and Japan. Now you know why you don't have to take either argument seriously. Plus, if things do get better, you would think the Weimar worriers would have some faith that Fed chair Ben Bernanke would do the right thing against inflation and raise rates expeditiously. However, the simple truth is that the analogists can never be appeased. There is always some negative analogue lurking that makes it so you'll feel compelled to sell. I say sell when our fundamentals are faltering, not when they are getting better, and have some faith in the Fed chairman. He's gotten it dead right since the severe part of the downturn began.

20. **Learning the wrong lesson from the crash of 2008 can be more dangerous than learning nothing at all.** I worry about some of the ideas that investors, especially people who were new to the game, took away from the crash, an experience that brutally shocked all of us into rethinking some of our core assumptions about investing. Whenever the market gets torn to pieces for a sustained period of time, it always produces a cohort of disillusioned investors and former investors who jump to the wrong conclusions and wind up hurting themselves or at least missing out on some much-needed upside. Huge losses in your portfolio are the greatest teachers in the world, but if they teach the wrong lesson plan, you're in a lot of trouble. What's the incorrect takeaway? It's almost always some variation on "they fooled me once, but they aren't going to trick me again." Guarding against being too credulous when the situation improves then becomes the most important priority for all of these people. Something similar happened after the dot-bomb collapse, where a lot of people came out of the experience believing that gravity applied to stocks: what goes up really far and really fast must be a sham stock, and it will therefore come down again, because that's what happened to a lot of stocks from 2000 to 2003. The lesson wasn't true, and it was one of the things that kept so many people out of Google's massive, multiyear run after it came public in 2004.

What's the wrong conclusion to take away from the latest crash? When they look back at the crash they blame it on the fact that things were much worse than they appeared to be, and then when everyone realized the true extent of our problems, something that happened with incredible speed, stocks got crushed. The lesson they learn? That the market's appearance is deceiving because things are often much worse than they seem; therefore you have to be wary and suspicious of anyone with a positive outlook, anyone who says the fundamentals are sound or at least getting better, and you always have to keep your eyes peeled and one foot out the door to be ready for the next huge sell-off, which could be right around the corner.

Of course, none of this is actually true, but the scenario is very compelling to a lot of people because it's based on recent and intense experience. So having one finger on the sell trigger seems the only rational approach to investing, especially in an era where GM goes belly-up, AIG needs three fed bailouts, Washington Mutual and Wachovia Bank fail, and so many other companies become wards of the state. However, as I said in 2008 when the market was in free fall, once the systemic risks, the big problems like Citigroup and AIG and Lehman Brothers and General Motors were solved, no matter how badly or poorly they were solved, the resolution makes for a better, not a worse stock market, because investors abhor indecision and uncertainty. But you could have fooled most people, as investors simply became so abused by the market that they couldn't accept the notion that the pain would ever end. Yet the fact that we went through a period of time where the next major pullback was always just around the corner does not mean that stocks will always behave that way. Investors who didn't understand that blew a great opportunity in March 2009 when the crash finally ended and the rally began. Just because the banks and brokers turned out to be in much worse trouble than most people expected and stocks performed far worse than anyone had imagined in 2008 doesn't mean that things will be worse than expected now. Dealing with a vicious bear market for months trains you to handle difficult times, and dealing with a healthy bull market, well, that trains you to take advantage of better ones. You can't generalize from how the market behaves at one time and expect it to behave the same way at all others. That's just absurd. Some people are always fighting the last war, which makes them ill-equipped to handle the current one.

One more point: when stocks crash, it's always because things turned out to be worse than people thought or because something bad happened, even though it had seemed unlikely. If everyone realized how bad things were beforehand, stocks would already have taken their tumble. What I'm about to say may be difficult to accept or let yourself believe, but trust me, if you swallow your pride and listen, it will help you make money and hopefully get back to even. Just because the situation turned out to be worse than *you* thought it was doesn't mean it was worse than *everyone* thought. If you got it wrong—and there's no shame in that, as most people did—don't assume that your mistake was universal. Don't overcompensate for the fact that you didn't see the crash coming or realize how dire the situation was in the past by assuming things have to go wrong in the future and try to figure out why. A lot of people just can't bring themselves to accept that the pain is over, so they come up with a dozen justifications for their negative outlook, then throw them at the wall and see what sticks. If you have one takeaway from a market that fell 53 percent from peak to trough, it should be that things would have to be worse than during the Great Depression, with 25 percent unemployment, most banks failing and 35 percent decline in production, because the only time the market has fallen harder in a multiyear period than it did between October 2007 and March 2009 was the great crash that began in 1929 and didn't come to an end until 1932, when we were well into the Depression. Simple distillation: Don't worry about the crash; it already happened!

21. **Listen to everyone, not just the "experts." You might learn something!** As someone who prides himself on his skill at security analysis and his understanding of what stocks should trade higher on the fundamentals, I tend to be too closed-minded toward people who know businesses but not the stocks that are sup-

posed to trade in synch with them. I can't tell you how many times I have had a chief executive officer from a big cyclical business like a machinery manufacturer, or a home builder, or a clothier, come on my show and start telling me about how things are going great at his company, and I have had to burst the poor guy's bubble, telling him right back, on the air, "enjoy it while it lasts, 'cause the cycle's coming and it's a grim reaper." No, I never know the business better than its CEO, but I always know the stock better, and when a stock is rolling over while the CEO's crowing, I expect that business is about to fall off a cliff. Stocks are pretty good predictors of the future and they tend not to lie, while even the most honest CEOs tend never to be bearish. This is a pretty toxic stew for those who take their cue from what the bosses say on TV, instead of from the market's almost always brilliant action.

Other times an executive from a soft goods company, a consumer staple, will express amazement that his stock isn't flying high after a "better-than-expected" quarter, forcing me to educate him about the facts of stock investing life: that his company's very nature, its built-in consistency, would be working against him as the economy's heated up and he couldn't deliver an explosive upside surprise based on stronger business, just a manufactured one from small price hikes and tiny lay-offs that weren't in the numbers. When the world's getting better, nobody cares if a food or drug company beats the numbers. There will be other "dog has its day" companies with truly blow-away earnings that will dwarf anything that even the best soft goods company could ever make versus the estimates.

But that doesn't mean you should dismiss people out of hand when they understand the business side but don't understand stocks, particularly when it comes to forecasting what the consumer might want. In fact, if you're like me, it means that you just have to work harder to find other people who know more than you do about the customer's likes and dislikes, because, in the world of stocks, their knowledge can have a much more powerful effect on the multiple that investors are willing to pay for a company's earnings. You remember the basic arithmetic: to arrive at the price where you think a stock deserves to trade, you need first to figure out what it might earn, then determine what investors will pay for those earnings, the price-to-earnings multiple—and as the name suggests, you multiply the earnings by the P/E multiple to get your price target. Sometimes the exercise is easy: I know what multiples to put on cyclical stocks by looking at previous points in history. I know how the market tends to value consistent earnings and how it tends to value earnings that fluctuate with product cycles, like the tech stocks. I can evaluate how a stock that produces oil or gas should be judged versus the commodity.

But I have always been confused about what the so-called fickle consumer would do whenever I try to project the earnings of companies that sell high-priced goods to the public. Call it the blind spot of simple living. It's the flip side to my rule number 3 from *Jim Cramer's Mad Money: Watch TV, Get Rich*—don't be a snob or you will miss the run on Darden (DRI) because of strong sales at Red Lobster or the Olive Garden, two places no snob would be caught dead in, or perhaps you lock yourself out of a rally in a Carnival Cruise Lines (CCL) just because you wouldn't be caught dead on one. I have to adjust to the ways of those whom I will politely call the "nonfrugal." These are the people who pay $400 for True Religion (TRLG) jeans, a stock that I thought was a great short until I found demand accelerating as rich kids simply couldn't part with their expensive denim pants. Same with Aeropostale (ARO), a casual teen apparel store with merchandise that to me looked no better than Abercrombie & Fitch, or even Old Navy, but to others, particularly "more discerning" younger people, merited substantial price premiums over the clothes sold in those foundering competitors. Silly me.

That's why when I read *Setting the Table,* a book about hospitality by my favorite restaurateur, Danny Meyer, who owns famous

New York eateries like Union Square Café and Gramercy Tavern, plus Blue Smoke and the Shake Shack, the preferred fare at the new Citi Field, where the Mets play, I knew I had to have him on *Mad Money*. Danny didn't really know it until I had him on the show, but he can divine the multiples of the high-end stocks that give me so much trouble without even knowing he's doing it. He can measure the secret sauce that explains why someone with a "nonfrugal" attitude is willing to pay more for an experience, or a product, or a service than someone like me, who often can't figure out what the fuss is about. Just witness my obliviousness about True Religion and Aeropostale, the two hottest apparel stories of 2008–2009.

Danny pointed out that some companies, such as Whole Foods (WFMI), Chipotle (CMG), and American Express (AXP), had developed such strong customer relationships and were so hospitable to clients that when things got tough those clients would stick with them and perhaps do even more business than the Wall Street models would ever indicate.

Because I will always be a stock guy first, I laughed when I first heard the suggestions. But Danny and I put together an index of the companies that fit the bill, companies like the ones just mentioned, and matched them against the S&P 500 right in the teeth of the garden-variety depression. Wouldn't you know it, the outperformance—the amount these stocks beat the average by—was extraordinary. Meyer knew what people will still pay for in a downturn; he knew the hospitality equivalent of Aeropostale and True Religion. He nailed huge gains in Whole Foods and American Express and Apple and Goldman Sachs with his hospitality thesis. I put his index up on my show periodically to remind me that just as you don't want to be a snob about stocks, you don't want to be too plebian, either. Just when I thought everyone was trading down to Wal-Mart or Taco Bell, Danny knew better. The moral? Listen to everyone, especially to people who know more about consumer behavior that's different from your own. Otherwise you will miss out on what look to be some totally impenetrable gains. Wouldn't you rather understand them, and take advantage of them?

22. **Keep it simple. If you're worried about the market, don't try to hedge using put options or ETFs; just swap out of stocks and into cash or gold.** For most of you, trying to protect your portfolio with hedging strategies is a waste of your precious time and even more precious money. How come? Hedging is basically just taking out insurance on a stock or on your whole portfolio. What could be wrong with that? Isn't the idea of buying something like a put option or an exchange-traded fund that can reduce your risk a worthwhile one? Why wouldn't you want to keep a product on the books that limits your potential downside? Given the horrible experience of the crash, what kind of maniac would want to discourage you from using hedging techniques to give your investments an extra layer of protection?

Nah, I am no maniac. I just know—through experience—that the costs you would incur from trying to hedge your portfolio against a major across-the-board decline in the market absolutely outweigh the benefits. And by costs I'm not just talking about the price of the hedge, which is huge, like fire insurance premiums when several arsonists are striking nightly. I mean the opportunity cost. If you're worried about a lengthy sell-off and you decide to hedge your whole portfolio against it, let me review the typical "wrong" options that brokers suggest you use to cushion losses. First, you can short stocks that are like the stocks that you own. This strategy exposes you to unlimited losses on the upside and capped gains on the downside. Of course, no two stocks are exactly alike, because no two companies are alike, so I think this strategy is a point-blank loser. Second, you could buy put options on all the stocks you own, a very cumbersome and expensive proposition that has "friction" costs to it. These costs could very well lose you more money than you wanted to protect in the first place, particularly if you are buying the put options in a down market, for the simple reason that insurance gets very expensive when everyone wants it at once, so the premium is outrageous. Third, you could buy puts on an index that you think mirrors your portfolio, although every time I tried to use this brand of insurance I ended up losing money on both, because nothing ever mirrors your portfolio closely enough to do the job. Or you could find an ETF to short that suits your needs—one that mimics the Standard & Poor's 500 or the Wilshire 5000 Total Market Index, for example, if you thought the whole market was coming down, again a potentially inefficient method that won't match your portfolio.

Or how about buying the most heavily promoted tool for "hedging" out there? You could always get one of these brand-new common stocks that purport to be instant shorts against individual sectors and the whole market, known as inverse ETFs, which, for reasons I'll delve into in greater depth in chapter 10, dealing with the new world disorder, simply hedge you for a day, and one day only. You see, these inverse ETFs rebalance their holdings at the end of every day, which means their longer-term performance is increasingly determined by volatility rather than what you would expect to make if you actually went to the trouble of shorting the indices that these products are *supposed* to be shorting for you. That daily distortion makes them totally undependable. These are all obvious but faux choices, as the accepted wisdom of hedging simply does not work except for the people who can follow the market tick by tick, and even then, rather than giving you peace of mind, many of these strategies can still be vastly inefficient, adding to your headaches and creating still more crises, as I know oh so well from my years and years of trading. Oh, but your brokers will make a ton promoting these strategies at your expense, so I guess someone makes money off hedging after all.

Don't make investing more complicated than it really is. All of these hedges will require more than an hour of homework, because your potential losses from shorting are infinite as the potential downside is unlimited, and the puts are too expensive and typically too short-fused to keep you out of trouble for long. These aren't just hedges, they are investments that fill up another spot in your portfolio. If it's there as a placeholder just in case the market goes down, you're better off spending your time researching a new stock. And if you're reacting to a sense of more imminent danger, if you're hedging to protect yourself from a decline that's staring you right in the face, why the heck do you own a bunch of stocks that are about to fall in the first place? In order to offset the declines in the rest of your portfolio, you'd have to make that one short position about 50 percent of what you own, but all you've done in that case is hope that the two sides cancel each other out.

As I indicated, usually they don't work like that, and you can end up losing money in both because of how inefficient and mismatched they are. That's a pretty silly and circuitous thing to do when you could just sell everything, which you're supposed to do anyway if you think the market's about to tank, as per my rules for protecting your money. Once you've done the selling, then keeping your money in cash, even with very low rates, will give you a better return than you'd get with a portfolio where all the losses in your stocks are being canceled out, but not surpassed, and again, that's only in the best case scenario, if things go right with the hedges. Remember, this is the successful strategy I recommended on TV when I told you to sell at Dow 11,000 and Dow 10,000 and then come back in more than 3,000 points lower. Dodge the bullet, don't hedge against it.

23. In abnormal times, don't expect technical indicators to point the way, no matter how accurate they usually are. "This time, it's different" is the most notoriously suspect phrase in the history of investing. Throw those four words into an argument and you're

guaranteed to induce instant skepticism in just about anyone who manages money for a living, for the simple reason that just about every time, it's the *same*. This fact is actually one of the main things that separates picking stocks from gambling; the odds are much better with stocks because they move in observable patterns and those patterns repeat themselves. Some are so regular that they can predict the direction of the market with a high degree of certainty, especially the classic technical indicators such as the put/call ratio or the ratio of stocks hitting new highs to stocks hitting new lows. Ordinarily when these indicators reach positive extremes, you can count on the market to pull back, and a rally is almost always in order when they hit negative extremes. Even if they don't make sense to you or seem like the worst sort of Wall Street gibberish—what the heck is an oscillator?—their accuracy is so stunning that it seems almost magical. Almost. Because they don't *always* work, sometimes the technicals will betray you, causing you to take agonizing losses or miss wonderful gains. That's why you can't rely on them as articles of faith.

But you know what? You don't have to be a rocket scientist to recognize many of the moments where the technicals are useless. These indicators are only reliable in the first place because stocks tend to behave the same predictable way almost all the time. So when things are really out of the ordinary, the technicals won't work, and you shouldn't expect them to. They're predictable because the market is predictable, but when the situation deviates too far from the norm, they will only mislead you. And that's exactly what we saw during the crash, and it's what we saw during the market's extraordinary rally after it bottomed in March 2009. Nobody had to tell you that both of these events were different from the market's usual action. Even investors who blindly follow the technicals, something you should never do, could have recognized that their tool kit was useless in both situations.

This is something we all had to learn the hard way when our

totems just didn't do the job. We can't give up on them, but we have to accept the fact that they have their own weaknesses and that they are fallible when we use them in the future.

All these indicators reveal sentiment. They tell when sellers usually become unwilling to keep dumping stock and when buyers balk at paying higher prices. But when people are willing to sell at any price or when they'll buy at any cost, the last thing you should do is expect investors or stocks to behave the way they normally would. For example, take the overbought/oversold oscillator (actually there are multiple oscillators, and they all cost money to subscribe to because they're proprietary; I like the Standard & Poor's oscillator and the one devised by Helene Meisler, my colleague at TheStreet.com), which measures whether the market has moved too far, too fast in one direction as a result of more buying or selling than the market could handle. Traditionally people use a minus 5 on the oscillator, indicating fairly extreme selling, as a sign that the market is ready to bounce, and historically that's been a very reliable predictor of oversold rallies. But anyone who followed that playbook during the crash got slaughtered as stocks just went lower and lower and the reading on the oscillator sunk to minus ten and below.

It also led you astray in the mega-rally off the bottom. About two weeks into the rally, the oscillator was at plus 7, indicating an incredibly overbought market, something that almost always presages a pullback. However, since it was no normal rally, the oscillator kept steering you out of stocks when you should have been staying in. The sentiment measure would also have caused you to sit out the huge 2009 summer rally. The oscillators registered extreme danger levels of bullishness, but no sell off ensued. Same story with the put/call ratio and the number of new lows to new highs. These two usually useful indicators of sentiment didn't work on the way up or the way down, for the same reason as the oscillator—neither move was normal, so indicators that tell you about how stocks normally move are of very limited use in an abnormal situation such as we have experienced.

Extreme markets mean we have to adopt other indicators. After this battle with the bears the only truism that held up was the worth of dividends, especially the accidentally high ones discussed at great length in chapter 4, as our normal dashboard of technicals simply ran us off the road. Relying on dividends as our indicator, we will certainly go more slowly, but at least we'll reach our intended destination.

24. **The money has to come from somewhere.** This is more like a codicil than a rule, one specifically put into place for this particular market, where we believe that the overall direction of the economy—and therefore the majority of stocks—is up, but it will get there in fits and starts. Also, you never want to be lulled into thinking that all is well when the fragility of the economy is going to be with us for some time. This is why you have to understand the concept of fuel, and where it has to come from in order to power the majority of stocks higher. When retail investors are taking their money off the sidelines and putting it back into the stock market, when the waves of buying by mutual funds never stop and the hedge funds are desperate to get long so that they don't get lost, whenever you can put these three things together, you're in the land of the thousand bull dances and you don't need to worry about where the fuel for a rally is going to come from. As long as more and more dough is flowing into the market, it's easy to find groups of stocks that can go higher, and when that money is flowing into the stocks at the same time as the businesses are turning around, you've got to buy the dips each time they occur. But as we've seen, it takes a great deal of time for regular people to become accustomed to putting their money in stocks again after a serious decline, and the hedge funds can be absolutely tenacious with their negativity, a negativity that the media unfortunately

feeds on because it's so sexy and sells a lot more papers than good news.

Even with no money flowing in, or even with outflows, you can still have powerful moves in the stocks and sectors that are trying to assert leadership. But the money to make those moves happen can't just come out of thin air. It has to come from somewhere. If people are still reluctant to invest, then the money will simply be pulled out of the least exciting, least interesting groups of stocks as investors swap out of them and into sexier names with more lift. People who own food and drug stocks will happily sell them in order to raise cash, the market's version of rocket fuel which makes it possible for the more economically sensitive stocks to move higher.

There's just one problem in this scenario: the advance becomes zero sum and, ultimately, you can run out of fuel. As soon as the selling in the staples comes to an end, the leaders also run out of steam—there's just nothing left to drive them higher. And when investors on the sidelines are still reluctant to commit capital, something even worse can happen: you can get a rally in the wrong stocks. The food and drug names that were used as fuel can become the market's new leaders, and all of the cash that investors pulled out of them can be poured right back in, because the big money thinks another economic downturn must be ahead or else the foods and drugs would still be going lower. No matter that it just might be because these nondurables are getting so cheap they represent great value. The big boys take their cues from the action, and when the action turns benign for the soft goods, the money will flow right back to them unless there are inflows from the sidelines. You never really want to see any of the consumer staples roaring higher because it means the big hedge- and mutual-fund managers think the economy's either going to get worse or simply stay in awful shape for a long time to come. In fact, it's even more self-fulfilling: as long as the food, beverage, and drug stocks stay strong, you won't see much money come in from the sidelines.

There must be a few more signs that the market's health is improving, because even if retail investors and the mutual funds and the hedge funds all think the coast is clear, they won't buy heavily without some evidence of a rally. To get that rally, these stocks must go lower to provide the cash to finance such a move.

That's why one of the most horrifying things you can see in the stock market is a powerful rally in the so-called "wrong" stocks, the Cokes (KO) and the Pepsis (PEP), the Kelloggs (K) and the Heinzes (HNZ). When people are betting on an economic recovery in the near future, a rally in safety stocks usually means the recovery's been pushed out or is nowhere to be found. I put quotes around the word *wrong* because if you own them, they obviously aren't wrong to you, but they are certainly giving off negative clues about the economy when they go higher.

25. **Become your own strongest critic and constantly challenge your own ideas.** If your opinion about a particular stock, or about all stocks, is wrong, don't wait for the market to deliver its verdict and punish them brutally. Every investor has to figure out the right time and place to change his or her mind about a single stock or the whole market, but very few will even come close. People who don't learn how to change their opinions in response to new facts end up becoming perma-bulls or perma-bears, two of the least credible and most absurd groups out there.

Why wasn't I thinking about this rule in previous books? That's a great question. The answer has to do with the changing nature of this stock market. Hedge funds, not mutual funds, now dominate trading, and they are the ultimate herd animals. They take stocks to extremes. When things are good in a sector, all the stocks in it go up and up and up, and there is no price the hedge funds won't pay for the group. And as soon as there is any negative change in the fundamentals, there is no price at which they won't sell. Worse, if the hedge funds begin to lose money, their impatient investors then pull their money out, and the stocks go into free fall, not stopping at any level until the hedge funds finish their forced selling—no matter how hideously undervalued their stock may get on the way down. When you get run over by panicky hedge funds, it can do so much damage to your portfolio that even a diversified investor may not be able to handle the pain. This binary action that characterizes how so many stocks now trade is so completely different from the way the market used to operate, where patient mutual funds would sit with companies for quarter after quarter until their cycles came back. The mutual fund managers who used to set the tone didn't worry about the movements of the herd. Now every single change of direction is a cause for action. You can't afford to be swept under the hooves of a rampaging herd of hedge funds.

The most extreme and eventually the most dangerous kind of "herdthink" was hard to miss in the natural resource stocks, particularly the copper and natural gas stocks, as long as you knew what to look for. Copper stocks like Freeport McMoRan (FCX) doubled virtually overnight as the commodity was in tight supply. Then the moment the supply of copper overwhelmed the demand for it, many mineral companies were cut down by at least 75 percent, with Freeport itself taking a 90 percent dive from peak to trough *in just six months*. Natural gas? Same story—as long as the commodity kept going higher, the stocks doubled and doubled again. But then natural gas peaked and literally in a matter of weeks they lost two-thirds of their value—totally unthinkable moves before the ascendancy of hedge funds as the marginal buyers and sellers of stocks, the ones who move stocks aggressively and, at least in the near term, determine their prices. So we have to be able to anticipate these waves in order to get in and out ahead of them whenever the fundamentals change. We can't afford to ride them out. No one is that rich or that inured to losses.

That means you need to be willing and able to discard your thesis about a given stock or sector. Of course, changing our opinions just isn't something that comes naturally for most people, as we're too good at self-deception. It's also hard to admit when you're making a mistake, and harder to sell a stock or turn on the market when, so far, your strategy has been making money, and even harder still to catch yourself before it's too late and the damage has already been done. That's why I'm always telling you to stay flexible, to keep an open mind, and not to dig in your heels, but those things are all easier said than done. In reality, most people stop agonizing over their decisions almost as soon as they've been made. No matter how rigorously you debate the decision to buy a stock, as soon as you put in a bid, your objectivity goes out the window and you join the ranks of the stock's rabid defenders. That makes it pretty hard to tell when something is really going wrong with the business.

Being a good investor demands a level of intellectual honesty that's really hard for most people to achieve. Who wants to admit that he's been wrong about the market's direction or about one of his favorite stocks? It's just too easy to play down the importance of evidence that's contrary to your views and filter out the strongest arguments for why you might be wrong, or to simply go into denial about the facts when they go against you. That kind of bias will always be a problem, but if you keep trying to find the holes in your thesis, and you go through all the things that could cause either the market or your favorite stocks to topple, there's a solution somewhere.

What you have to do, at the same time as you're buying the stock for the first time or you start making other buys based on your forecast for the market, is compile a list of the things that would invalidate your thesis, negatives that would make you feel that owning the stock might be a mistake—essentially, anything that you believe would change your mind about the market or the stock. With that list, you're set. It says you must sell if any of the hypothetical events it mentions as being harmful actually happen. This is similar to something I used to do at my old hedge fund, that all good money managers do, examining everything, looking everywhere to see if we might have been mistaken about the market, to check for any holes in the thesis. If you're wrong about one of your stocks or the direction in which the market's headed, then being able to recognize that fact quickly allows you to avoid big losses and catch great opportunities that you otherwise would have missed.

You make the list at the same time as you start to like the stock market, and while you can update your concerns afterward to stay up to speed, it's very important that you lay down the criteria for failure early, not just for individual stocks, but for the market, so if it occurs, you are ready and can take action and cut and run, if necessary.

This kind of thinking goes both ways, bull and bear. Consider how right the bears were in the fall and winter of 2008 as our financial system looked like it was going to collapse; we were in our garden variety depression and China had pretty much shut down, slowing economies all around the world. We had no idea when any of this would end—that's the situation where the bears decided stocks were no good no matter what. Then the depression ended and we went back to a good old-fashioned recession, the banks found a firmer footing than anyone could have imagined, and China started picking up again. None of that mattered to the bears. They had their downbeat view, and even though many good things had happened since they became that negative, that didn't make the perma-bears any happier. It sure didn't make these bearish investors change their minds, not even close. When things got better, they just raised the bar in terms of what they would need to see before they believed anything had improved.

My method could have worked for the bears if they'd tried it. I know because I basically used it to foresee the bottom in March 2009. On my TV show I would make all kinds of lists about what could happen to make things better, and kept telling people that if we got any positive new material facts, we would get a genuine rally. I had a bearish view of the market until then, but I knew exactly what had to happen to change that view. Bull or bear, you have to make your list of things that would make your thesis about the market, or a sector, or just a stock, totally wrong, and if those things happen, you automatically know to back away—no clouded judgment involved in the decision at all. If you decide ahead of time what would invalidate your thesis, don't come up with new reasons to stick with it. Abort or lose big money: your call.

11

COPING WITH THE
NEW WORLD DISORDER

Beyond the strategies, the stocks, and the new strictures that we've already covered, there's one last thing you can do that will really help accelerate the pace at which you rebound from your losses, one final piece of advice that can ensure you get back to even much sooner than you had ever expected. From now on you have to be more opportunistic as an investor. We know that there are going to be roadblocks and other impediments holding you back; we know that in many ways investing has become more difficult, and that holds true even after the phenomenal bottom in March 2009, even after the incredible rally that came next; and we know that getting back to even by investing what's left of your capital in stocks can be a very choppy and daunting process.

I've given you the best advice I know to help you navigate your way from dire losses back to huge profits, but you'll still make mistakes and get blindsided by the unexpected from time to time—that's just the nature of investing in stocks. However, I saved for last this idea that you need to become more opportunistic. The reason? While there are many ways in which investing has become more difficult than it was just a few years ago, the current environment—the new world disorder—is also almost constantly creating new chances for you to make what's essentially free money, chances that didn't exist before in any of my thirty years of investing. In fact, I don't even think it's much of an exaggeration to say that there are a whole lot of circumstances where Wall Street is literally giving money away. In some cases, I wouldn't even be surprised if the brokerage houses that facilitate and advise on all the opportunities actually see what they're doing as part of a broad strategy to entice regular retail investors back into the stock market by handing you some easy wins that pump cash into your bank account and make you feel good about equities again. They know how discredited stocks have become as investment vehicles. They don't want to lose their lifeblood; they don't want to lose you.

When I tell you to make yourself more opportunistic, that means something fairly specific, and in the current environment, it's even more detailed. First of all, you don't just decide to be more of a stock market opportunist. Being opportunistic isn't an attitude or a style, it's really a skill set. Just because you know it pays to be an opportunist doesn't mean you can do anything useful with that knowledge. It certainly won't help you find these huge giveaways I just mentioned, let alone evaluate them to make sure they're safe. Being more opportunistic means knowing how to identify these opportunities as well as how to analyze them, and it also means being able to tell the difference between a genuinely great way to make money and the financial products that are just heavily advertised, extremely overhyped ways to lose money, not make it. (Don't worry, I have a whole section coming up devoted to warning you about the dangers of the newfangled products that have been issued in the last few years that allegedly protect you from the downside of stocks and sectors but in reality pulverize your savings.)

The best way to capitalize on the new world disorder is to take advantage of the wounded nature of the bond and loan markets, also known as the credit markets, and the public companies that can't tap into them and have to raise money by selling stock directly to you. I'm talking about the jaw-dropping number of secondary offerings that were a constant for most of 2009 and should continue for a good while going forward. Just as we have too many people with too much debt, we have far too many indebted companies in this country. You've probably heard the word *deleveraging* more often than you'd have liked over the last couple of years, but if you want to see classic examples of deleveraging, of companies reducing the debt on their balance sheets, then look no further than all of these secondaries you see being launched every week.

Secondaries are stock offerings of existing publicly traded companies, as opposed to initial public offerings (IPOs), which are considered "primary" offerings. Companies hire brokers to sell additional shares in big blocks—the secondaries—and use the funds to retire their old debt. The credit crisis has been so severe that it has been almost impossible for some businesses to borrow anywhere to refinance debt that was coming due or soon to come due. But now that the stock market has moved higher, many companies are taking advantage of more bountiful stock pricing to issue stock to repay banks and bondholders what they owe. If you own the stock of a company that files a secondary, this can be painful in the short-term. The announcement of the new supply typically causes a stock to take a dive immediately. Plus, new stock means dilution, as more shareholders get to share the profits. We have all been conditioned to look for companies that have the cash to buy back stock and shun companies that need to issue new stock to raise depleted capital. You have to be wondering how anything good could come from a company that's frantically issuing stock when we prefer to buy stocks that have the cash to reduce the amount of shares outstanding, not increase them! As we shall see, though, that's where the best opportunities for you surface.

Cash-strapped companies that file secondary offerings often become wrapped in a virtuous circle. Their share prices immediately dip on the announcement of the secondaries. But then, once the companies raise the capital, they refinance their debt, which takes a lot of worry off the table, and that, in turn, sends their stock price right back up to where they announced deals, or in many cases, much higher than they were before they filed their offerings. For a long time, it wasn't just the bond market that was frozen; the stock market was sinking so fast that investors had no appetite for any new stock, and no deals of any sort could be done to raise money. We had a huge clog in the system that created a major backlog of heavily indebted companies that may have wanted to do a secondary, but not at the prices the market was offering, not in such a bearish environment. Now, though, the stock market has improved just enough for them to launch secondaries. In fact, if a company with lots of debt hasn't filed a secondary by the time you read this, it's likely that its balance sheet has deteriorated further, or that something ugly, like a big pile of debt coming due, has come even closer. Therefore, the time is right for the company to issue stock at a huge discount to current prices, and for you to profit because you have the money it needs. Its desperation equals your best opportunity to get back to even quickly.

Remember, corporations don't borrow money the same way you or I do. A public company doesn't just go down to the local branch of Bank of America or Wells Fargo—two banks, by the way, that each did their own bountiful secondaries—and say "I need to borrow $700 million, please help me." When corporations need to borrow, they go to a different kind of bank, an investment bank that will help them issue bonds, either in a private placement or a public offering. The company will then sell the bonds, and pay its bondholders—its moneylenders—interest every year on the money it borrowed, called the "coupon," an arcane term that, to me, makes this process even more difficult for laypeople to understand. The nomenclature, by the way, comes from the original paper bond that was issued, when investors would literally clip a coupon off the physical bond and send it in to get the interest back. Fortunately, now you are paid automatically and electronically right into your account. This repayment process goes on until the bond matures, which is more jargon that means when the principal comes due. With most bonds, the entire amount of the principal has to be paid back on the maturity date.

If that sounds too complicated, just try thinking of most corporate bonds in terms of mortgages, something most of you are probably much more familiar with. Bonds aren't structured like an ordinary thirty-year fixed-rate mortgage, where you pay back some of the principal on the loan every month along with the interest. Instead they're more like the interest-only mortgages that let you skate by with lower monthly payments made up solely of interest until, usually after five or ten years, the principal has to be paid back, in full, all at once. Just like the homeowners who took out interest-only loans, and had to refinance or face foreclosure when they reached the end of the line, where they would have to pay back the entire amount of the loan, a company with a lot of bonds that are about to mature has to refinance, too, unless it has enough cash on hand. But very few companies with that much debt due have that much cash to pay it off, so they have to go borrowing again, hat in hand, to roll over the debt.

Although the credit markets may have thawed, they're still real cool, uncomfortably cold, which you can measure by the sky-high amount of interest that bondholders demand for companies to roll over maturing debt, that is, if the prospective bondholders have any appetite to buy new bonds at all. Rates are still too steep for almost all but the most creditworthy companies to issue bonds. These almost uxorious interest charges would wipe out the vast majority of companies that have to roll over debt. Often the rates quoted are the same as you would get on your credit card, so you can imagine how onerous that can be! Avoiding those charges makes doing a secondary offering much more appealing than a bond offering for most companies, the chief reason why these secondaries have been coming so fast and so furious.

You want to be able to find the secondaries that allow you to make quick but still significant gains in stocks, even the stocks of companies you don't particularly like, or to use secondaries as opportunities to buy stocks that you would genuinely want to invest in at a nice discount. Unfortunately, despite the fact that there have recently been a lot of secondaries that turned out to be very profitable for the buyers, you can't just assume that the next one will work. So keep in mind that not every secondary offering is a fabulous opportunity to make a very fast gain, but at the same time, don't assume that past performance isn't predictive of future success—in this case, we can learn a lot from the secondaries that have been the most profitable for their investors. I'm going to teach you how to analyze a secondary in just a moment, but first you need to know some basics, like the fact that keeping an eye out for the best equity offerings and doing the right homework on each of these deals will require more time than just managing a plain old five-stock portfolio. But if you do it right, your gains will be so instantaneous that the time invested will be well worth it. So many of these offerings have effectively amounted to huge giveaways where, in a matter of days, or sometimes even hours, the stock rises far above the print price—that's the price where the secondary happens, the price you would pay for the stock if you got in on the deal. It's almost enough to make you feel like you're taking advantage of the suckers who priced their stock so low. That's how badly the new capital is needed.

You probably don't know about this secondary windfall because this is one totally crazy market where the action is completely at odds with how things normally work. These stocks, post offering, shoot up as if they were fresh-faced IPOs and not mature companies pumping more supply into the system. Consider the trajectory of two amazing secondaries of recent vintage: U.S. Steel and Vulcan Materials. Normally when an old-dog company like U.S. Steel prices a secondary offering at $25.50, you don't expect to see the stock levitate almost $17, taking it to $42, giving you about a 66 percent gain over a few weeks' time, but that's just what happened. Usually if a boring rock and asphalt maker like Vulcan Materials offers stock at $41, you wouldn't anticipate that the stock would jump immediately to $47.25. Yet that move occurred in one day—yes, that's right, one day—after the huge chunk of stock was priced.

These discounted deals, which were almost like the red-hot IPOs of 1999–2000, are among the most difficult and counterintuitive to spot, because right before the offerings, both U.S. Steel and Vulcan

Materials substantially lowered their earnings estimates, slashed their dividends, and indicated that if they didn't raise oodles of money they could run afoul of their credit provisions. In other words, bond and bank creditors had stuck guns to their heads to raise cash. But it is precisely because of those dire circumstances that these deals worked so well: you were the beneficiaries because the brokers who priced the merchandise knew they could virtually extort the companies to benefit their own institutional and retail clients. And make no mistake about it, these deals weren't just for the big boys. Brokers love to give stock to smaller investors because they are less likely to "flip" the stock. Why does that matter? Deals "work," meaning that they go up after pricing, if they are placed in the hands of people less likely to want to dump the stock as soon as they get it. The managers of these deals believe that retail investors don't flip, they like to own stocks, not flit in and out of them.

If brokers gave stock to nothing but hedge fund managers, these quick-draw traders would be likely to sell the stock the moment it lifted above the offering price, as they often are happy to make a dime or two and move on. That kind of flipping would make the secondary "heavy," which would damage a brokerage firm's credibility with its other important constituency, mutual funds, which are traditionally very large buyers of secondaries. The big mutual funds pay massive amounts of commissions and expect to be rewarded with healthy chunks of good deals, not bad ones, where there's a risk of losing money. But the deals won't be good if they are filled with flippers. So the "syndicate desks," which allocate stock on each deal, are very particular about the kinds of investors they want to parcel stock out to. The syndicate people know that if they can price the offering at a big enough discount to the last sale, many buyers will come in to them and ask for much more stock than is available. That's why these stocks tend to rocket higher after the pricing, because the big clients who asked for a lot of stock get just a fraction of what they need and then go into the open market to get the rest of their position. A combination of retail investors who don't trade out of stocks and mutual funds that want to build gigantic positions and get started on the deal is the perfect recipe for a successful offering because the former hold on to the stock and the latter just keep buying until the position size is meaningful enough to move the needle for their investors.

That's what happened with the incredibly successful Ford secondary, another company that needed to raise money lest it be seized by bondholders or, even worse, the government—talk about a gun to its head, that's a howitzer! Ford's stock was trading at $6 and change when it announced that it would do a secondary to keep the creditors at bay. The brokers quickly placed 500 million shares at $4.75, an irresistible value even if you hated the autos. Soon after the deal was priced and the merchandise distributed, Ford's stock traded right back up to where it was, as many institutions were cut back on their allocations and had no choice but to put in buy orders at dramatically higher prices to get the rest of the stock they needed. Everyone who bought on the Ford offering made fortunes on a percentage basis betting on this household name and those who held on for a couple of months caught nearly double in the automaker's stock. The same thing has happened with bank secondaries. In about one month's time we saw seventeen straight offerings in the bank stocks and fifteen of them made you money immediately, almost all with double-digit gains. Only two deals failed to deliver a profit—Capital One, the big credit-card issuer, got hit with a series of anti-credit-card-fee speeches by President Obama right after the deal; the other, Bank of New York, had a nasty lawsuit hanging over its head that scared people. You would have lost a couple of points in Capital One and broken even in Bank of New York, barely denting the profits you would have made by participating in all of the other bank stock offerings, especially when you consider that in secondaries, unlike regular stock purchases, the issuer pays the commission, not you. These opportunities weren't hard to find. They included offerings by giants like Bank of America and Wells Fargo, both of which gave you 25 percent gains with breathtaking speed.

So how do you get in on these winning, often free-money secondaries? What are the tricks of this new-world-disorder trade? Let me tell you how I would approach them back at my hedge fund, because the tactics are still relevant today. First off, you have to watch the news tape; you have to hear or read that a secondary has been filed. It helps to have a full-service broker alert you to these deals and aid you with these as each secondary has a manager who runs it, typically one of the major banks, such as Goldman Sachs, Morgan Stanley, JPMorgan Chase, or Bank of America. But you can do it on your own with an electronic broker if you are uncomfortable working with a full-service house. When you hear about a secondary, you have to do some fundamental analysis of the company, the same kind of homework I have explained to you over and over again in other chapters as well as in my other books and on *Mad Money*. Even when Wall Street is giving away free money, I would never, ever buy the stock of a company I hate or a company I don't trust, even at a discount. For example, at the height of the secondary offerings, the same day that the bountiful Ford deal took place, Fortress Investment Group, a publicly traded hedge fund that had been losing gobs of money, offered stock at $5 a share, about a 15 percent discount to where it had been before the filing. I immediately railed against this deal in my Real-Money blog, because we basically had no idea how Fortress was really doing or what they would do with the money. The company has been a disaster ever since it came public and there was no reason to think that this time would be different. Sure enough, right after the deal was set at $5, the stock "broke price," meaning it didn't hold where the deal came and dropped 20 percent virtually immediately. It was a big win for Fortress and a total disaster for anyone who bought on the deal. So if you hate a company and think it has disappointed shareholders, there's no reason to speculate with its secondary.

However, there are a ton of other companies offering stock I might have disliked at a higher price, but liked lower, especially when the company is a good one, but needs money to be able to refinance debt or pay its bondholders and would normally have no problem paying back that money if the credit markets weren't closed or nonfunctioning. These are what I call "binary" plays, companies that could be worthless without the deal but extremely solvent once the deal is done. These represent the best buys in this market, especially when the deal's done "in the hole," well below the last price. The Ford deal I just described is a good example. Here is another: a late spring 75-million-share-offering for BB&T, a troubled southeastern regional bank alluded to earlier. Before the banking crisis, I thought BB&T was a great stock with a terrific dividend. But then when the economy stumbled, the company lost its discipline and made a lot of bad loans in Florida, loans that defaulted rather quickly. Because of those bad loans, BB&T had to borrow more than $3 billion from the Troubled Asset Relief Program, or TARP, and cut its dividend drastically. Once BB&T took federal money, it became a binary situation. If the bank could raise money in the public markets so it could repay TARP and take charges against its bad loans, it could survive and even thrive. However, if it couldn't raise this money, it might succumb to government pressure and become a Citigroup, a near ward of the state, where the government comes close to seizing the company, diluting all shareholders and ruining your investment. BB&T's stock was trading close to $30, where I disliked it because of its bad loans and its TARP exposure, when it announced that it was going to sell 75 million shares to fix its balance sheet and pay back TARP. That got my attention, and everyone else's for that matter, because the stock immediately dropped to $25 since the market sensed that the brokers "running the books," who were in charge of raising the money, had BB&T in a vise and could price the deal where it would benefit the brokerage clients, not the bank. Now, here's where it gets interesting. When you see that dramatic a fall, take particular care in noticing who the stock managers are for the deal. Their names are always announced right along with the news of the stock offering. If you have an account with one of them, call your broker at that firm and tell her that you want in on the deal and give an indication of the size of your order. If you want

100 shares of BB&T, indicate it right then and there. If you do not have an account with one of the deal runners, you are going to have a very hard time getting the intelligence you need to play the secondary game, but you might want to play anyway if you follow the guidelines I am about to give you.

This pre-deal sell-off is what creates the real opportunity. Some of the decline is caused by original holders of the stock who sell it to dodge a bullet, knowing that they can get their stock back at a lower price. Some of the selling pressure comes from hedge fund traders selling the stock short, betting they can get in and "cover" on the offering, meaning that they can buy back the stock they shorted on the deal at a lower price for a quick profit, something that is technically illegal but is done by many funds because the government has, for years, looked the other way at this kind of shenanigan. You shouldn't care how the stock gets knocked down. Both groups, the longs who sell and the sellers who short, simply ensure that the deal will go better because they both have reasons to buy when the secondary is priced, and they will keep buying if they don't get the number of shares they want. I like to consider this phase as "softening" the stock, the way an invader may soften the enemy's defenses with artillery before going over the top or landing on the beach. The more the stock drops before the deal, the more likely it is that the stock will rebound in your favor and the deal will make you a quick and big return.

The next stage is the actual pricing of the deal. On the day of the pricing, the stock tends to break down even more. In this case, BB&T's equity plummeted to $22, dropping 3 more points from the closing the day the deal was announced. When you see that kind of decline occurring, you, intraday, should ask your broker to check with the syndicate desk, the people in charge of parceling out the stock, to see if the deal is "tight," meaning there are a lot more buyers and it is not likely the deal will fall apart after it is priced. Your broker might suggest doubling the indication of interest you have to get what you want if he finds out it is tight. Sometimes I would tell brokers that if the deal were to be priced at an even bigger discount than $22, say $21 or even $20, I would like even more stock. As we get closer and closer to the pricing of the deal, your broker should be updating you regularly on the prognosis of the offering so you can change your indication of interest and get the maximum amount on what could be a great bargain. These deals typically get priced after the close of the market, and the BB&T deal was no different. When the 4 P.M. bell rang, the dealers immediately announced the pricing of the 75 million shares at $20, down another 10 percent from where the stock had closed that day, and off more than 25 percent from where it was right after the deal was announced. Now that's a terrific discount. When I see that kind of bargain from where the deal was first announced, I immediately try to get even more than my 100 shares, perhaps doubling or tripling my indication. But it is more than likely that when free-money deals like this occur, you will be cut back severely and not get the stock you want. That's why it is good to indicate the size of your order as early as possible as the brokers reward Johnny-come-earlies and shun the Johnny-come-latelies who indicate interest only on the night of the deal, when it is obvious that the pricing is far more advantageous to the buyers than the seller.

On this BB&T deal you made 15 percent on your money almost instantly, within a couple of hours of when the stock opened for trading the next day. Even if you didn't care about BB&T beyond the deal, you could have sold at the opening at a point higher than where the deal was priced because there was so much demand from institutions that were severely cut back at the $20 price and needed more stock to make the BB&T position meaningful. Remember, these funds manage billions and billions of dollars and if they get "only" 100,000 or 200,000 shares, it is entirely possible that is not enough to be considered a full position, meaning that it's not big enough to be meaningful to their performance. Then they have to go into the open market to buy enough to make the whole exercise worthwhile. Either way you could immediately ring the register for a monster one-day gain.

As you can see, this whole pricing strategy is incredibly important for you to understand. Had the last price, $22, been used, and not the $20 ultimate price, you may not have made a lot of money on the deal, although I believe a profit would have been virtually assured because of the previous decline. If you decide ultimately you don't like BB&T after you've gotten your stock, get rid of it quickly. If you do like the company, you have just gotten a great entry point to a bank you just might want to ride back to where it was when it was announced, if not higher. Either way, you could trade out of the stock with minimal risk and the chance for a heck of a lot of reward, which is almost always the case in these binary deals, that is, deals where the company could be worthless without the stock offering but solvent with it.

For most of my investing life, secondaries were simply a crapshoot, even after I used the tactics I have described. But for as long as we have dislocations in the stock market—and I think that will be a very long time, owing to all the damage that was done to the credit markets, the stock markets, and the economies of the world—I believe that secondaries, far more than IPOs or any other opportunities, give you the best chance to accelerate your climb back to even. So get ready, watch the tape, stay close to the markets, do your homework, and grab some of that free money Wall Street is throwing your way in order to entice you back to the casino that, for once, favors you, not the guy on the other side of the table.

Taking advantage of the wave of secondary offerings is a fantastic and fairly reliable way for you to quickly generate substantial gains in the current investing landscape, but it's not the only way or even the best way. Guess where we can find rival and even sometimes better returns? In the primary market, which is what we call it when companies directly issue common stock for the first time, in what I've mentioned as the initial public offering, or IPO.

You've learned what secondaries can do to help you get back to even, and do it quickly. Getting in on the right IPO can be a whole lot better, and when you know how to play an IPO, when you can tell the difference between an about-to-be-public company that will soar and one that will go down in flames like the *Hindenburg*, then you should be able to rake in profits ranging from large to totally stupendous in size. And unlike dealing with the aftermath of a great secondary, you don't have to wait weeks or months for the stock to climb high enough to sell for a colossal gain. When you get in on the right IPO, one where the stock soars almost instantaneously as the shares begin to trade on the open market, you can walk away with a 20 percent, 30 percent, even upwards of 50 percent gain after only a few minutes, based entirely on the difference between the offering price and where the shares actually started trading. For example, if you got a piece of restaurant reservation website OpenTable's (OPEN) IPO, you paid the company $20 a share. The stock closed at $31.89 for a 59 percent gain if you sold at the end of the session, and that was after it had gone as high as $35.50 during the day, up 78 percent from where the IPO priced.

Unfortunately, in the first half of 2009 there were only a handful of IPOs. But I am certain that, over time, when the stock market and the economy become more hospitable, we will see more deals, and I want you to be ready for them. As only a handful of American companies are going public each month, your odds of finding a great IPO opportunity are much, much slimmer than they used to be, when we had substantially more of them. But because of the damage done to the psyche of most investors by the gigantic nature of the declines in the market, the brokers are anxious, as with the secondaries, to put some money in your pocket to rebuild the trust of equities as a reliable source of profit for burned investors. That's why I am predicting we will have a flood of fresh-faced IPOs by early 2010. There are lots of good companies owned by venture capital or private equity outfits, companies that these owners should be willing to take public now that the stock market has bottomed and it feels like the economy is starting to turn. Just as the seemingly endless procession of positive secondary offerings practically popped out of nowhere to become a part of the market's current environment, the coming torrent of IPOs will be unexpected to most, even as these offerings quickly settle in as an important characteristic of the new world disorder. Because of what I am about to show you, you will be ready for them and will know to how to spot them and profit from them better than anyone else.

The next crop of IPOs will not be orchestrated solely to help these newly public companies raise money, because the investment banks that underwrite all the deals have their own agenda: enticing regular retail investors back into the market. One of the things I learned in my many years on Wall Street, both hawking stocks and bonds at Goldman Sachs and managing money for myself and for rich people in my hedge fund, is that when the market turns south, when it becomes really difficult to make money and people start pulling out of stocks altogether, the brokers like to throw investors an easy win. After the recent crash we are in deep-south territory. So I believe the industry will give you many easy wins for the next year, layup IPOs that are intentionally underpriced so they will pop when the shares start trading. Why would they underprice the deal and shortchange their investment banking clients? Because it's very important to the brokers, long term, that their other clients, the ones who pay them commissions whenever they trade stocks, come back into the stock market. For most investors, the gains from a sweet, underpriced IPO are a great reason to feel good about owning stocks again. As long as you take the free money for exactly what it is, you can look back and see what I mean. Back on March 19, 2008, an entire year before the market bottomed, the forty-one investment banks and boutique brokerage houses that underwrote the largest IPO in U.S. history, Visa's IPO, did exactly what I just described. At the time the IPO market had been truly crummy, the market miserable, and the brokers just wanted to give their clients a slam-dunk. So they underpriced Visa, one of two large credit-card issuers, at $44 a share, causing it to pop as high as $69 during trading that day before closing at $56.40, for a 28 percent gain if you got a piece of the IPO. The brokers knew that Visa would be "hot," the term for an IPO that opens substantially higher than it is priced, in part because they knew that the market loved MasterCard, Visa's rival. They also knew that if they priced Visa substantially cheaper than its comparable rival—lower price-to-earnings multiple for a stock with an equal growth rate—investors would throng to the offering and maybe even get MasterCard stockholders to swap their positions for Visa. Although the new issue was the biggest in stock market history, the brokers tightly controlled the supply, parceled it to accounts that they believed would not flip the stock, and gave out just enough to the large mutual funds that they would be able to start, but not finish, their positions. That way, the mutual funds, appetites whetted, would come into the secondary market and bid up the stock to get the rest of their positions.

Never forget that the trick to why these deals work so well is the rationing process. The syndicate desks know how much the big mutual funds ultimately need to have enough of Visa to affect their performance. So they give them a percentage, usually about a third to a half of what they need, and that forces them to complete the size of their position in the aftermarket. Of course these institutions could flip the positions themselves, but the brokers have ways to monitor who takes that quick money, and those institutions will be punished by not being allowed to get big allocations the next time around. You benefit because the syndicate desks almost always save a lot of stock for retail investors since brokers know they are not likely to play the flipper game. I am indifferent to whether you do either. I advocated taking the Visa gain at the time of the deal when I talked about it on *Mad Money*. I just want you to make money. But I never want you to go into the aftermarket and buy stock. If you don't get in on the deal, forget about it, as the desperate mutual funds will pay too much for the rest, knowing that their basis won't be all that horrible because they can average their aftermarket price with the cheaper IPO price. You are in a much better position than that of a mutual fund because you don't need to buy a lot of stock well above the offering price in order to be assured that you have enough of the company's shares. The amount you get on the offering should suffice.

As helpful as those freebie profits can be, don't let the brokers trick you into believing that buying *every* IPO is a great way to make money. Wrong, wrong, wrong! Some initial public offerings aren't worth investing in. The brokers will try to slip in some clunkers after they have lulled you into thinking that all the deals work, something that should become increasingly clear as the flood of new IPOs begins. Now, partially because the performance of newly public stocks tends to be all over the map, especially on their first day of trading when the gyrations in each individual stock can be maddening, and because there simply isn't that much information available about newly public stocks beyond the prospectus, there's a tendency to assume that the success or failure of a given IPO is mostly a question of luck—also wrong. You can accurately figure out which IPOs to write off as uninvestable and which ones deserve to be researched more carefully and potentially bought. Separating the IPO wheat from the chaff isn't about luck, it's about analysis, the kind that professional money managers do all the time but retail investors too often ignore, and not because it's too sophisticated or difficult. I know the pros have it right because every day I would analyze stocks the exact same way back at my old hedge fund, and that's how I still do it to this day. I made a great deal of money at my hedge fund gaming IPOs, and I will tell you so you know exactly how I did it.

Even if you can do a bang-up job of analyzing a company that's about to come public, even if you think it looks like that company's stock could rocket higher when it starts trading on the open market, even if the fundamentals appear to be terrific, or at least what counts as terrific among newly public companies, which tend to be much smaller and far less profitable than the average company, as they've only just entered the big leagues; in short, even if you have all the evidence you need to believe that a given IPO will work out well, that still might not be enough to ensure a profit. IPOs can be difficult and dangerous, so you need a consistent method to make sure you don't get torn to pieces by something that you don't understand or can't fathom. So here's your primer on analyzing hot from cold and safe from dangerous.

The first and most important thing I look for isn't what the company does; it's the company's pedigree. I care about who the managers are, who the investors are, and most important, who the broker doing the deal is. The first cohort, the managers, can be a relative unknown, and, strangely, represents the least important of the pedigree elements. That's because many of the best deals these days represent technology companies and the companies revolve around an invention. Take the Google deal, for example. You would have avoided it like a disease. Think about it—who were Sergey Brin and Larry Page but a couple of twenty-something wild men. I do care if there is one seasoned player in the midst, and in this case, the company had hired Eric Schmidt as its chief executive officer, a man with a long history of shepherding along Silicon Valley companies from infancy to formative stages.

My second check, the investors, is more of a negative check than a positive one. Sure, when it comes to tech, I would like to see in the prospectus that some of the venture capitalists have a long history of bringing successful start-ups to fruition. You can see that by looking at the principals in the prospectus and their backgrounds, as each will have a short squib about what he or she has accomplished. But that kind of background check really matters only for tech companies because venture capital doesn't always play a role in companies coming public. For example, in the Visa deal, you needed to know only the name, the brand, and the fact that the people behind it had been instrumental in implementing the company's success. No, I am far more concerned that you might get caught up in another kind of investment, one that is funded by private equity companies eager to cash in on a better market. Private equity firms, like Blackstone, KKR, Thomas H. Lee Partners, Carlyle Group, and Cerebrus, have bought dozens of companies in the last few years, in many cases paying far too much for them. They need badly to offload these companies into the open market so they can get them off the books and get a return on the investment they have made in these companies. Some of these

IPOs will barely be profitable; others will simply be stinkers that the brokers will try to entice you to pick up with the hopes that a stronger economy will lift all boats. These deals, almost as a rule, cannot be trusted.

If they are so bad, why are they allowed? Why doesn't the government or the brokers stop them from coming public? First, the Securities and Exchange Commission does not ever purport to judge the quality of an offering. The government wants companies to disclose as many facts and financials as possible so you can judge for yourself. The brokers, in the case of the private equity firms, are deeply conflicted. Take it from me as someone who worked at a brokerage house, these private equity firms (then called leveraged buyout firms) do so much business that it is hard for the big brokers to say no to them. Consider that a private equity firm pays an investment house a huge fee to raise the money and advise the client in any transaction where it first takes a public company private. Then when the company is about to go public again, the private equity firm pays large amounts to the investment house to take it public and gigantic fees to issue new bonds to refinance the entity once it comes public. The bankers are often compromised by the immense amount of money these going-private-and-then-going-public-again deals bring in, so they bend over backward to help private equity brokers, not the brokerage client. I have long known this to be the case, yet now and again I get fooled. In the spring of 2006, for example, KKR brought public Sealy, the mattress company, using a host of respectable firms to do so. I mistakenly recommended the stock on air, as I liked the brand and the housing market was quite hot, the relevant end market for Sealy's products. The deal came at $16, quickly traded to a small premium, and then began the sickening descent down to the low single digits, trading at $2 as I write. I should have known better. Let Sealy be a lesson to you when you look at the next crop of IPOs. If you see private equity money involved—as was the case with Sealy—just take a pass, no matter how enticing it sounds. Sure, you might miss out on some winners, but, trust me, there will be more losers from this crowd than big paydays.

Finally, I look at the brokerages bringing the deal. I want them to be major firms of the Goldman Sachs, Morgan Stanley, Credit Suisse ilk. Why is that important? Because they have their reputation on the line with each deal. They are typically unwilling to bring a company public just for the fees. Once you have cleared the hurdle that it is not a private equity firm behind the IPO's finances, you can take the brokerage name as a good seal of approval for the enterprise. Why do I know this to be a fact? Let me tell you a story. In the 1980s, as a broker at Goldman Sachs, I had personally helped work with the finances of the investors behind a young company started by some brilliant people out of MIT called Thinking Machines. This company's claim to fame was that it had a computer capable of calculating more data faster than any other. I had done so much work with the principals that when they decided to bring the company public I was able to convince them to use Goldman Sachs as their deal manager. There was only one problem: I couldn't convince Goldman Sachs to put its name on the deal despite the immense fees that that an IPO brings to a firm. The research analyst at the time who would have followed the company for Goldman Sachs, Dan Benton, pored over the financials and looked at the product and made a judgment that the company, while having short-term momentum, would not have any staying power. I was aghast. I stood to make a big six-figure ticket for bringing the deal to Goldman Sachs. Benton simply wouldn't budge, reminding me that this was Goldman Sachs, not some schlock firm that would put its name on any company just because it was hot. Sure enough, Goldman Sachs passed, and within a couple of years the company failed, a victim of better technology and poor financial management. So, take it from me, that's why the brokerage pedigree matters and why I would skip deals done by firms that you have never heard of that have little or no track record with successful underwritings.

Only after I have gone through that three-step vetting process would I then actually consider what the company does or what it makes or how it has done in the past, in part because it is so difficult to judge these issues with a company just coming public, and I would rather use the quick filter above before I even crack the books on the company.

My next step is to assess what the company makes and, more important, how big is the company's end market. The former can be easy if it is a consumer product, a Visa, or an Under Armour or a Heelys, to name a few of the deals that have come public in the last few years. But it can be more difficult if it involves a sophisticated product, like something connected to broadband or the Internet or wide-area computing, the hot trends that have some staying power. If it is a consumer product, first ask yourself if you like the product. That does matter. I, for example, didn't care for a product created by a red-hot company named Heelys that came public in December 2006. Heelys made shoes with wheels on them and, to me, as a parent, I despised these toys and figured the whole wheel-on-shoe craze was just a fad. I suggested people get in on the deal but then skedaddle quickly. Sure enough the deal came at $22 and popped to the $30s but you had to sell it immediately as the infatuation with this product ended soon after the company came public. It dropped to $2 a few years later.

Under Armour (UA) was different, a profitable company with a product competitive to Nike and with solid financials. That made the deal mouthwatering and I knew the steak would be equal to the sizzle, and not just because my very athletic eldest daughter and her teammates all loved the stuff. Here's one I urged people to hang on to, even after it popped on its first day from $12 to 25. Why hang on? Because even at that higher price it was valued comparably to Nike, but it was growing much faster than Nike, a classic example of stock market mispricing that you could take advantage of. It then proceeded to triple a year later. Alas, all good things come to an end, as was the case with UA. Why? Because of the addressable market issue. UA came public with the hopes that it could challenge Nike for the athletic clothing market. It very quickly took a large share and began to trade at a premium to Nike, meaning a much higher valuation. That was fine as long as it was a dominant clothing player. But then it decided to expand beyond clothing as it had saturated its addressable market and went after Nike's bread-and-butter footware division. This made no sense to me, given how powerful Nike's brand is and how it cherishes its turf and had repeatedly thrown back all comers. Sure enough, you had to sell UA on that challenge and never look back. Its growth hopes faded and it just became another apparel and shoe company in a long line of clothing companies that have tried and failed to dislodge King Nike.

Sometimes a company is thrice-blessed, a profitable entity with lots of room to run in a market that looks very big, and a great brokerage house sponsoring it. That was the case with Lululemon Athletica, a deal that Goldman Sachs brought public at $18 in 2007. I advised people that given the unique product, specialized yoga-based natural apparel for women, it was worth taking a flier on. The stock tripled quickly, but then it became absurdly valued to Under Armour and Nike and it, too, ran out of room to expand. The stock had to be sold once growth peaked, further hurt by some bad publicity that its clothes weren't as naturally made as advertised. It never recovered. So, the trick in all three of these situations is to recognize the size of the market, the power of the competitors, and to try to figure out how the company is valued versus these comps. As long as Under Armour and Lululemon considerably exceeded the growth rate of competitor Nike yet were valued relatively similarly, they were fine to hold on to. Once their growth rate slowed and their valuations were superior to Nike's, they had to be sold.

That kind of analysis works for every company, including the abstruse tech companies that come public: look at the addressable market, the competitors, and the historic growth rate of the company versus the growth rate of the market itself. If the company is profitable and the brokerage pedigree is good, you should put in for the deal. Sure, these deals are harder to understand, but that shouldn't prevent you from trying to capitalize on them if you follow the rules and don't pay too much for them. No matter what, I never want you to put in any aftermarket orders to get more stock. You will ruin your average price and possibly end up sacrificing the easy profit. While Lululemon and Under Armour did power higher after the initial first-day pop, those are the exceptions to the rule. Most deals are like the Heelys fiasco, one-day wonders that can hardly live up to their billing because they are faddish yet are so much more expensive than the seasoned players in their markets. On most deals we must follow the old adage of the Steve Miller Band and take the money and run!

My final concern is, as with secondaries, the pricing of the deal itself. Brokers love to entice you by announcing a very low initial range for every deal. This process is exactly the opposite of the secondary, where they start with a high price and work down. The brokers are trying to make a deal look hot by enticing clients to think they are getting a bargain. But as the deal gets talked up and management goes around the country touting itself—you can see the road show, as it is called, online, since the SEC has forced brokers to open up the process—the syndicate managers begin to raise the range of pricing the IPO. Typically the range slowly and subtly moves up, from $9 to $11, to $12 to $14, to $14 to $16 and so forth, to the inevitable, $19 to $20, which is the trajectory of the vast majority of IPOs in this well-orchestrated display of "hotness." Sometimes the ranges of the really hot ones double or even triple from the initial price talk, but those are rare. That's a sign that things are so hot that you can expect to get very little on the deal but it sure is worth trying to get some. However, on the typical deal you have to compare the company to other seasoned stalwarts in the industry. The process is the same as you would typically do before you buy any stock. You assess whether you are getting a bargain—is the growth rate higher but the price-to-earnings multiple lower than its competitors? Is it growing faster than its industry? Is it in a business that has great secular growth, like mobile Internet, or is it hostage to the growth of the economy and therefore shouldn't be paid up for? Once you figure out what it should sell for, you should tell your broker that you will pay a particular price, but not more than that, for the stock. You must be willing to pass up deals if you think you are getting caught up in the hoopla and are about to pay too much. The process is a stampeding one, so keep your head and don't get trampled.

IPOs are sexy, they are written about endlessly, they always seem like great deals, but take it from me, they are only great as enticements to get you back in the casino. Rarely do they bring you long-term rewards, even if they have the good seal of approval of major investment banks and track records, however long—and usually they aren't long at all. Stay close to them, try to get in on them. Don't turn up your nose on the boring or obscure ones if they are brought by major brokerages; those can be priced tightly enough, too, to make you some quick change. But I don't want you obsessing about them because you will most likely never get enough stock on the hottest ones to get you back to even. Nevertheless, they are a tool in your recovery arsenal and now you know what to look for, and what not to, in the coming thicket of IPOs that I expect will happen when the economy returns to normal and healthier levels.

We've covered two of the most important, most demanding methods you can use to make easy money quickly, to become a more opportunistic investor, but now we need to examine something of even greater significance so that you know to steer clear of it. Perhaps the most powerful change happening in the world of investing right now, a trend that threatens to actually take over trading in individual stocks, is the increased buying and selling of exchange-traded funds, or ETFs, and the rapid rise in the number and kind of ETFs available to investors. These pools of stocks that trade just like stocks, with far less hassle than investing in most active or passive mutual funds, are generally thought to be the ideal way for investors to get diversification and exposure to stocks without picking a clunker in a sector that you want to be in. I understand the need for these from the point of view of people who simply do not have the time to pick among a sector, like, say, the oil-drilling cohort to find the best driller, yet want exposure to higher oil prices and know that this group is acutely sensitive to the ebb and flow of the price of crude, far more so in fact than the oil stocks themselves.

I like the ETFs that track the prices of some of the commodities—but not all, as you shall see—particularly the GLD, which is a way to take advantage of the physical price of gold without having to own and store the bullion. That ETF literally buys gold for you, so as I indicated earlier you are going in lockstep with the direction of the precious metal, something that is more of a sure thing than owning a gold stock or two or even a gold stock index because gold stocks do not even purport to track the actual metal and are more plays on low finding costs and good production growth. I am comfortable with the ETFs that allow you to invest in countries that otherwise you would not be able to buy stocks in, particularly some of the Asian countries that don't allow U.S. investors to buy stocks directly. For my charitable trust ActionAlertsPlus.com, I have purchased the ETFs that allow you to track Chinese indices, particularly the I-shares FTSE Xinhua China 25, which is a way to diversify among twenty-five of the largest Chinese companies so you don't buy a fly-by-night Chinese equity or two—there are many in that notoriously poorly regulated market—and miss a great countrywide move. All of those ETFs make sense to me.

But I don't recommend the stock sector ETFs for anyone who actually has the smarts and the time to pick the good stocks from the bad. If you have come this far, I bet you know how to do that. I always feel that I can divine which stock is the best in a sector and would much rather own that particular equity than be forced to own all the bad with the good in a sector ETF. After all, I am first and foremost a stock picker, not a sector picker. Even when I play "Am I Diversified" on *Mad Money* on Wednesdays, where I tell callers whether their five-stock portfolio is diversified, I can't resist offering qualitative opinions on each stock, too. You want exposure to oil drilling? You want Transocean and Schlumberger; the rest are second-rate. You want exposure to steel? Why buy a steel ETF when you can own Nucor, a vastly superior steel company with great management and a terrific dividend. I can go on and on for just about every sector ETF. I am also greatly concerned that people who buy sector ETFs actually think they are therefore diversified among many stocks. Of course, the opposite is true; you are putting all of your eggs in one basket. People who choose this method should be choosing five ETFs among different sectors if they actually want to be diversified. (For the make-up and quality judgments on the representation of ETFs and the sector, read Don Dion's excellent work in TheStreet.com. He is an invaluable guide to the ETF thicket.) No matter, people have fallen for these ETFs, in part because they perceive that the alternative is to buy sector mutual funds, and those are horribly inefficient, with high costs and, often, restrictive terms on how you can enter and exit the funds. Those rules, set up to avoid the gaming of mutual fund timing, make sense if you are going to use sector mutual funds as a *long-term* diversification tool, but they are impractical as a way to quickly allocate capital from one sector to another. So, the industry created sector ETFs to fill that vacuum, allowing investors to get sector-wide exposure without sacrificing flexibility. At this point, these products have become so popular that, on some days, ETFs will represent close to 35 percent of the volume of trading at some of the bigger brokerage houses. I know I can't fight them—and to be fair, most of the uses people put ETFs to aren't objectionable. But I can help police the most dangerous of them for you, because not all ETFs are created equally; some are a heck of a lot more equal than others.

The rise of ETFs as a means of diversifying your portfolio is fairly harmless, but the widespread and conventionally accepted idea that you can use ETFs to hedge risk is incredibly hazardous to your financial health. ETFs are constantly being promoted for zillions of different purposes, and they come in numerous different varieties, but if you remember only one thing about them, remember this: don't try to use ETFs to hedge risk—especially the ones that are most commonly suggested for just that role, because many of them don't do what you, or most nonprofessional investors and even some pros, think they do. And nothing is more dangerous than buying something that you believe you comprehend only to later realize you were completely wrong about what was happening.

You see, there are two kinds of ETFs: the ones that simply track sectors, and the ones that track sectors and allow you to make a leveraged bet, short or long, on that sector. The former are fine; the latter are toxic and should never have been invented, and certainly never been permitted by the Securities and Exchange Commission. In fact, I have tried mightily to have them banned, but it has been an uphill battle, since the issuers of these leveraged ETFs somehow managed to convince the SEC that the public understands the risks and hazards of using them. I would laugh at the absurdity of this notion if it hadn't already lost people so much money.

First, so you can really understand the stakes, let me give you some background. After the crash of 1929, the Federal Reserve decided that one of the precipitating causes of that massive decline came from the reckless use of margin. People didn't understand that when they borrowed money to make purchases they could end up owing more than they owned if the stocks went down. So to protect you the Federal Reserve limited the amount of leverage you could use. The rules can be changed by the Fed but the essence is simple: you typically can't borrow more than 50 percent of what you own.

However, the creators of the ETFs hit upon a truly ingenious way to get around the margin rules. They created products that were already juiced: ETFs that could give you double or even triple the amount of buying or selling power for each dollar you put down. Unfortunately, the SEC didn't seem to understand the power of these instruments or how they even worked, and it began to bless one leveraged ETF after another, until they have proliferated like cockroaches. I regard these leveraged ETFs, which are ostensibly supposed to help you hedge risk, as weapons of financial mass destruction, aimed directly at whatever poor, misinformed investor buys them and makes the perilous mistake of assuming these products do what most of us expect them to. (The Fed, which should be policing margin in the system, seems to have delegated it completely to the SEC, which doesn't seem to care at all about the consequences to the little guy.)

What do I mean when these double and triple ETFs don't do what you think? How about I give you some facts and let you decide for yourself, okay? You're about to see why I think these ETFs, in combination with their ever-growing popularity, are so important and so darned dangerous. Let's take an example that I've often used on *Mad Money*. It's my absolute least favorite member of the entire leveraged ETF cohort, the UltraShort Financials ProShares or SKF, its ticker symbol. People look at this ETF, which is what is known as a double-short fund, and see something that lets you put down a dollar and have the SKF give you $2 of short exposure to the Dow Jones U.S. Financials Index. So, theoretically, the SKF is the kind of ETF you would want to buy if you owned some financials, were worried about a decline, and wanted a hedge against the potential downside. And that would make perfect sense, except that that's not actually what the SKF, or any of the double- or triple-levered ETFs, really do. You would think that if the Dow Jones U.S. Financials Index declined by 10 percent, well, then the SKF would advance by 20 percent, right? Isn't that intuitive? That seems to be what everyone thinks when they look at these ETFs. Yes, it's what most people think, but it's completely wrong. The leveraged so-called inverse, meaning short, ETFs, simply don't reflect the opposite of the index as most people believe.

What do they actually reflect? Well, I can prove it's not the opposite of the indices they track multiplied by 2. Let's take four leveraged ETF examples. Suppose you made the best four investing decisions of your life back in 2008 and decided to short real estate, Chinese stocks, and the oil and gas stocks in addition to the financials—four of the worst-performing sectors in the market that year by far, utter disasters, frankly. Anyone outright short them should have made a fortune and could have retired immediately after those fantastic bets. Now, suppose you decided to short each of these areas with one of the UltraShort ProShares ETFs? There's already the SKF, the UltraShort banking ETF, the FXP, the UltraShort China ETF, the DUG, which does the same for oil and gas, and then the SRS to double-short real estate. How do you think you would have done if you not only bet against the year's worst four sectors, but also doubled down? Well, if you used those ETFs, altogether they would have produced a 30 percent loss over the course of 2008. That's right, a loss. A megaloss! These instruments that purport to capitalize on the downside fell hard—they didn't rise straight up, as investors thought they would, even though oil, real estate, everything else had been completely pulverized and laid to waste. Now, if you had simply shorted each of the four indices that these ETFs claim to hit with double the selling firepower, then that would have given you a 48 percent gain, which would have become a 97 percent gain if you had truly been able to double-short everything. To put it another way, going negative on the banks, on China, on real estate and on oil and gas in 2008? Those could have been life-changing wins and career-making calls for most professionals. But instead of a 97 percent gain, these absurd ETFs, although they don't directly mislead anyone because they are marketed as daily hedges, managed to fool both professionals and amateurs alike into thinking they were going to be protected or be profiting from the downside.

How the heck does that happen? How could you lose money on both your hedge and what it was trying to protect? The SKF, SRS, FXP, and DUG all were pretty imperfect hedges, and, in fact, there had never been any serious evidence that these things worked or made sense to hedge with in the first place. These products obviously have some relationship with the indices they're supposed to be shorting with massive leverage, but the strength of those relationships seems to erode over time. The thing that became most important, surprisingly enough, was the market's volatility—the more volatility, the more it eats into the returns of these double-bear inverse ETFs. How does that work? Remember, all the UltraShort ProShares ETFs are supposed to be short various different passive indices, and each ETF needs to be reset daily so it can be rebalanced to reflect the makeup of the index. That rebalancing can take a major bite out of your returns, and the more volatile the market, the larger your volatility-related losses from these double-short ETFs become, something that's been documented extensively by Eric Oberg, my colleague at TheStreet .com, a man who spent seventeen years toiling in the derivative vineyard of Goldman Sachs before retiring as a managing director. What we see here is that all of these leveraged ETFs are meant only for day traders, because they simply do not work over any longer period, as the volatility warps their performance.

Not only are they bad hedges, they're about as bad as it gets. ProShares and Direxion, the two main producers of these insidious leveraged ETFs, acknowledge that their products are only for tracking daily changes. They recognize in the prospectus of their products that daily changes will not correlate with long-term changes because of the need to rebalance the index every day to reflect the losses or gains of the index companies. So basically each instrument starts at zero every day and can't possibly work as longer-term hedges the way shorting the individual stocks would. Many day traders understand that these are just daily wagers on the indices, but the vast majority of people I talk to and who call in on *Mad Money* or email me at The Street.com are simply baffled at best, and far more often furious that they lost money both on the investments they are trying to hedge and the hedges themselves.

So, if you work at a bank and own stock in your company and you want to protect it by shorting the finance sector, the last thing you want to do is play with one of these double shorts. If you are worried about the stock of your company your only hope is to be as diversified away from it as much as possible with your other holdings. If you simply own a bank stock, *do not* try to protect it with a double- or triple-short instrument. I am virtually guaranteeing that you will lose both ways.

In addition to the leveraged ETFs, there is one more variety of ETF that doesn't work as you would expect: ETFs that track oil prices. Again, I just want to help police the worst aspect of what's become a huge feature in the investing landscape. You would think that the oil ETFs essentially mimic the returns you would get by buying crude—that ETFs that track crude prices are simply an easier way for regular people to buy the commodity, just as the inverse ETFs with double or triple leverage should make it easy for people to short stock and evade the margin rules. In reality, that's not how the oil ETFs operate. The oil ETFs have consistently underperformed compared to the oil prices they're supposed to track, because of basic structural problems with the way these funds are put together. The most widely traded and most troubled in the group is the U.S. Oil Fund, USO.

What's wrong with the USO? Unlike, say, the GLD, the ETF that buys the physical gold with the money put into it, the USO buys futures, not actual oil. Owning the ETF may be easier than the owning the commodity, but you pay a price. When oil was going higher in its big multiyear run, you did much worse owning the USO to capture the upside than if you'd just owned crude. When it was going lower, you lost more money in the USO than you did if you owned crude. And now that oil prices have recovered, the USO is once again lagging. There is no reason for you to own this kind of ETF. The fund companies that create and sell these ETFs make tons of money from you, but they're not making money *for* you. So how the heck is it that an ETF that's supposed to track oil has managed to underperform the commodity so dramatically? It's all about how the ETF works.

The USO is designed to track the price of West Texas Intermediate light sweet crude, but it's not a direct play on oil. It doesn't own the oil. The ETF tracks light sweet crude prices by buying listed crude oil futures contracts and similar derivatives. The problem is that these futures contracts have a limited shelf life; they expire, making it impossible for the USO to remain indefinitely invested. Every month USO has to roll its contracts forward—so once a month, over a period of four days, the USO sells its expiring contracts and buys new ones for the following month.

That's where the underperformance comes from. In periods where the oil futures market is in what's called *contango*—an important piece of Wall Street gibberish meaning when the price of a commodity for future delivery is more expensive than the spot price, that is, when future oil costs more than the oil that's selling right now—then the USO is buying futures contracts that are more expensive than the ones it's selling, month after month, cutting heavily into its performance. That's a built-in friction problem, and it's why the USO and all the other oil ETFs should be avoided. It's not nearly as bad as the leveraged inverse ETFs like the SKF, but it's still a pitfall of the new, ETF-filled environment to be shunned like a leper. The people running the USO aren't doing anything wrong. They warn investors about this in their prospectus, but I bet most of the people buying this thing don't read the prospectus, and I'm sure anyone buying the leveraged ETFs for more than a trading day hasn't even glanced at a prospectus. In this case I'm doing the homework for you to spare you the pain so you can focus on making money opportunistically in secondaries and IPOs, and avoid loser ETFs.

There are plenty of other ETFs to be wary of, including all of the newfangled ones that seem to pop up for every single fad out there. When wind and wind turbine stocks were hot, the ETF creators quickly put together an ETF of the hottest wind stocks, something that's just a cheap trick to capitalize on a trend that, by the time they whip it up, has almost always peaked. I don't mind those, if only because anyone stupid to buy into fads well after they are defined and exploited deserves to be taken to the cleaners. I just worry that unless the government steps forward and demands that these double and triple ETFs be reined in or closed so long as they fail to do what people think they do as well as skirt the margin rules that are meant to protect people and the markets from willy-nilly volatility, these instruments will plague investors and our markets for years to come and will drive the unsuspecting investors out of the game. These ETFs are creatures of the days of deregulation under the SEC chaired by Christopher Cox, days when anything went and the playing field, leveled by years and years of regulation, became heavily tilted again toward the big boys, particularly the short sellers, leaving regular Joes unprotected. Protect yourself. Don't use them. They don't work. They are the surest things to stop you from getting back to even that man has ever created, and let's hope the regulators come to their senses and shut 'em all down.

The new landscape is treacherous but filled with opportunity. If you can avoid the pitfalls and exploit the gifts, you'll get revenge in a profitable way. But if you fall prey to false products and the snake-oil salespeople who produce them, you will never get back to even.

AFTERWORD

I dedicated this book to Ben Bernanke for a simple reason: without him I don't think we could ever hope to get back to even with our finances. The Federal Reserve chairman has done so much to nurse a deathly ill patient—the U.S. economy—back to where it has a chance of thriving again that I am now confident we can make money, not just lose it, by buying the right stocks and ridding ourselves of the wrong ones. But the damage that came from Bernanke's being late to recognize the dangers of the calamity, plus the lassitude and indifference of the Bush administration toward the looming financial meltdown, have left us with an investing landscape that's been changed, and it isn't for the better.

Hopefully with this book we've learned that no matter what awaits us—a return to the bear, a continuation of the bull—the investing world has become far more difficult to fathom than the pre-crash era. There are opportunities galore, as I have tried mightily to show you, but we must never again view stocks as some sort of cash machine that will be ready at a moment's notice to pay for our important purchases or for our imminent retirement or for those extras in life that we deserve after working so hard and taking home less and less, a legacy of our nation's profligacy and the subsequent need for our government to balance its books.

I hope you have discovered that in this new kind of environment, old lessons such as buy and hold and inactive management of your money no longer work. They have failed us—definitively failed—as anyone who simply took a beating the last few years, relying on such simple and misguided precepts, can tell you. Instead, I have tried to replace them here with a new ethos, one based on buying and doing homework to see if the situations we invest in have changed for the worse, as so many companies have failed to measure up to this brutal environment. I have made the case for sidestepping the financial wrecking ball when we have the ability to see it coming. I have tried to give you the grounding to face the facts of this much more daunting firmament and given you new rules to help you adjust to it. You've been presented with the stocks that can and have weathered the storm, as well as those that I believe will be the best ways to play the inevitable recovery that Ben Bernanke has steered us toward. I have stressed the worth of dividends as a way to measure a stock's health in this more fluid, more dangerous time, as well as offering you those stocks with yields just bountiful enough to give you a return no matter how treacherous the future may be, even though I believe that the crash is definitively behind us. You now have the larger investing themes that you can return to over and over during the fits and starts of a stock market that will always accompany a sick economic patient being pumped back to life using governmental measures, not the strength of a hobbled private sector.

Last, I have opened your eyes to the most sophisticated weapons I kept in my arsenal at my old hedge fund, when I needed to get back to even and get back to even quickly with the least amount of risk and the most amount of reward, while showing you the pitfalls of other instruments that, though designed to get you there, will undermine your wealth, not augment it.

Now it is your turn to pick and choose, to figure out your tolerance and your trajectory for how and when you want to rebuild your capital. The ways needed are active, not passive, and far more time-consuming than any of us would like. But these are not ordinary times and may not be for years and years to come. The need for extreme caution has passed, the need to be opportunistic with intelligence and skill is upon us. Take advantage using these rules, these methods, these themes, these stocks, and we will work together to get us back to where our investments were, and hopefully restore our wealth, not overnight, but over time. As always with my suggestions and strategies, please do the homework. If you do not have the time or the inclination to employ the more difficult of my tactics, stock replacement and options insurance, please rely on the less challenging but just as rigorous work to benefit from the gift of dividends and the economic recovery that will always be in store for us.

I hope one day that investing will be fun once more and that my lifetime obsession with stocks can help you accumulate wealth with interest and aplomb. But I am realistic; no matter what Bernanke does, no matter what the federal government delivers, no matter what I do, getting back to even requires hard work and lots of pain before we can even get to gain. I do feel confident, however, that we can at last put the past behind us and start anew as better, more realistic and sophisticated investors, ones who will never again take for granted that the stock market alone will make us rich on its inevitable climb upward. We've lost too much to return to that level of complacency. We can't rely on buying and holding so-called blue chip stocks or investing in mindless indices to get us where we want to go. Hard work, skill, and perseverance are the only true ways to rebuild our capital to the levels we need to survive the post-crash era and rebuild our wealth as soon as possible with the least amount of risk and the most amount of reward.

ACKNOWLEDGMENTS

Once again, my thanks go out to all my viewers and readers, especially those of you who have taken the time to call or email or just walk up to me on the street to ask how the heck you can get through this mess without losing your shirt. I don't think I could do what I do—any of it—if not for your enthusiastic support. Let me make it clear: stop apologizing! You are not bothering me when you stop me on the road or at home; I love it and I will thank you for watching the show and reading me on the web. I learn from everyone, so keep teaching me.

While it might seem like everything I do is a one-man show, the truth is that there are multitudes of hardworking people behind the curtain who make it all possible. As ever, all the folks at Simon & Schuster who made this book a reality have my eternal gratitude, with special thanks to Bob Bender, the best financial editor on earth, whom I continue to have the pleasure of working with, and David Rosenthal, the publisher and the man who convinced me to start writing books all the way back with *Confessions of a Street Addict*. They both inspire and nudge, and believe me, I am always in need of both! I also have to thank all the other people who work for the best publishing house in the universe and deserve credit for making this book a reality: Johanna Li, Phil Metcalf, Tom Pitoniak, Victoria Meyer,

Judith Hoover, Rebecca Davis, Leah Wasielewski, and the always incredible Aileen Boyle, the terrific associate publisher who knows how get the word out about a new book better than anyone.

Thanks to everyone at NBC Universal and CNBC who, for whatever crazy reason, continue to give me a soapbox and a megaphone every weeknight with *Mad Money*, as there's nothing more enjoyable than having your own national television show. I will always owe a huge debt to Mark Hoffman, the fantastic CEO of CNBC, who gave us the backing to do a new and entirely different kind of show about stocks and investing, and not only has allowed the spectacle to continue but also has never stopped promoting or protecting the franchise. Thanks as well to the fabulous Jeff Zucker, the top dog at NBC Universal, for believing in *Mad Money* and standing behind both the show and me when it really counted. People say that there's no loyalty in the TV business, but Zucker is proof positive that the opposite is true. I also want to thank Jeff Immelt, the CEO of General Electric, who has been unwavering in his support of the show and is a staunch proponent of the *Mad Money* ethos of telling it like it is.

Put simply: I have the best bosses in the world. I hope you get to work for people as great as Hoffman, Zucker, and Immelt.

Thanks to all who make the show happen on a daily basis: Kyle Remaly and Keith Greenwood, who work their butts off to keep me sane "on the floor" of the show; Bryan Russo, our brilliant director, who is responsible for the show's "look and feel"; Laura Koski, who makes me up everyday and is responsible for my "look and feel"; Kat Ricker, George Manessis, Heather Butler, Chris Schwartz, Candy "Props" Cheng, Kate Welsh, Jackie Fabozzi, Tim Dewald, Kareem Bynes, Justin Johansky, and Henry Fraga, who come to play every day—I can't praise you guys enough. Special thanks as well to CNBC'ers Brian Steel, Jen Dauble, Tom Clendenin, and Steve Smith, who do so much to promote and defend the show and have our backs every minute of the day and night. And speaking of having our backs and defending *Mad Money*, few have done more at CNBC than Aisha Royall, who's always been there when it counted. I would be remiss if

I didn't express my endless gratitude to the wonderful and fabulous Erin Burnett for being such a fantastic teammate on *Stop Trading* every day and not treating me like a lunatic, no matter how much I might seem like one when I rant and rave. Most of all I want to thank Regina Gilgan, *Mad Money*'s executive producer, who is the heart and soul of the show, as well as the best new mom in the world. To put it simply, there would be no *Mad Money* without Regina.

Special thanks as well to Stephanie Link, the amazing research director for ActionAlertsPlus.com, who helps me deliver the best portfolio product in the world and is an exacting and disciplined analyst; to Sanket Patel, the show's chief researcher, and Dave Peltier, for their help on a day-to-day basis and their assistance with this book; and to everyone else at TheStreet.com, especially our new CEO Daryl Otte, who is leading us to new heights. Thank you to RealMoney's Doug Kass, for helping me call a once-in-a-generation bottom in March. Let's hope it stands! Special thanks to Bucknell professor and TheStreet.com board member William R. Gruver, one of my oldest friends, dating from the days when he taught me everything at Goldman Sachs. Bill's the hardest working director at any public company in America. Bill, I don't know how you do it. Thanks to Glenn Hall and Bill McCandless of TheStreet.com for their excellent editing and video skills. And of course, I don't know how I would do anything without the help of Deb Slater, who has been managing my hectic schedule and running my life—like a well-oiled machine—for years. Eric Oberg, Rick Bensignor, Ron Insana, and Don Dion, all great contributors to TheStreet.com, have helped me immensely in figuring out this difficult new landscape.

Much love as well to my fabulous agents, Suzanne Gluck and Henry Reisch: you two are simply without peer. Thanks as well to my lawyer, Bruce Birenboim, who has the hardest job in the world—keeping me out of trouble! A hearty thanks to Jon Gluck, my excellent editor for years and years at *New York* magazine.

A devoted thanks to Matt Horween, who provides common sense, humor, and an even keel about all things business and personal. Matt, my forensic accountant, has the best judgment of anyone in the business world.

Also to Lisa Detwiler, for once again putting up with me and all the angst that comes along with a project like this one, something that I consider to be the height of selflessness. She was nominated for sainthood after *Stay Mad for Life*, now *Getting Back to Even* secures the title. I promise the chaos that is writing a book will never happen again . . . until the next one. And of course, endless thanks to my father, Ken Cramer, for teaching me the important things about business and life from a very early age, and my sister, Nan, and her husband, Todd Mason, for always being there for me, another totally thankless job.

Best for last, thanks to Cliff Mason, my coauthor and head writer for *Mad Money*. There would be no book without Cliff. More important, without Cliff Mason, *Mad Money* would have disappeared a long time ago, and I would have just gone back to being a money manager. He makes all the effort fun, worthwhile, and smart. He is the show's minister of offense and my minister of defense. I'd just be a dollar sign represented by a man without him.

INDEX

accidental high-yielders, 31, 79, 88–91
acquisitions, 73
ActionAlertsPlus.com, 17–18, 55, 76, 110–11, 231, 279, 326
    newsletter for, 112
actively managed portfolios, criticisms of, 16–17, 18
Advance/Decline Index, 241
Aeropostale (ARO), 289, 290
aerospace, 50
Aetna (AET), 256–57
Africa, 114
Agnico-Eagle (AEM), 53–54
Agrium (AGU), 273
AIG (AIG), 6, 8, 31, 253, 254, 267, 285, 286
Alcoa (AA), 253, 262
Allende, Salvador, 53
Alliance, 259
Altria (MO), 76–77, 78
AMD, 201, 270
American Express (AXP), 138, 290
American Gold Eagle, 53
Anadarko, 270
Analog Devices (ADI), 231
Anheuser Busch, 62
Animal Farm (Orwell), 44
annual reports (10K), 37, 50
Apache, 270
Apple (AAPL), 27–28, 33, 227, 228, 229, 230, 231–32, 237, 263, 264, 266, 269, 270, 271, 290
Archer Daniels Midland, 62
Asia, 116, 122
asset-backed securities (ABS), 141
AT&T (T), 68, 105, 231

"at-the-money" call, 176, 178, 179, 181, 185
Australia, 127
auto loans, 141
automobiles, 265

Bair, Sheila, 21
balance sheets, 37–39, 115, 117, 121, 127, 134, 136
balance-sheet test, 95, 97–98, 115
Baltic Dry Freight Index, 240–41, 273
BankBoston, 144
Bank of America (BAC), 143, 144, 158, 260, 262, 270, 275, 278, 305, 309, 310
Bank of New England, 143, 144, 153
Bank of New York, 309
Bank One, 143
bankruptcy, 39
banks, 2, 51, 106, 140–63, 234, 257, 271, 282, 301
    call for nationalization of, 278
    dividends paid by, 75
    failures of, 140–41, 143–44
    key metrics of, 150–51, 152
    regional, 143–44, 146–63
    stress tests on, 148, 278
BB&T (BBT), 276, 311–14
bear markets, 247–49
bear raids, 81–82, 235
Bear Stearns, 6, 32
Bensignor, Rick, 244, 260
Benton, Dan, 321
Berkshire Hathaway, 184
Bernanke, Ben, 37, 275, 284, 335, 336
Best Buy (BBY), 266, 270

Bethlehem Steel, 35–36
BHP Billiton (BHP), 126–28
Biggie Smalls, 62
Big Lots (BIG), 260
BlackBerries, 228, 229, 231
Blackstone, 319
Blake, Frank, 131
Blank, Arthur, 131
blue chip stocks, 6, 7, 8, 15
Boeing, 145
bonds, 2, 58, 76, 93, 106, 164, 210, 212,
    221, 240, 278, 303, 305–6
  in 401(k)s, 216
  risk of, 208
  stocks vs., 85, 207, 208, 213
  see also Treasurys, U.S.
BP (BP), 89, 124, 270
BP Prudhoe Bay Royalty Trust (BPT),
    217–18
Brin, Sergey, 319
Brinker, 64
Bristol-Myers Squibb (BMY), 103
Broadcom (BRCM), 231, 269, 273
brokerage houses, 303, 320, 321, 323
Bucyrus International (BUCY), 273
bull market selloffs, 29, 270–71
Bunch, Charles, 123
Burger King (BKC), 264
Burke, Kevin, 104
Burlington Northern (BNI), 273
Bush, George W., 158
BusinessWeek, 170
buy-and-hold strategy, 7, 9–11, 16, 17,
    20–21, 23–24, 29, 36, 43, 44, 118,
    147
buy and homework strategy, 7–8, 43, 45,
    54, 61–62, 63–64, 109, 118, 166, 235
buybacks, 126, 238, 256–58

"calendar" spreading, 203
call options, 164, 165, 167, 169, 172,
    173–87, 190, 191, 192–96, 197–200,
    201, 202–3, 221, 233, 235
camera, 229
Canada, 53, 116, 125, 130, 132
cap-and-trade, 104
capital appreciation, 15, 41–42, 74
capital gains tax, 214
Capital One, 138, 309

capital preservation, 41, 42, 74, 213
Carlyle Group, 319
Carnival Cruise Lines (CCL), 289
cars, 22, 38
Case-Shiller Home Price Index, 279
Cass, Doug, 262
Caterpillar (CAT), 113–16, 117, 132, 262,
    273
cell phones, 228
Cerebrus, 319
certificates of deposit (CDs), 21, 93, 213
charge-off-to-loan ratio, 154, 157, 161
charitable trust, 17–18
Chevron (CVX), 55, 89, 125, 270
Chili's, 64
China, 110, 114, 116, 120, 123, 125, 126,
    127, 130, 132, 218, 240–41, 272–73,
    300, 326, 329, 330
China Unicom, 231
Chipotle (CMG), 290
Chittenden, 161
chloralkali chemicals, 122
Chrysler, 131
Ciena, 269
Cisco, 26, 227, 270
Citigroup (C), 6, 15, 30, 253, 254, 262, 278,
    286, 311
climate change, 104
CNBC, 11, 58, 222
coal, 104, 127, 241
Coca-Cola (KO), 297
Colgate (CG), 36, 37, 264
college funds, 5, 13, 22, 25, 40
commercial loans, 148, 151
commercial real estate, 142
commodities, 2, 265, 299
commodity collapse, 243–44
competition, 93
compound interest, 84
computers, 129, 130, 228, 266
Congress, U.S., 104
ConocoPhillips (COP), 55, 123–26
conservative strategy, 165–66, 187–88
Consolidated Edison (ED), 104
contango, 333
copper, 127, 244, 298–99
Corning, 266
corporate bonds, 58, 212, 305
corporate earnings, 109, 111

corporate taxes, 217
Costco, 123
Countrywide, 148
coupon, 305
coverage ratio, 96
Cox, Christopher, 333
CPI, 211
Cramer Berkowitz & Company (hedge
     fund), 2, 4–5, 6, 17, 45, 157, 162–63,
     165, 235, 240, 246, 250
credit cards, 1, 43, 141
     see also Visa (V)
credit crisis, 12, 140, 141, 145, 160,
     264–65, 304
credit markets, 303–4, 306
credit rating, 98
Credit Suisse, 321
CSX (CSX), 273
current liabilities line, 38
cycles, 69
cyclical stocks, 35, 36, 57, 79, 111, 112,
     115–16, 145, 227, 287–88

Darden (DRI), 64, 289
deadbeat ratio, 151, 152, 154, 157, 160–61
debt, 306, 310
"deep-in-the-money" call, 185–86, 187,
     190–91, 198, 200, 221–22, 235
defense, 51
deleveraging, 304
Dell, Michael, 27
Dell (DELL), 27–28, 129, 227, 263, 264
deposits, 150–51, 152
Dershowitz, Alan, 170, 171
Dimon, Jamie, 134, 136, 149
Dion, Don, 327
Direxion, 331
disability insurance, 39, 44
discretionary stream of investment, 24, 80
diversification, 42, 49–51, 54–58, 60, 113,
     138
     ETFs and, 325
     for retirement money, 215
dividends, 11, 43, 54, 73–107, 111, 126,
     171, 209, 218, 234, 311
     of bank stocks, 155, 156
     buybacks vs., 256, 257–58
     cuts in, 90, 93
     of health care companies, 256

historical yield of, 87
moderate-to-large, 74
outsized, 31
as paid by mature companies, 76
payout of, 76
of PPG, 121
of preferred stocks, 106
reinvestment of, 22–23, 83, 84, 86, 96
by sector, 75, 101
tax breaks on, 93
taxes on, 214
as technical indicator, 295
yield support of, 80–82, 98–99, 257
     see also yields
Dividend Stock Advisor (Peltier), 101–2
Donne, John, 59
dot-com boom and bust, 6, 27, 226,
     285
double-short funds, 329
Dow Chemical (DOW), 121, 122
Dow Jones Industrial Average, 2, 4, 8,
     23, 31, 116, 222, 224, 247, 253, 255,
     261–62, 293, 329
Downey Savings, 148
Dreamliner, 145
drug companies, 238, 296, 297
dumb money, 245–47
DuPont (DD), 121, 122

earnings, 266, 288
earnings coverage, 96–97
earnings growth, 225
earnings per share, 33, 99, 236, 237, 257
earnings test, 95–96
Eaton, 90–91
eBay, 269
economic growth, 94, 109
economic recovery, 108–9, 120, 121, 128,
     188, 273
economists, 277–79
Eldorado Gold (EGO), 53, 54
electricity, 104
Electronic Data Systems (EDS), 129–30
Eli Lilly (LLY), 102–4
email, 229
EMC, 227
emerging markets, 118
Emerson Electric (EMR), 87–88, 89, 91,
     117–19

EnCana (ECA), 125
energy, 50
energy trusts, 216–17
Erbitux, 103
Ericsson, 230
Europe, 114, 122
exchange-traded funds (ETFs), 52, 53, 102, 105, 106, 240, 290, 291
  inverse, 292, 328–30, 331
ex-date, 77, 78
exports, 283
Exxon (XOM), 124, 125, 171–72, 173–74, 175–76, 177, 178, 179, 181–82, 184, 185, 193–97

F-5, 269
Fair Disclosure (Regulation FD), 235
Fannie Mae (FNM), 8, 32, 267, 268
FDIC, 21–22, 140, 143, 146, 148, 149, 150, 153, 154, 155, 159, 160, 161, 162
Federal Deposit Insurance Corporation (FDIC), 212–13
Federal Home Loan Bank Board, 268
Federal Realty, 220
Federal Reserve, 93, 94, 111–12, 141, 145, 148, 151, 197, 204, 211, 212, 328, 329, 335
fertilizer, 244
fiberglass, 122
Fidelity, 22, 259
Fifth Third (FITB), 153, 278
finance, 50
First Company, 152
FirstMerit (FMER), 153–55, 162
First Niagara Financial Group (FNFG), 155–57, 162
Fitzpatrick, Dan, 260
$5 rule, 185, 186, 187
529 plan, 24–25
flat glass, 122
Fleet Bank, 143–44, 145, 146, 147, 149, 153, 156, 157, 162
float, 72
food companies, 238, 296, 297
Forbes, 170
Ford (F), 35, 57, 276, 309, 311
Fortress Investment Group, 310
4G (fourth generation) semiconductor patents, 231

401(k)s, 1, 7, 12, 15, 16, 24–25, 43, 214
  employers' matching of, 215–16
  IRAs vs., 216
  management fees of, 216
  tax breaks on, 214, 215
Freddie Mac (FRE), 8, 32, 267, 268
free cash-flow test, 95, 96–97
Freeport McMoRan (FCX), 127, 243, 298–99
fundamentals, fundamental analysis, 60–65, 72, 73, 170, 229, 242, 259, 261, 271, 274, 285, 299
  of IPOs, 318
  for options trading, 166
  for secondary offering, 310
fund-of-fund managers, 243

Galbraith, John Kenneth, 14
Geithner, Tim, 37
General Electric (GE), 15, 262
General Growth Properties, 220
General Mills (GIS), 32, 36, 37, 57, 255
General Motors (GM), 6, 8, 14, 23, 30, 31, 253, 254, 267–68, 285, 286
generation Y, 82
Germany, Weimar, 212, 281, 283–84
Glacier Bancorp (GBCI), 150–53, 162
glass computer screens, 116
GLD, *see* SPDR Gold Shares
gold, 2, 16, 51–54, 58, 59, 222, 239–40, 290, 326
Goldman Sachs (GS), 18, 52, 118, 134, 149, 162, 244, 261, 290, 310, 316, 321, 323, 331
Google (GOOG), 167–70, 184, 202, 203, 227, 269, 271, 285, 319
  options on, 168, 169, 184–85, 186–87, 197–200
  volatility of, 168, 184, 185, 197
grain, 241
Great Crash, The (Galbraith), 14
Great Depression, 1, 13, 14, 24, 25, 43, 90, 109, 136, 224, 257, 287
Great Plains Energy (GXP), 98
Greig, Paul, 155
gross domestic product, 69, 94, 109
Grove, Andy, 228
growth stocks, 101, 225
growth-to-value risk, 226

Halliburton, 270
Hansson, Herbjorn, 219, 220
hardware, 129
Harleysville National, 156
Harvard Law School, 170
health care, 50, 51, 104, 116
health-care stocks, 20
health insurance, 39, 44
hedge funds, 2, 4–5, 6, 17, 45, 55, 59, 66,
    67, 68–69, 81, 112, 134, 142, 146, 157,
    162–63, 165, 190, 203, 221, 235, 240,
    242–43, 244, 245, 246, 250, 252,
    254–55, 284, 296, 297, 300, 310, 312
hedging, 51–52, 290–93, 328
Heelys, 322
Heinz (HNZ), 34, 36, 297
Hewlett Packard (HPQ), 128–30, 227, 270
HMOs, 257
Home Depot (HD), 72, 130–31
home equity loans, 156
Honeywell (HON), 88, 89
house flipping, 40
housing bubble and crash, 1, 3, 4, 13, 22,
    40, 51, 82, 209
housing-related stocks, 63
Huntington Bancshares (HBAN), 153
Hurd, Mark, 128
hyperinflation, 212, 283–84

IBM, 227
ImClone, 103
index funds, 17, 18, 19, 40, 42–43, 44
India, 123
indicators, 238–42, 293–95
individual retirement accounts (IRAs), 1,
    12, 15, 16, 24, 43, 53, 74, 101, 214,
    215, 216, 220
  401(k)s vs., 216
  tax breaks on, 214, 215, 218
Indonesia, 125
industrial manufacturing, 50
IndyMac, 148
inflation, 51–52, 53, 81, 100, 128, 211–12,
    239–40, 283–84
information, 63–64
infrastructure, 50
initial public offerings (IPOs), 304, 307–8,
    314–25
  ensuring profits on, 318–24

In Motion, 230
Intel (INTC), 26, 28, 76, 145, 201–2, 227,
    228, 270, 276
Intel 486 microprocessor, 227
interest rates, 21, 81, 93–94, 100, 111–12,
    151, 197, 212
Internet, 228, 231
"in-the-money" call, 176, 177, 181–84,
    195, 204
inventory, 264–66
inverse ETFs, 292, 328–30, 331
investment bank, 305, 316
iPhone, 28, 105, 145, 228, 229, 230,
    232, 237
iPod, 27, 145, 237
iron, 241
I-shares FTSE Xinhua China 25, 326
iTunes store, 28, 143, 230

Janus, 259
Japan, 281–83
*Jim Cramer's Mad Money: Watch TV, Get
    Rich*, 289
Jobs, Steve, 27, 230
Johnson & Johnson (JNJ), 36, 92,
    255
Joy Global (JOYG), 273
JPMorgan Chase (JPM), 32, 134–36,
    138, 142, 143, 148–49, 162, 261,
    262, 270, 310
Juniper, 270
Justice Department, U.S., Antitrust
    Division of, 155–56, 158

Kellogg (K), 32, 33, 36, 92
Key (KEY), 278
key metrics, 150–51
Keynes, John Maynard, 261
Kimberly-Clark (KMB), 36, 62
Kinder Morgan Energy Partners (KMP),
    106–7, 217
KKR, 319, 320
Kodak, 6
Kraft (KFT), 34, 36
Krugman, Paul, 278

Latin America, 114, 116, 122
Lehman Brothers, 6, 8, 23, 31, 32,
    61, 149, 255, 272, 278, 286

leveraged buyout firms, *see* private equity firms
liabilities, 38
life insurance, 39
LINN Energy (LINE), 217, 218
loans, 141, 148, 150–51, 152, 155, 156, 159, 303
long-call, short-common, 191–204
long-term investments, 26, 47, 61, 72
Lowe's (LOW), 130–31
Lukoil, 125
Lululemon Athletica, 323, 324

McDonald's, 264
Macintosh, 230
Mad Money (TV show), 8, 12, 18, 21, 29, 33, 41, 44, 49, 58, 62, 71, 74, 84, 88, 90, 98, 111, 123, 131, 158, 214, 219, 222, 245, 266, 269, 289–90, 310, 317, 326, 329, 331
  "Am I Diversified?" segment on, 50
  at colleges, 224
  "hedge funds gone wild" series on, 245
  "Off the Charts" segment on, 259–60
  "Outrage of the Day" segment on, 29–30
  "sell block" on, 190
  sound effects on, 46
  Wall of Shame on, 30, 121–22
Mad Money: Watch TV, Get Rich, (Cramer), 2, 236
Madoff, Bernie, 12
manufacturers, 116
Marcus, Bernie, 131
market-capitalization-weighted portfolio, 106
Marvell Technology Group (MRVL), 231
Masco (MAS), 98, 99–100
mass selling, 69–70, 74
MasterCard, 316–17
master limited partnerships (MLPs), 106, 216–17, 218, 222
medical REITs, 220
Meisler, Helene, 294
Merck (MRK), 103
Mexico, 130, 132
Meyer, Danny, 289–90
Microsoft (MSFT), 26, 28, 68, 76, 227
Middle East, 114
millennial generation, 82

Minnesota Mining and Manufacturing, *see* 3M (MMM)
MIT, 321
mobile Internet, 228–33
momentum-driving buying, 225
money managers, 65, 68
Monsanto, 62
Morgan Stanley, 149, 310, 321
mortgage bonds, 2
mortgages, 151, 270
Mosaic (MOS), 273
Motorola (MOT), 263, 264, 270
MP3 players, 28
multiple, 32, 33, 34, 35, 36–37, 289
multiple contraction, 225–26
multiple oscillators, 293, 294–95
municipal bonds, 2, 58, 210
music players, 229
must-own date, 78
Mutual Fund Monday, 246
mutual funds, 7, 22, 23, 59, 67, 68–69, 92, 112, 246–47, 259, 296, 297, 308–9, 317
  fees for, 10, 18

Nardelli, Bob, 131
NASDAQ Composite, 4, 26
National City, 153
National Oilwell Varco (NOV), 244, 270
NationsBank, 143
natural gas, 104, 123, 124, 125, 127, 217, 244, 261, 288, 299, 329
net interest margin, 151, 152, 160
NewAlliance Bancshares (NAL), 157–59, 160, 162
New York Times, 5, 268
New York Times Company (NYT), 258
nickel, 127
Nike, 322–23
Nikkei 225, 282
Nissan, 123
Nokia, 230, 270, 273
nonperforming loans, 150–51, 152
Nordic American Tanker (NAT), 219–20
Norfolk Southern (NSC), 273
Norstar Bancorp, 143, 144
North America, 122
North Face, 132, 133
Nucor (NUE), 89, 92, 327
NVIDIA (NVDA), 276

Obama, Barack, 20, 103, 104, 148, 158, 255, 309
Oberg, Eric, 331
Occidental (OXY), 125
oil, 37, 50, 55, 63, 66, 123, 124, 125, 127, 172, 178, 195, 217, 218, 219, 244, 254, 270, 271, 273, 288
    ETFs for, 326, 329, 330, 332
oil tanker stocks, 217, 222
Olive Garden, 64, 289
Only the Paranoid Survive (Grove), 228
ON Semiconductor, 270
OpenTable (OPEN), 315
opportunism, 303
options, 164–65, 168, 169–70, 171, 189–205, 221
    call, 164, 165, 167, 169, 172, 173–87, 190, 191, 192–94, 197–200, 201, 202–3, 221, 233, 235
    fundamentals for, 166
    monthly cycles of, 174
    pricing, 173
    "pumping" of, 184, 202
    put, 190–91, 290–91
Oracle, 26
Orwell, George, 44
oscillators, 293, 294–95
"out-of-the-money" call, 176–77, 179, 181, 195, 200, 203

Page, Larry, 319
Palm (PALM), 228, 229, 230, 270
Panera Bread, 64–65
"partial" selling, 203
Patterson, Peyton, 158, 159
paychecks, 39, 210, 224
payout, 76
Peabody (BTU), 273
Peltier, Dave, 101–2
pension plans, 15
Pentium, 145, 227
People's United Financial (PBCT), 158, 160–62
Pepsi (PEP), 255, 297
perma-bears, 298, 301
perma-bulls, 298
Permian Basin Royalty Trust (PBT), 217–18
Pfizer (PFE), 68, 103

phantom income, 196
phones, 229
Pitney Bowes (PBI), 96, 97, 98, 99
Pittsburgh Plate Glass, *see* PPG (PPG)
plastic, 117
PNC Financial, 143, 153, 156
Poe, Edgar Allan, 259
Post-its, 116
PowerShares Financial Preferred Portfolio (PGF), 105–6
PPG (PPG), 121–23
Pre, 228, 229, 230, 231
preferred stocks, 105–6
premium, 198
press, 279–81
price-to-earnings multiple, 32, 34, 35, 36, 75, 87, 115, 132, 288, 317
price-to-earnings-to-growth rate, 33–34
"primary" offerings, 304
printers, 129, 130, 227
private equity firms, 319, 320–21
private placement, 305
Procter & Gamble (PG), 36, 86, 92, 255, 264
product cycle, 227–33
profits, 36
proprietary products, 28, 33
public offering, 305
pullbacks, 270–72, 286, 293
"Purloined Letter, The" (Poe), 260
put/call ratio, 293, 295
put options, 190–91, 290–91

Qatar, 125
Qualcomm (QCOM), 231, 232, 263, 264, 270, 273
quarterly statements, 37, 236

raw materials, 50, 51
real estate, 50, 58, 142, 177, 192, 240, 265, 282, 329, 330
real estate investment trusts (REITs), 217, 220–21, 222
Real Money (radio show), 50
RealMoney.com, 204, 260, 262
Real Money: Sane Investing in an Insane World (Cramer), 2, 165, 236
recessions, 108–9, 110, 117

record date, 77–78
recovery stocks, 112–39
red chip stocks, 8
Red Lobster, 64, 289
refinancing, 38, 39
regional banks, 143–44, 146–63
Regulation FD (Fair Disclosure), 235
regulators, 267, 268
Research in Motion (RIMM), 228–29, 230,
    231, 269, 270
residential loans, 148, 155, 156, 159
residential real estate, 142
restaurants, 50
restricted shares, 72
retail, 50, 51
retail inventory, 265
retirement, 3
retirement savings, 1, 4, 5, 12, 13, 58, 80,
    82, 206–22
  bonds important for, 207, 208, 210, 221
  deep-in-the-money call options for,
    221–22
  see also 401(k)s; individual retirement
    accounts
return on assets, 154
Reversal of Fortune (film), 170
RF Micro Devices (RFMD), 231
risk profile, 48–49, 80
risk reward, 63, 110, 166, 167, 172, 190
road signs, 116
Rohm and Haas, 121
Roosevelt, Franklin D., 3–4
Roubini, Nouriel, 278
royalty trusts, 218–19
rule of 72, 84, 218
Russell 2000, 255
Russia, 125

Safeway, 264
Samsung, 230
SanDisk (SNDK), 231
savings, 3
savings accounts, 7, 20–21
savings and loan crisis, 142–43, 144, 146,
    149, 153
Schlumberger (SLB), 55, 254, 270, 327
Schmidt, Eric, 319
Scotch tape, 116
Sealy, 320

secondary offerings, 304–5, 306–10, 324
sectors, 50–51, 54–55, 58, 60, 69–70, 113
  dividends by, 75, 101
  equal weighting of, 56
secular growth stocks, 36, 57, 92, 227–33,
    258
Securities and Exchange Commission
    (SEC), 37, 235, 257, 268, 320, 324,
    328, 329, 333
sell list, 300, 301
sell-side analyst research reports, 64
semiconductor cycles, 145, 266
Setting the Table (Meyer), 289
Shawmut, 144
Shell (RDS-B), 124
short interest rebate, 196–97, 201
short-sellers, short-selling, 29, 68, 81–82,
    190, 193, 194, 199, 203, 204, 250–51,
    255, 312
  risk of, 190, 193, 291
  uptick rule and, 235, 257
short-term earnings, 242
SigmaKalon, 122
Simon & Garfunkel, 59
60 Minutes, 275
Skyworks Solutions (SWKS), 231, 270
smartphone, 228, 229, 231
Social Security, 80, 82
software, 129, 130
SPDR Gold Shares (GLD), 52, 53, 54, 58,
    59, 326, 332
Spitzer, Eliot, 252
spot price, 333
spreads, 164
Sprint (S), 275
Standard and Poor's 500, 2, 4, 15, 16, 17,
    29, 34, 43, 83, 96, 106, 115, 216, 247,
    253, 255, 256, 290, 291
Stanford bank, 21
Starent Networks (STAR), 231
state pensions, 67
State Street, 259, 270
Stay Mad for Life (Cramer), 2, 209, 236,
    244
steam, 104
steel, 244, 273, 327
Stephenson, Randall, 105
stimulus packages, 51–52, 111, 114, 116,
    117–18, 126, 211–12

stock brokers, 23, 320
stock market, 4, 6–7, 9
  breadth of, 153
  pundits with dislike of, 249–53
  skepticism regarding, 19–20
  see also dividends
stock market crash of 1929, 14
stock market crash of 1987, 2
stock market crash of 2000, 4
stock market crash of 2008–2009, 1, 12,
    13, 16, 19, 43, 48, 57, 74, 79, 82, 94,
    108, 162, 168, 189, 206, 207, 209, 223,
    291, 302
  as boon for young people, 222, 223, 224
  lessons from, 284–87
stockpickr.com, 244–45
stock replacement, 184–85, 191, 193, 202
stocks:
  author's choice of, 102–7, 112–39,
    150–63
  bonds vs., 85, 207, 208, 213
  "cheap," 31–37
  cyclical, 36, 57, 79, 111, 112, 115–16,
    287–88
  depressed prices of, 25
  fast-growing, 73–74
  five as minimum number to own, 54
  five stages of grief and, 29–31
  flipping of, 308
  in 401(k)s, 216
  growth, 225
  high-yielders, 31, 75, 79, 81–82, 84,
    85, 88–91, 92, 95, 103, 164, 209, 212,
    216
  insurance on, 191–92
  momentum-driving buying of, 225
  predictions of future of, 59–60
  preferred, 105–6
  for recovery, 112–39
  as risky, 211
  short-term fluctuations in prices of,
    45–47, 61, 65–70, 72, 147
  speculative, 73
  zombie, 267–69
  see also dividends
streams of investments, 34–35
stress tests, 148
strike price, 164, 172, 173, 174, 177, 180,
    181, 185–86, 198, 202

student loans, 141
subprime loans, 156
Sunrise Senior Living, 80
syndicate desks, 308, 317

Taco Bell, 290
Taiwan Semiconductors, 266
takeunders, 32, 140
tangible-capital-to-assets ratio, 154, 161
tangible common equity ratio, 157
taxes:
  capital gains, 214
  corporate, 217
  dividend, 214
  income, 24
  retirement plans and, 214, 215
TD Bank, 158
technical analysis, 239, 258–61, 293–95,
    323
technology, 50, 128, 265, 271
tech stocks, 26, 27, 29, 75, 145, 209,
    226–33, 288, 319
telco equipment cycles, 145
10-K, 37, 50
10-Q (quarterly statements), 37, 236
10X changes, 228
Term Asset-Backed Securities Loan
    Facility (TALF), 141
Texas Instruments (TXN), 231, 266, 273
TheStreet.com, 45, 78, 102, 133, 244, 260,
    280, 294, 327, 331
"They Know Nothing" rant of author, 11
Thinking Machines, 321
Thinsulate, 116
Thomas H. Lee Partners, 319
3M (MMM), 116–17, 262
Tier One capital ratio, 152, 154, 157, 159
timber REITs, 220
time premium, 181
Today (TV show), 8, 11, 14
Tokyo Stock Exchange, 282
"too late to sell" philosophy, 26
Top Gun Trader, 244–45, 260
Toyota (TM), 57, 123
traders, 17, 43, 47, 200
"trading around," 203
trading diaries, 181, 185–86
Transocean (RIG), 55, 254, 270, 327
Treasury Department, U.S., 278

Treasury Inflation-Protected Securities
    (TIPS), 211–12
Treasurys, U.S., 2, 16, 21, 43, 58, 79, 82,
    85, 203–4, 210, 211, 222
Tribune Company, 215
TriQuint Semiconductor (TQNT), 231
Troubled Asset Relief Program (TARP),
    141, 152, 153, 157, 159, 161, 311
T. Rowe Price, 259
True Religion (TRLG) jeans, 289
Twain, Mark, 58

UltraShort ProShares ETFs, 329, 330–31
Under Armour (UA), 322–23, 324
unemployment, 3, 39, 69, 109, 150, 160
Union Pacific (UNP), 119–21, 273
UnitedHealth Group (UNH), 256–57
university endowments, 67
uptick rule, 235, 257
U.S. Bancorp (USB), 148–49, 270
U.S. Oil Fund, 332
U.S. Steel (X), 14, 35, 273, 307–8

valuation, 31–32, 35, 36, 111, 115, 141,
    225–26
value-oriented investors, 81
venture capitalists, 319
Verizon (VZ), 80–81, 105, 231
VF Corporation (VFC), 132–34
Visa (V), 46, 47, 136–38, 316–17, 319, 322
Vista, 227
VIX, 241
Von Bulow case, 170, 171
Vulcan Materials, 307–8

Wachovia Bank, 106, 148, 285
Wal-Mart, 123, 264, 290
Washington Mutual, 31, 135, 148, 149, 285

Web browsers, 229
Webster Financial, 158
WellPoint (WPT), 256–57
Wells Fargo (WFC), 136, 148–49, 158, 162,
    254, 261, 270, 305, 309
wheat, 244
white chip stocks, 8
Whole Foods (WFMI), 264, 289–90
Wilshire 5000 Total Market Index, 17, 291
Windows, 227
wireless infrastructure, 231
Wiseman, Eric, 132
Wood, Donald, 221
Wyeth (Wye), 103

Yahoo, 26
Yahoo Finance, 78, 173
yields, 76–77, 79, 80–82, 84, 85, 87, 88–91,
    92, 93, 95, 100, 101, 102, 103, 164,
    212, 219
    of AT&T, 105
    of BHP Billiton, 127
    of Con Ed, 104
    of Conoco, 125
    of Eli Lilly, 102
    of Home Depot, 132
    of Kinder Morgan Energy Partners, 107
    of PowerShares, 105, 106
    of PPG, 123
    superhigh, 90
    of TIPS, 211
    wide scales based on, 90–91
yield supports, 80–82, 98–99, 257
young people, 222–26
YouTube, 11

zombie stocks, 267–69
Zyprexa, 103